WE MOVED THE EARTH

We Moved the Earth

GORDON BROWN

Zenith Publishers Ltd

First published in 1996 by
Zenith Publishers Ltd
25 Shelton Street
Covent Garden
London

ISBN 1 900794 00 4

Typeset by Carnegie Publishing, 18 Maynard St, Preston
Printed and bound by Bookcraft (Bath) Ltd

Contents

Acknowledgements

AFTER THE COLLAPSE of Brown Group International plc in mid-1990, it has always been my wish to place the true facts surrounding the rise and fall of Brown Group International on record to help people, particularly those in the farming and construction industries who supported us through the good and bad times, to have an understanding of what happened.

I have done my utmost to portray a balanced view, without bitterness, but do forgive me if from time to time some anger shows through. There were, of course, people who were let down by this event, but I trust that they will have a better understanding of what actually took place if they can find the time to read my book.

After hours of spilling out my thoughts on to paper, I have now completed my book and I would like to dedicate it to the following people, who were so supportive. I would like to thank my wife, Liz, who has stood by me through thick and thin, and who transcribed my thoughts. Special thanks are due to my daughter, Tina, who gave up so much of her time, and played such a large part in the production of my book. Thanks also to my sister, Dot, who gave up so much of her younger life to look after my mother after she had her stroke. I would also like to thank my two brothers, Freddy and Ron, for without them I would not have led such an interesting and enjoyable life; and also for their support throughout our career together.

Last, but not least, I would like to thank all the people who worked alongside me in the Brown Group and who helped to make it so successful until events overtook us in June 1990.

Prologue

LOOSENING MY BOOTS, I stretched my legs out and leant back on the sun-warmed terrace chair of the mountain café. Squinting, I cast a glance at the splendour before me. The mighty Matterhorn, magnificent in the winter sun, dominated my view, its overhanging north face loomed like a crippled limb. The pistes sprawled like a spotless backcloth, stained only by the descending skiers whose presence peppered the mountainside. Closing my eyes to the glare of the winter sun, I inhaled deeply and injected my lungs with a dose of the purest mountain air. 'This is the life,' I thought. 'This is what it's all about'.

It was 27 December 1987 and a new era of my life was just beginning.

The beauty of the Alps fuelled my mood. For the first time in twenty-five years I felt totally at peace with the world. The week prior to the Christmas of 1987 had been hectic. However, after intensive negotiation, we had secured one of the most important deals of our business life, paving the way towards a bright future. We had bought one of Britain's premier excavator manufacturers and I felt certain that this was the final piece of the jigsaw, the platform on which to build a European construction equipment company.

Twenty-five years earlier, three brothers, Freddy and Ron and I, had sown the seeds of a new business. We always dreamed that one day Wharfedale Agricultural Services Ltd (WAS), as it was then known, would blossom into a force to be reckoned with. Here we were twenty-five years on, our dream come true: we were at the helm of Brown Group International plc with offices in Germany, France, the USA, Norway and the UK. We manufactured, distributed and serviced a comprehensive range of earth-moving equipment across the globe. We had even diversified into air transport. By 1987 we were employing 1,800 people. The institutional shareholders were happy, the banks were confident, and the future looked bright.

It seemed only a short time ago that we had made the enormous leap from distribution into manufacturing. We were, at heart, country boys about to take one of the biggest steps of our lives. Moving into manufacturing in itself was a big step but we were going to manufacture in a foreign land, using a foreign currency and a foreign language – we really had the odds stacked firmly against us. People said that we could never succeed, that we would never become a serious threat to the mighty powers of earth-moving equipment manufacturers, Volvo and Caterpillar, but they were wrong. By 1987 we were manufacturing 700 articulated trucks a year and were joint number two in the world market place, second only to Volvo.

When we bought Moxy, the dumptruck factory in Norway, we decided that a wise investment would be an aeroplane. At that time, the scheduled flight from Leeds-Bradford Airport to Molde took a whole day. This single aircraft was the foundation stone for Capital Airlines which by 1989 had a small fleet of nine aircraft, including two jets, and was responsible for carrying 40+ per cent of traffic in and out of Leeds-Bradford Airport.

Reaching further back into my subconscious I recollect the early days, the 1970s. Britain was growing rich on the discovery of North Sea oil. In 1974, short of work, my farming colleagues and I found ourselves heading north to Scotland in search of the Klondike. It is funny how these things stick in your memory, I remember that it was 1974 because it was the year that Don Revie left Leeds United after ten years of glory and Brian Clough stepped into the breach for 32 days!

Casting my mind back further, I recollect the 1960s. Happy days. When Freddy, Ron, Tony and myself worked together in the interests of the family farm contracting business. Spring, summer and winter were taken up with seeding, fertilising, grass cutting, baling and manure spreading. Armed only with lunch box and vacuum flask, we worked hard from dawn until dusk.

Stirred from my thoughts by the bustle of the lunchtime crowd I reached forward to fasten my boots. Who would have thought all those years ago that one day my brothers and I would have been at the helm of a company with a gross turnover of £160 million a year, holidaying in Zermatt and enjoying such trappings. How lucky we were! However, in my ignorant bliss, I did not realise this was to be the calm before the storm. Little did I know that I was just another coal fuelling the fire of Margaret Thatcher's overheated economy in the UK, and that I would only have one further year enjoying the rollercoaster ride before events in Norway would start the downward spiral of a one-year nightmare, which abruptly brought to an end twenty-seven years of hard work. On 27 June 1990 I became one of life's failures.

PART I

The Early Years

CHAPTER I

The Early Years

I WAS BORN IN NORWOOD (or Norud, as those who lived there called it), a small sprawling farming village set above Fewston reservoir in the Washburn valley, five miles south of Harrogate. The youngest of eight children, I had three brothers and four sisters – Frederick William (Freddy), sixteen years my senior, was the eldest, followed by Winifred Mary, Nona Margaret, Gwendoline Amy, Ronald (Ron), Dorothy (Dot), Tony and myself. By the time Ron was born my mother was running short of second names so Ron, Dot, Tony and I were rationed to just the one.

My father was Fred Brown. He was a strict man who believed strongly in the work ethic and instilled this belief into his children, especially his sons. He worked for the local council. In the summer he drove a steamroller and in the winter he worked as a 'lengthman', looking after a small stretch of road, filling in the potholes, digging gullies for drainage and spreading grit when necessary. In 1938–39 when the war started Council steamrollers and wagons stopped working as no money was available for road repairs. As this meant that my father would have to revert to being a 'lengthman' and using a brush and shovel, he thought this would be a major step backwards and decided to go it alone. He bought a small lorry and embarked on his first business venture. This was a coal round, not only delivering coal but also working with the Forestry Commission delivering pit props to Glossop in Derbyshire. This sort of journey, with the equipment he had, took up a substantial part of the day.

My father was single-minded, very hard working, and seemed to be well respected in the local community. He was always smartly dressed and wore a brown smock, an item of clothing which I never felt was particularly appropriate for the job he was doing, but it was the norm for all truck drivers and farmers at that time. I suppose that in some ways he shook off his council image when eventually he joined the elite farming community in Norwood by taking over Watson House Farm in 1944.

I was closest to my mother, Ivy. Her principal occupation was to produce and raise her children. She made and patched our clothes, cooked our meals and pandered to our needs. This sort of life was not unusual. Many farming families were large and while the men toiled and provided for their families, the women cooked, sewed and cleaned. Looking back, my mother had a hard life. She was a kind woman, very easy going, taking most things in her stride and acting as mediator in our frequent family differences.

When I was about nine my mother suffered a stroke which left her with a speech impediment and paralysed down her right side. She never recovered from this cruel blow and it was left to my elder sisters, especially Dot, to raise Tony and myself. Dot left school and took over the running of the family home. Freddy, Winnie and Nona were already married. Ron and Gwen were grown up, but Tony and I were still young and Dot looked after us all; and as my mother could do very little for herself Dot nursed her as well. She spent all her time cooking, cleaning, washing and baking.

Even before my mother had a stroke, Dot used to help my mother with the raising of her youngest sons. I still have vivid memories of Tony and myself, under the close supervision of Dot, wallowing in Freddy and Ron's used bath water. Four people using the same bath water! But this was the norm in the Yorkshire farming community in those days. Imagine trying to fill by hand a bathtub eight times; not only would it be tiresome but also uneconomical and repeated on a daily basis would probably result in the complete draining of Fewston reservoir!

My clothes too were a cast-off from my elder brothers. Being the youngest in the family my clothes were normally somewhere between fourth- and

My father, Fred Brown (front left), with the rest of the road-making gang.

eighth-hand and little of the original garment could be seen under the array of patches and darns. No one in the village had new clothes so I did not feel badly done by or out of place. I would probably have stuck out like a sore thumb and provided the local bully with ample ammunition if I had worn anything else.

Norwood was and still is a small village with the usual village bobby, vicar, sweet shop, pub and so on. Fortunately for us the sweet shop was ideally located near to our home. Our house, Bland Hill, was a semi-detached farmhouse and nearby lived Mr and Mrs Stubbs. It was not a sweet shop in the conventional sense of the word; Mrs Stubbs simply had a large cupboard full of sweets. For a lad of my vintage – only five or six years old – it was like entering Aladdin's cave. My eyes would pop out and my stomach ache at the sight of the chocolate delicacies before me. I have often thought what a marvellous business the confectionary business is and kicked myself for going into the wrong trade. The sweets in Mrs Stubbs's cupboard were exactly the same as those we buy today – Mars Bars, Kitkats, Polos and Smarties – the product doesn't seem to have changed in fifty years; even the packaging, as I remember it, was the same as today.

The vicar in the village was a Mr Clegg. Looking back, I remember the importance of this 'man of the cloth', his 'presence'. For a long time I was convinced that Mr Clegg was actually God himself and was rather pleased that he had chosen to live in Norwood, Yorkshire, England. Mr Clegg had the free run of the village. He tended his flock on a daily basis, sauntering in and out of our houses at will. He would arrive unannounced and unexpected. He never knocked; he just entered. I don't think anyone dared refuse entry for fear of eternal damnation or something equally unpleasant. I know it was not just our village; all over the country the vicar was considered to be a sort of demi-God. Mr Clegg lived in a huge house – the vicarage – overlooking the reservoir, he drove a huge car and was brimming over with wisdom and advice. Life revolved around Mr Clegg. Sentences began and ended with his name and it was a name that was never taken in vain.

The next most important person, or so it seemed at the time, was Mr Snailham. He was the village policeman. He lived in various lodging houses in the Washburn valley and did his daily rounds with his motorbike and side-car. He was an awesome chap, absolutely enormous, and made brother Freddy look like a super-waif. His face was set in a permanent scowl and sent tremors of fear though Tony and me and our school friends. Mr Snailham, like Mr Clegg, entered houses unexpectedly and unannounced. Parking his motorbike, he would stride out up the garden path towards the front door. Without knocking he would come straight in, hitch up his coat, thrust his hands deep into his trouser pockets and plunge his formidable backside into the warmth of the fire. His immense rear eclipsed the burning embers and ensured that we shivered while he glowed. Mr Snailham was a gossip – he always arrived armed with sackloads of tittle-tattle. Nearly all his sentences would begin, 'Don't say anything but . . .' or 'I shouldn't really tell you this, but . . .' Such secrecy would have been admirable but for the fact that Mr Snailham spent the whole day visiting house after house sharing the same secret with anyone willing to listen. To a small boy of eight, this pointless exercise was one of life's imponderables. How could a secret that everybody knew about still be a secret!

Not only did I fear the man but I also feared his powers. If he had the power to enter the house without knocking what other powers might he have? I worried myself to sleep in the knowledge that Mr Snailham might one day uncover our deep, dark secret, the secret that hung high up in the attic. To a boy of eight, this secret was dark and sinister. In hindsight, the crime that my father was committing would not have resulted in three life sentences or death by hanging but at the age of eight, I considered it to be incredibly naughty and concentrated hard on keeping my mouth shut. For quite a while after the war food was still rationed. Fred Brown along with many other farmers provided extra food for his family, thus short-circuiting the law.

Instead of consuming only what his ration book permitted, my father used to kill some of his pigs in the outbuildings. The meat was salted, cured

My parents (right) at Nona's wedding. My mother's calliper is just visible.

and hung in the attic ready to be brought down when required. When Mr Snailham dropped in on one of his frequent visits, Tony and I would be instructed not to mention the ham and bacon. Sitting nervously on the floor (we had to sit on the floor, because when there was a full house we were always two chairs short), we would concentrate on not blurting out the truth. We concentrated so hard on not saying it that we almost did say it! We would listen in trepidation to the conversation, terrified that someone would slip up and mention the bacon and hams curing above. I had visions of the motorbike and side-car disappearing into the distance weighed down with my father, Mr Snailham, two sides of bacon and four cured hams, to rot inside a dark cell and never to be seen again. In later years, it occurred to me that Mr Snailham, being the size that he was, could have been a party to this activity and, being an accessory to the crime, did not arrest my father. I cannot possibly believe that a man that large could have been satisfied by the food allocated to him by the state.

Another character in the village was Albert Spence. He was a farmer and was always asking questions and wanting to know all about everything. He was not a nosey man, simply thirsty for knowledge. As I too was thirsty for knowledge I was given the nickname of 'Albert'. At the other end of the village was a pub, the Sun Inn. But this was not my father's local; he preferred the Hopper Lane which was on the Skipton Road. My father, along with most other husbands and fathers, would descend on his chosen pub every night. My father would leave the house sometime between 8 and 9 o'clock and religiously return home at 10.45. My mother only accompanied him once a year for the 'darts and dominoes' dinner. In those days it was not done for women like my mother to go to the pub. She would stay at home, feed her clutch and make sure the younger ones were ready for bed. Once we were tucked in she would turn her hand to needlework. She spent many of her evenings sewing. I don't know whether she made our clothes out of necessity or whether she enjoyed it. I suspect it was a mixture of the two. Whatever the reason, she had an indisputable talent for dressmaking. She made most of our clothes as well as rag rugs to scatter round the house. Such was her talent with a needle and thread that she could not only start but finish a garment in a single evening.

Going back to the subject of the Sun Inn: from the age of eight until I was about fifteen, this was forbidden territory. Under Fred Brown's strict regime, pubs, like towns, were considered evil to his children. Tony and I would hide in the woods opposite the pub and watch the comings and goings of the busloads of people and listen to the frivolity of the folk inside. When I was really young some people called the Bells had the pub. However, the most memorable landlord was Frank Beecroft. Frank Beecroft was of greater interest because not only did he have a son for me to play with but he also had two daughters to hanker after. Dennis was about three years younger than me and became my instant playmate. Pat was four years older than me and Catherine, four years younger. Catherine, who was only about four at the time, was obviously of little interest. However, Pat, whom I, at the tender age of eight, considered perfect was rather more interesting. Unfortunately she wrote me off immediately, saying I was too young for her – it seemed that I couldn't win. The only two girls in the village who were exactly the same age as me and therefore qualified as possible girlfriends were Winnie Marston and Ella Noble. Both were certainly 'interesting' but not as 'interesting' as the lovely and unattainable Pat.

At the other side of the reservoir, high on the Blubberhouses Moor, lay the small village of Timble. Like Norwood, Timble was a collection of farms and outbuildings with a small chapel and a much frequented ale house. We shared the same Mr Clegg and the same Mr Snailham. While Fred Brown was raising his family of eight at one side of the reservoir, Albert Victor Ogden was raising his clutch of six at the Timble Inn. We were two large families, living two miles apart. My father was a farmer/contractor, Mr Ogden was a publican – our lives were separate and our paths infrequently crossed. However, as time went by our careers ran parallel. In later years, the Ogdens were to become one of our major competitors and a formidable force in the construction industry.

The entire Brown clan attended Norwood village school. I use the word 'attended' in the loosest possible manner as our presence there was often spasmodic. As I have mentioned earlier my father instilled the work ethic into all of us. There was no time for schooling and education. Fred Brown wanted his children to work hard on the farm not in the classroom. Consequently my attendance level was not great. Baling, ploughing and lambing normally took precedence. Anyway, when we did attend the school it was under the watchful eyes of Miss Heaton and Mrs Gill. Miss Heaton was a strict woman with short hair and glasses. To my young eyes she looked very old and forbidding but I suppose she was probably no more than forty. She lived in the school house in Norwood and apparently had a boyfriend. There was once much lively gossip in the village when it was reported that the cleaner had found a pair of men's pyjamas in Miss Heaton's bedroom.

I was more afraid of Miss Heaton than I was of my parents. The school itself consisted of little more than two rooms. As a five-year-old I began my education in the smaller of the two rooms, taking my afternoon nap in the sewing box, and at the age of seven I was upgraded to the larger room where I stayed until I was eleven. There were only about fourteen of us at

Tony, Dot, Ron and me (at the front), about 1948.

the school. Being so small, there were no prefects, just the two teachers. About twice a year they were summoned to Harrogate to refresh their teaching skills and attend a Ministry of Education course. One of the older pupils was told to look after the rest of the school and to send us home at 3.30 p.m. However, the moment Mrs Gill's Ford Popular left the premises anarchy broke out.

Tony, Malcolm Rayner and myself were just beginning to take an interest in what girls were made of. I was about eight and Tony would have been about ten. Being of farming stock, we had spent many hours watching father sorting out the tups (male) from the gimmers (female). We thought it would be a good idea to apply these tried and tested methods of sorting out to our school colleagues. Malcolm and I would rearrange the desks to make two pens. We would herd all the school into one pen and then set about the task of catching our classmates, especially girls, and checking that they were in the right pens.

Tony and I were very close as children. He was much braver than I was and I always tended to follow his lead. As youngsters we would disappear for hours at a time, causing my mother a great deal of worry. My father

Our class at Norwood School. Ron and Dot are at the left of the back row; Tony is on the right of the front row; I am the little one third from the right.

always comforted her by saying that once our stomachs began to grumble we would return, and he was right. We were like the 'Bisto Kids', drawn home by the smell of cooking.

We never had any pets. We had cats but they were employed to curb the ever-growing mouse population. We didn't have sheepdogs because my father considered eight children could do the job just as well as one dog. We once inherited a fluffy mongrel called Sandy, but she was not a pet as such, and was not smothered with affection. She simply lived with us and was fed. Animals, to my father, were only worthwhile if they could be sold later, for profit at an auction.

Having said that we had no pets, we did in fact have one, a donkey called Nairobi. When Freddy, Nona, Winnie and the others were young, my father bought Nairobi as a kind of pet-cum-lawnmower. However, as they grew older, they lost interest in her. Tony and I were still young and had grown very fond of the donkey. But my father decided she would have to go, being 'good for nowt but taking grass in at one end and shitting it out of the other'. She would be taken to the auction and Tony and I went along with my father and the poor donkey. She caused quite a stir. At the cattle auction, there was no great call for donkeys and poor Nairobi had to wait until all the serious bidding was finished. The sight of our ageing, scraggy donkey caused much hilarity. My father announced that she would be a good buy to anyone who wanted her because she was in foal – 'a two for the price of one' concept. Once the cattle were all finished with, the auctioneer moved onto the task of selling Nairobi. After five minutes he stopped the bidding, saying:

'Are you sure she's in foal?' I had to admit that she didn't exactly look fit to burst; perhaps there was something I didn't know. Anyway, I decided that father knew best.

'Course she is,' replied my father. The bidding started again but in a matter of minutes the auction was stopped again.

'She's too old and thin – are you sure she's in foal?' questioned the auctioneer again.

'Well, when ye sold t'old thing to me eight years ago, she was, and nowt's come out since then,' smirked my father.

'Well, in that case, it must be in there somewhere,' blushed the auctioneer and carried on the bidding.

I have fond memories of our country life. From Bland Hill, the farm where I was born, we had panoramic views of the surrounding countryside. Tony and I would have made ideal characters for an Enid Blyton novel. We would set off on a morning through the local farmers' fields. My father would often forbid us from walking through certain fields because he and the farmer would be on bad terms. However, this was like a red rag to a bull to Tony. These fields would become prime targets for our adventures. Tony would almost go out of his way to cross the prohibited areas in order to satisfy his sense of adventure. Tree-climbing was one of our favourite activities. Tony would always climb too high and I would spend the rest of the day trying to get him back down. Another pastime was rabbiting: we would inspect our home-made snares on a regular basis. We also collected eggs. Once home, Tony would put a hole in either end of the egg and blow the contents out; he would then wrap it in cotton wool and put in a box along with the rest of the collection.

Often while on our great expeditions we would be struck by a call from nature. Miles from anywhere, we would note a distinct lack of 'facilities'. Neither Tony nor I had many inhibitions in this area, but the lack of such luxuries as toilet paper did present something of a problem. Creative young men that we were, we would assist each other by rolling up dock leaves which provided a comfortable cleaning device. Once, to add a little humour to the occasion, I slipped a nettle in amongst the dock leaves. Tony was not amused.

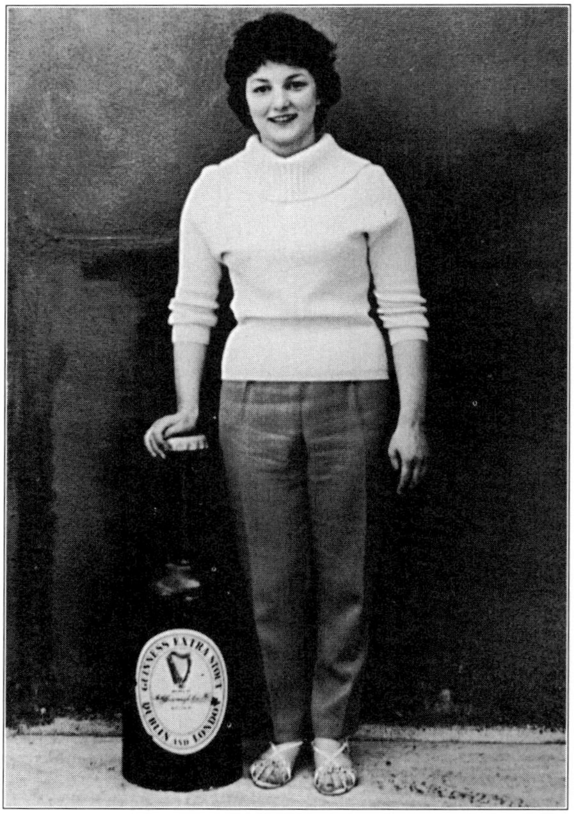

A young Dot.

I remember the day my mother had her stroke. I was nine or ten at the time and still at the village school. My mother had suffered the stroke during the night. She had tried to wake my father to get help but was paralysed. It was not until the morning when my father awoke that he discovered what had happened. I was sent to school as usual; it was best that I was out of the way as I was too young to understand how ill she really was. To take my mind off what had happened, Miss Gill, who knew the severity of my mother's condition, took me and the other children on a nature walk. I remember running home in the afternoon expecting to find my mother going about her daily chores, wearing a plaster or something until she got better. I was looking forward to telling her about the nature walk and my day at school, but that, sadly, would have to wait.

It was three months before my mother was allowed home, and she never once complained. She gradually learned to stand again, to put all her weight on one leg, to dress herself, and to go about her daily chores. She was not forced to do those tasks. She loved her family and simply wanted to continue as best she could being a mother and a wife but despite her efforts, she never regained the use of her right side. My sister Dot, despite being married and having a family of her own, continued to look after her until the day my mother died over twenty-five years later.

CHAPTER 2

School

MY LITTLE WORLD was truly blissful until I was eleven. But then the big day arrived when I was unceremoniously plucked from my quiet village existence at Norwood and sent to 'big school' at Otley.

To an eleven-year-old country boy whose whole existence had encircled simply his mother, father, seven brothers and sisters and several hundred cows and sheep, Otley, six miles to the south, really was 'the big smoke'. I had been there several times before, with my father and Tony and Dot, to see the auction mart. Once there he would seat us and command us to stay 'put' until he had finished his business and returned. I would sit contentedly watching the activities of the market, bemused by the hustle and bustle of it all. Several hours later my father would be back to collect us and take us home.

But now at the age of eleven, this was not a pleasure trip any more: this was school. Miss Heaton and Mrs Gill had done all they could with me, they had tried their best, taught me all they could, shared their knowledge of maths, English and history and given me an ample dose of the moral teachings of the church. Now it was time to move on, time to study bigger and better things.

I had taken my Eleven Plus and, not to anybody's surprise, failed it. Thus I was duly dispatched to the local secondary modern. Unfortunately the term 'secondary modern' seemed to carry a kind of stigma and conjured up the image of an excessive number of backwards children with not a lot between their ears. I prefer to think of us as those people who 'could have done better, if only they'd tried' or 'had a lot of ability but didn't apply themselves' and not as 'thick as two short planks'. If anyone asked which school I went to I would answer that I was at school in Otley and hope that they would assume I meant the grammar school, thus avoiding any unnecessary embarrassment on my part or theirs.

I was rated as a 'C' class student, not brilliant but not as bad as being rated a 'D'. We all know what that stood for.

Norwood village school didn't really prepare me for 'big school' and the secondary modern opened up a whole new world to me. Every day the lovely Pat Beecroft, Malcolm Rayner, Tony and I would catch the Wrays six-mile journey to Otley. At the secondary modern, there was a notable lack of academic ability and so the emphasis was on 'using your hands'. Practical subjects such as metalwork and woodwork were the norm – we were to be the builders, joiners and plumbers of the future. Maths and English were taught but as you can imagine, for the teachers it was rather like banging their heads against a brick wall. None of us had the basic knowledge on which to build and expressed no sort of interest in doing so.

My time at Otley secondary modern was put to good and practical use. In the metalwork class, much to my father's delight, I would make tractor drawbar pins. In the woodwork class I made a table. It was a highly technical piece of furniture with a swivel top which, when turned, allowed two hinged side-flaps to be released, so that they hung neatly at either side. It was a good sturdy piece of work – everything matched, legs were the same length, hinges well screwed on, the top was spirit-level flat and so on. I was rather proud of my handiwork. However, years later, after my father's death, I found the table in his house. His second wife had left shortly after his death, taking all the furniture and fittings, in fact just about anything and everything that was not nailed down. The only thing she did abandon was my table. I found it standing solitary in a corner – obviously she was distraught by my father's death and didn't recognise a fine piece of craftsmanship when it was set before her.

At school, I always remember the 'hygiene class'. You may well ask 'what was the hygiene class?' Did we learn how to bath and wash our hair? Did we learn how to use detergent around the house? No, this was the code name for that most secretive of subjects – sex education. Hygiene class was a lesson about the 'birds and the bees'. The drawback was that it was for girls only: the boys were banned. If a teacher was away, relief teachers were not brought in. Instead we were told to join another class. Guess where I went! Tubby Darnbrook, Colin Smith, Malcolm Rayner and myself on numerous occasions tried to gatecrash; we felt it was a vital and necessary part of our education and our apparent exclusion was just 'not cricket'. However, the teachers were not of the same opinion. We were sent back to woodwork and the clandestine sessions were completed in our absence.

I'm afraid my attendance at secondary school was again pretty spasmodic. In the local villages it was a common belief that education began and ended on the farm: in fact the whole of life revolved around the farm. The farm was the school of life and any knowledge gained in classes other than woodwork or metalwork was thought to be superfluous to requirements.

There was never a great hullabaloo if my brothers or I took the day off school. In fact in the early spring and summer months, there were barely enough hours in the day for my father's men to carry out their never-ending workload. The contracts would come in thick and fast with the local farmers demanding that *their* work be done first, and yesterday if possible, at a ridiculously knocked down price. Short of time and men, my father was only too happy that his brood should skip school and help the Ellisons and Frank Wade carry out these formidable tasks.

As a youngster, I idolised great tractor drivers, machine operators, lorry drivers and flat-capped farmers, not poets and mathematicians. Shakespeare would have aroused my interest only if he had been an experienced chain-harrower or needed our baling services. Donnie and Geoff Ellison, the best tractor drivers in the Washburn Valley, were my heroes, not Tennyson and Wordsworth.

Donnie and Geoff and their brothers Alec and Phil all worked for my father. Donnie could do no wrong; he always had time for me. From him I learned important things, things that mattered, things that would expand my farming knowledge, that would offer me the respect of my father and make me the envy of my school friends. Donnie always had time to talk, to answer my never-ending stream of questions, my constant querying and my relentless desire to learn more. He would teach me about farming, operating machinery and driving tractors. I felt that what Donnie didn't know was not worth knowing. Donnie taught me how to start a 'grey Fergy': I would start it on petrol and then switch it onto TVO (tractor vaporising oil), a much cheaper fuel. The time of the changeover was crucial and to a twelve-year-old boy it was an impressive and highly skilled operation. I always wanted to capitalise on Donnie's seemingly endless farming knowledge, learn and expand my horizons and, in doing so, gain respect from all those around me.

At the age of twelve I was given my first driving lesson. My father approved of my learning to drive the old 'grey Fergy' because it was one of the safest tractors around. Its starter mechanism was really quite revolutionary. The gear lever itself actually activated the starter, thus ensuring that it could never be started while in gear.

There was a tremendous feeling of competition among all those who worked on the farm; not malicious rivalry but rather a driving desire to be the best. Donnie taught me how to plough, for ploughing is an art and he was easily the most talented for miles around. He showed me how to open a furrow and close a 'rig', the term for the first strip of land ploughed. It is essential that the rigs are exactly parallel. They must be parallel because, having cut a rig, the land must be ploughed in one direction only, circling the rig. If the rigs are not parallel, a small patch of land between them, called a 'gaze', is bound to be left unploughed. A gaze is an unacceptable sign of failure in ploughing. A man cannot hold his head high knowing that

Hero Donnie sitting behind the driver next to my sister Nona. Behind Nona is Gwen and next to Gwen is my other hero Geoff Ellison.

he has exposed a gaze. Such incompetence would have been round the village like wildfire. It really was a sin; and I was determined to perfect the art of ploughing.

The farming year could be split into the four seasons, with summer the highlight of the calendar. The six-week summer holiday was certainly not a time of rest. Fred Brown capitalised on his expanded workforce by sending all his children out to work in the fields, with contract haymaking the major activity. Dot was in charge of the telephone. On the window-ledge near the telephone, she kept two lists, one for those who needed our services for grass cutting and the other for baling. It was a period of non-stop work – from dawn through to dusk.

The whole family would be involved in the grass cutting. Ron or Freddie would drive the tractor with the mowing machine, cutting the grass ready for haymaking, while Nona, Gwen, Winnie, Dot, Tony and myself would be involved in 'raking off'. This involved raking the grass back so that the cutting blade of the mowing machine was not hindered from doing its job. 'Raking off' was a great novelty at the start of the summer but its appeal was short lived.

Everyone who worked for Fred Brown had to serve an apprenticeship before they were offered the great honour of driving the Massey Harris 701. This was an ungainly baling contraption, capable of picking hay up from the ground to form a bale which was then dropped out of the back. The bale could then be lifted onto the back of a trailer by a single man. In previous years, old stand-balers had been used. With these machines, the hay had to be swept to the baler and then forked into the machine in order to produce the bale rather than the baler travelling along the row of hay to be baled. Much manpower was required.

By the age of fourteen I had served my apprenticeship, and it was now my turn to sit behind the wheel of the mighty Massey Harris. I felt so proud to be at the helm of this revolutionary machine for not just any Tom, Dick or Harry could win this privilege. I was now in Donnie's league, I thought. And I have distinct memories of the source of power at the front of this cumbersome monster – the Armstrong Siddeley engine. This powerful engine drove a series of belts which in turn drove the donkey-like head to force the hay down into the baler. As the bales churned out one by one behind me, I remember my feeling of real achievement, for I knew my father let only those whom he trusted drive this machine. That meant a great deal to a young lad of fourteen.

As autumn approached, the work changed. Haymaking finished and harvest approached. Most of the haymaking was north of Harrogate, around Skipton, whereas we worked on the straw in the Wetherby area to the south. Tony, Donnie, Ron, Frank Wade and myself would set off early in the morning in our old Commer van. My mother always prepared some sandwiches and flasks of tea and coffee. The sandwiches were always filled with either banana or tomato, a bit repetitive, but always good.

With the onset of winter, the cold, dark months cast a shadow over the farm work. Contract jobs were few and far between and my father found it difficult to occupy his men. The Brown clan became obsolete; so, no longer needed on the farm, we returned to school. Life on the farm was never dull; there was simply no time for boredom. I would return from school in the evening, jump off the bus at the end of Smithson Lane and dash back to Watson Lane Farm in search of Donnie. If I couldn't find him I would help his brother. Geoff, a real disciplinarian. Geoff was an ideal teacher – strict and thorough. If I was to become a good all-round labourer, Geoff was the man to teach me. On wet days my father struggled to find work for us and we would often end up either cleaning out the sheep's feet or whitewashing yet another outbuilding. However, on the really wet days, we would be rented out to clean other farmers' cattle-yards.

Forming a line the muck would be shovelled from one man to another and finally chucked out of the window on to the midden heap below. Five or six of us would be involved and the lazy one among us would be put nearest the window. In that position he had to work as fast as the rest of us or else he might find himself two feet under. All the time we would exchange bawdy jokes, discuss the local talent and brag about our conquests, not that I had much to brag about. We were a small and close community with the same interests and goals. The hours were long and often cold but we were a cheerful bunch. I never woke up filled with gloom at the prospect of a day on the farm – quite the opposite, I relished the thought. I suppose it is fair to say that work has always been my hobby. If I didn't work what would I do? When I was fifteen work on the farm was a hobby; it was something I did when I was not at my day job, at school. Work was always sociable and we cherished the group spirit. Rivalry, where it existed, was of a constructive rather than a destructive nature. It was healthy competition for we all wanted to be the best: the best farmer, the best contractor. Office politics did exist but rather than concentrating on who had the biggest office or the best car, we would turn green with envy at the sight of Malcolm Wilson in his new Fordson Major.

At the risk of perching on my soap-box and sounding opinionated, I would say that with the coming of the computer, increased mechanisation and the overall speed with which business is now conducted, work for many people has become a drudge. Perhaps it always was; perhaps I am looking back through rose-coloured spectacles, or perhaps I am just blessed with a perverse liking for labouring. Whatever the reason, it often seems to me that work for many is just a slog, concerned only with profit margins and the so-called 'bottom line'. The enjoyment has gone, group spirit has been extinguished and destructive rivalry has reared its ugly head.

Anyway, at the age of fifteen I left school. I collected my now infamous folding coffee-table, picked up my tractor drawbar pins from the metalwork room and entered the big wide world of work. At the time I thought I had pretty well wasted the last ten and a half years of my life trying to be an academic. And that attitude was nurtured by my father, I am afraid. Now my friends and I believed we were about to do something really useful at last. We all had at least one job to choose from, and some of us were often spoilt for choice. Many of my friends took up apprenticeships, and all of us had acquired the skills needed to begin a proper career. I was proficient in tractor-driving, Richard Thompson could drive a lorry and Tubby Darnbrook was a dab hand at shearing sheep. The slogan at that time was, 'You've never had it so good'. How true that was. But I don't think we really appreciated just how lucky we were.

CHAPTER 3

Work

MY WORKING LIFE started the moment I got off the school bus for the last time. My father and I skipped the interview stage, simply agreeing that I should start in the morning. There was no contract of employment and my hours were broadly defined as 'you can go home when it's finished'. Fred Brown had my life mapped out for me. In fact, he had Freddy's, Winnie's, Nona's, Gwen's, Ron's, Dot's and Tony's careers in hand as well. The girls, Freddy and Ron were to be involved in the contracting, coal and transport business. Tony and I were to be kept on the farm with Geoff Ellison as our mentor. I had always enjoyed working on the farm but by this time I was ready to move on.

My first wage was about £5 a week and my ambition was to save up to buy a van. In 1957, Tony, who was two years older than me, passed his driving test – so he and I were no longer dependent on the others for our transport. On a Saturday night, we were given permission by my father to drive to Harrogate to the fish and chip shop on Harlow Hill. However, we were under strict instructions to drive no further. My father wanted to protect us from that most evil of places, the town centre, and perhaps more important, we needed shielding from those most evil of beings – 'townies'. As usual, when asked not to do something, we disobeyed. Tony, with his mechanical expertise, would park outside the fish and chip shop and disconnect the speedo cable. We would then venture into forbidden territory – the exclusion zone. Saturday night was reserved, as Tony most eloquently put it, for 'pulling birds'. After a quick trawl round town, whistling at the local talent through the car window, we would return to Harlow Hill, reconnect the speedo, and return home.

In those early days, the various businesses in which we were involved consisted of haulage and contracting, the shop, the farms and the coal round. The coal round was the responsibility of my uncle Arthur and Tommy Kendall. On the days when work was slack, I went along with uncle Arthur to collect and buy hay. Hay days were long days. We started at 5.30 a.m. We would go down to Thorne, on the Trent side near Scunthorpe, and examine the goods. My uncle showed me how to examine the hay and check whether it was of a quality suitable for our customers. With our cargo on board, we would return, arriving at Lancaster at milking time. Uncle

Arthur was another one who made time for me. He had an endless store of jokes and tall stories. I remember he was always full of advice on the art of seducing women. As a fifteen-year-old, I was not blessed with suave sophistication, essential qualities if I were to be a 'hit' at the Friday-night village dance. Uncle Arthur would suggest that I picked the plainest girl there, as no one else would want her. It made sense. It was useful advice and in moments of desperation I took it. Another heart-warming thought, highlighted by my uncle, was that those girls who were less attractive at the start of the evening would become better looking by home time, so if I had been repulsed at 7 p.m., with the aid of several pints of intoxicating fluid, little Miss Plain would turn into Marilyn Monroe by 1 a.m. He was right again. Tommy Kendall and Uncle Arthur passed many pleasant hours plotting how I might tackle the local talent. They certainly kept me amused but suggestions were never more helpful than those I have outlined above.

Around this time, my father had acquired two other wagons, a Bedford, driven by Frank Wade, and an Austin, driven by my eldest brother Freddy, to add to the two ex-army Bedford vehicles and the two vans we already had. Their job was 'catchwork', delivering on a daily basis mangles, hay, straw and so on.

Agricultural contracting was our other source of income. All four tractors were driven from time to time by an Ellison – Donnie, Phil, Geoff and Alec. The four brothers were kept busy haymaking, straw-baling, and ploughing; every season provided us with a new job. I often worked alongside the brothers, with Donnie or Geoff appointed as my teacher. We would meet early in the morning outside Watson House Farm. Our first job would be to feed the cattle; then, under instructions from my father, Geoff would drive me and my tractor to Harrison Wards at Blubberhouses. My task for the day would be 'discing'. How can I define this? Basically I would drive up and down the ploughed field towing behind me a piece of equipment which had disc-like attachments. These attachments would rotate and break up the ground.

Geoff would set me going: the first pass was always a pretty unpleasant experience, rather like sitting for ten minutes astride a bucking bronco. Having made the first pass, I would attach more discs, and travelling in the opposite direction I would embark on the second. As the discs did their job, the ride became easier. The contracting price allowed for three passes by which time the field would be ready for sowing.

Those were solitary days. I would be alone from early in the morning until late at night, armed with a flask of cold tea and a box of tomato sandwiches which invariably I would have consumed before the clock struck 10 o'clock. Occasionally, especially when the work was pressurised, my allocated chauffeur would forget to return at night to take me home. Cold and hungry, I would patiently wait. Out of fear of my father, I would never think of abandoning my post. My absence often went unnoticed for many hours and I would be retrieved only after my father, scrupulously counting his flock back into the fold, had noticed that young 'Albert' was missing. I have vivid memories of those cold, wet winter days. The tractors had no cabs and keeping warm was an art form. However, those dismal hours were more than compensated for by the balmy summer months. Then the cabless tractors were a godsend; during June, July and August we would acquire our 'agricultural glow' as the sun beat down.

However, the tractors were far from reliable and breakdowns were frequent. 'Breakdown', along with words like 'rest' and 'holiday', did not appear in my father's vocabulary. His workers would rather burn in hell than admit that they could not repair their equipment. Thus calling out my father to repair my machine was not an option; as a result, innovative engineering was needed on a daily basis. Frequently the tractor would overheat. I would then take my five-gallon drum and go off to fetch water from some nearby source, a trough or a stream. Setting the tractor running I would top up the radiator. This was a job that was repeated throughout the day. Another problem, I remember, was that the discs were always breaking down. I would scrabble around in the soil looking for the broken part and then find some wire or 'billy band' in order to make my repair.

Towards the end of 1959, my seventeenth birthday was rapidly approaching. With it came the excitement and the pressure of the dreaded driving test. 'Excitement', because soon I would have my own wheels under me; 'pressure', because failure was a sin worse than death. I had to pass to please not only my friends but also my father, who saw my driving test as an investment and rubbed his hands at the thought of another qualified driver. At least I would be able to drive his machinery on the road legally.

There was an awful amount at stake; my self-respect, my social standing, my success with the local girls – all were dependent on whether I passed or failed. I was the talk of the village, the focal point of the Friday night dance. If I passed I would be a man amongst boys, and infinitely more popular with the ladies. Driving lessons were scorned. One-up-manship was the name of the game. Credibility was given to those who had booked their test for 8 a.m. on their seventeenth birthday. Now that really was impressive: to pass your driving test on your seventeenth birthday. To fail first time was the ultimate embarrassment. Those in this category were ruthlessly ridiculed, never allowed to forget the humiliation of their failure. Respect was withdrawn for late applications (say, two days after your birthday) and for failure at first attempt. I was determined to pass first time. Unfortunately,

My brother Ron with his best friend Malcolm Wilson.

I did not. Life was unbearable: how could I hold up my head knowing my social rating was so low? I spent the next two weeks repelling the disgrace of my defeat. Time and effort were invested in proclaiming that it was someone else's fault (it always is) and that I had failed on some minor point (you always do). Eventually I passed and the ridiculing stopped.

I remember that at this time that no one could define whether you could drive a heavy goods vehicle (HGV) at seventeen or twenty-one. Under the almighty law of Fred Brown, it was seventeen. My father's law was edited to include the clause 'if stopped – plead ignorance'. With his team of young, enthusiastic, low-priced drivers, Fred Brown had the competitive edge.

Then Fred Brown expanded further into general haulage. Having hauled lime and slag in ex-army trucks, I was assigned the task of spreading it. By this time, my friends from school had joined the business, now known as Wharfedale Agricultural Services. Tony, Colin Smith, Derek Darnbrook and myself were the raw recruits. On the odd days that we were allowed to drive the HGVs, we were placed under the watchful eye of the old hands. These were experienced workers in their thirties: Dick Lodge, Donnie Ellison and Frank Wade were assigned to share their wisdom with us.

Our HGV training consisted of following Dick Lodge to Liverpool. We were told to get on the A59 and stay on it until we got to the Dock Road; we then had to ask where North Shore Mill was. Dick showed us how to 'sheet up' and make a 'pull knot'. The biggest worry on the return journey was climbing Sawley Brow at Clitheroe. I could not relax until I had safely steered my 'A' model Bedford with its Perkins P6 engine, carrying eight tonnes of cattle food, over the topside of this obstacle. Dick would tell me to stay in low gear, his advice was 'keep the revs up and, if it does peter out and you can't hold it on the brakes, make sure you get the back corner into the banking. If you have a problem get your chain out and ask another driver to give you a pull.' We all worked together, and the hauliers, McBays and Longsters of Pateley Bridge, were always willing to give us a hand.

I distinctly remember the day I received my first new lime-spreader. This customised piece of machinery was inventively created over a long period of time. First, my father purchased a Bedford QL wagon from a local army sale. The engine was taken out and replaced by a Perkins P6 conversion and a twin wheel conversion was set at the back of the chassis. This mongrel piece of engineering was then sent, on the final leg of its creation, to Robert B. Masseys at Market Weeton where its lime-spreader body was fitted. My pride and joy was registered 42YG and painted in white with a red nose. The maiden voyage highlighted the difference between the engineering of the 1950s and the engineering of today. Dougie Furniss (an army colleague of Ron's) and I set off at 5 a.m. to Dorman Long's Slag Works at Middlesbrough to collect our first load of slag. We had not gone two miles before the throttle fell off; but innovative Doug soon had us on the road again. By Ripon, the lime-spreader was at boiling point. Topped up with water, we hit the road again. After we had arrived at Dorman Long's and loaded six tonnes of slag, we noticed that one tyre was flat. Finally, after a long morning coping with one repair after another, we got back to Donald Ashby's at Norwood with the intention of spreading our slag. The wind had got up and it was too wild a day to achieve our goal. We had to park up for the afternoon and get on with some other task. I remember my father instructing us to get up at 5.30 a.m. the next day and spread the slag before the wind got up again.

It was in the late 1950s, in 1957 I think, the business seemed suddenly to jump forward. That was the year that Ron returned after completing his national service, and when he got back he provided us with two able engineers, Doug Furniss and Fred Balsdon. My father, of course, was the overall dictator; Freddy emerged as the administrator or deal-maker, when father would allow him the freedom. On Ron's return, he and his army

Ron in his army days.

pals were to be the repairers and engineers. Tony, myself and our school pals were the machine operators. Dot took the telephone inquiries, Gwen looked after the office administration and Nona and Winnie were married with families. Nona had made an excellent choice in my hero Donnie, and Winnie an equally good choice by marrying Frank Wade. However, it was not long before Frank left the business to start his own farm at Clifton, two miles out of Otley.

Father had done well, his small empire had grown from strength to strength. In addition to his coal, haulage and contracting businesses, he now had two farms, Watson House and Brown Bank, as well as an agricultural shop in Otley. From humble beginnings, he had achieved a great deal. However, his stubborn, inflexible nature was to prove difficult. The future success of the business depended on the wholehearted co-operation of Freddy, Ron, Tony and myself, but under his regimented dictatorship such loyalty and unity could not be guaranteed.

The business badly needed to be reorganised and my father dedicated more and more of his time to this. I can remember clearly one particular evening: Bill Morley, the accountant, my father, Freddy, Gwen, Dot and Ron were sitting discussing the future. Tony and I were in the bedroom above, listening intently. Father decided, without any consultation with Tony and me, that we should work on the two farms. This was a terrible decision. Tony and I had outgrown farmwork: we had worked on the farms from a very young age, by now we had acquired new skills, we could operate machinery and drive the HGVs, and we had new goals and aspirations. When the news was officially broken to us, we strongly objected. My father spent many hours trying to persuade us that it was a good idea, coining the cliché, 'One day, sons, all this land will be yours'. He would not listen to our point of view, to our ideas: there was deadlock.

As time went by, the family feuding grew worse. We argued about anything and everything. Father was stubborn: his favourite phrase was, 'We'll do it my way, whether it's the right way or not'. He seemed not to realise that he was no longer dictating to his children but to adults, who needed to be consulted, not simply told what to do. In 1955, when I was about fourteen, Freddy had walked out after a terrific row with my father and left the business to work for Addison Bulls. I can't remember what the row was about, how long he was gone or the sequence of events that brought him back into the fold. But what I do remember is that this was not an isolated incident; employees were laying down their tools left, right and centre.

As the years passed, my father grew worse, allowing his workers, and in particular his children, no freedom at all. Annoyed by the rebellion of his youngest sons, he threatened to sell off the whole business. Then in 1958,

Freddy at 40 Bondgate, Wharfedale Agricultural Services' shop.

he started to carry out this threat. In the July of that year he sold the coal round to Bob Thompson of Otley. But the arguments continued into 1959 and 1960. In 1961 Ron too was to leave the family business. This was a blow to those who relied on his engineering expertise. Eventually, in 1962, the day arrived when father could hold his family together no longer. He announced that the only fair way to divide the business was to sell out completely. This decision was met with disbelief. I remember it as a very sad period in my life but it must have been much worse for Freddy and Ron.

I was only twenty and had already given five years of my life to my father's business. Freddy had given twenty-one years and Ron fourteen. We were all devastated. But my father was unrelenting; his mind was absolutely made up. He would sell everything, buy a bungalow and treat my mother to the retirement that she deserved. The happiness of my mother was perhaps one of the few things that we all agreed upon. But as the months passed no takers could be found for the business. Potential buyers realised that without the Browns, there was no business. We were the business. During the winter of 1962, an acrimonious compromise was worked out. My father decided that he would sell the business to his sons. Listers, auctioneers and valuers in Otley were assigned to prepare the valuation, and it was agreed that we would pay £16,000. This sum was to be paid in regular instalments as we could not afford to pay a lump sum. Realistically it was decided that Freddy, Ron, Tony and I could only afford to buy what was to be called Wharfedale Agricultural Services Limited. So in April 1963 we opened a bank account at the Midland Bank in Otley, the first instalment was made, and we took control of our newly named company.

We took our new enterprise to 40 Bondgate, Otley. The premises were set in the town centre. The entrance was narrow, and we frequently brought the flow of traffic to a standstill as the lorry drivers skilfully negotiated this daily obstacle. I remember the corrugated iron roof. It had so many holes in it that the rain simply poured through. More rain came in than was kept out. The premises were totally unsuitable but they were all that we could afford at that time.

Freddy, being the eldest, the most experienced and with the most contacts, was naturally the managing director of our new company. Ron was in charge of the engineering side of the business. Working alongside him were Fred Balsdon and Doug Furniss. Tony and I, along with Colin Smith, Tubby Darnbrook, Donnie, Gordon Simpson and Frank Copsey, were the tractor drivers. Many of the old hands did not join us in Otley; for some it was too far, others preferred to stay with the farms. Geoff Ellison was one such. He and his wife moved into Brown Bank and continued to work for my father.

By 1963, all my brothers and sisters were married. Freddy had been the first, marrying in 1948, Winnie was married in 1952, Nona in 1954, Ron in 1961, Dot in 1962, Tony and Gwen in 1963. All of them had left the family home. Even my mentor Geoff, whom we strongly believed to be anything but the marrying type, had fallen in love. This momentous event had happened in about 1959. Romance blossomed between him and the grocery-van girl. It was a slow-moving relationship as they only met once a week, when she arrived to deliver the provisions. Every Wednesday, or whatever day it was, Geoff would cunningly ensure that his work kept him close to the house, so that he might catch a few stolen moments with Jackie. Before I knew it, Geoff too was married. That just left me single and hard up. I had not accumulated enough cash to buy the mini-van I wanted let alone get married and buy a house. Consequently I was given little option but to stay at home. When the business was sold, my father sold Gate House where we had lived since 1959, and we moved to Knaresborough. This was not a pleasant period in my life. My father bore a grudge. He was disappointed that we had chosen Freddy over him. He found it difficult to accept that I had not pursued the farming path that he had mapped out for me and was hurt that Tony and I had turned down his offer. Those conflicts added greatly to the strain of the next two years.

From left to right: Nona, Winnie and Gwen with Dot at the front.

Although not yet married, I was in fact courting the girl who was later to become my wife. Going back to 1961, my social circle consisted of Tubby Darnbrook, Colin Smith, Jim Noble, Keith Newall, George Tinkler and of course big brother Tony. We still attended the Friday-night Fewston dance, but realising that there were a lot of women out there just dying to meet us and being kind-hearted, generous souls we decided to subject the girls further up the Dale to the pleasure of our company. We adopted the Harrogate, Grantley, Pateley Bridge, Burnt Yates, Darley and Dacre Saturday night dances as our new haunts.

On a Friday evening we would finish work at a reasonable hour, go home and begin the gruesome task of extracting slag, silage, and so on from our bodies. The silage caused callouses on our hands, tattooed with the green tinge of the silage. And not only did the skin become discoloured, but the stench was ingrained in the cracks. I would scrub and scrub my hands to get rid of the affliction but it seemed to have no effect. I once complained to my father that I stank and that I couldn't go to the dance stinking of silage. He suggested I pick a farmer's daughter because she would stink the same! Scrubbed with silage repellent, we would all meet at Jim Noble's house. To save petrol money, six or seven of us would travel in one van. The dances were memorable occasions. I remember them being rather like a scene from the film *Grease*. The lads would all line up at one side of the dance hall and the girls would be collected in a gaggle in front of the band. We would stand eyeing up the talent, nudging each other and daring each other to cross no-man's-land to ask a girl to dance.

At the beginning of the evening, bursting with confidence, we would proposition the most attractive young ladies. After being refused we would lower our sights and take Uncle Arthur's advice. It was at these dances that we discovered a group of very attractive girls consisting of Muriel Brockhill, Jennifer Marshall, Susie Atkinson, Trisha Craggs and a certain Liz Holliday. We would come across several of these girls at the various dances we went to and eventually got to know them well. A kind of 'young farmer' friendship blossomed.

The selection process began to take place and I started to court the attractive Liz Holliday. Tony set the trend by marrying Margaret Tinkler, George's sister; Keith Newall then married Sue Robinson; and Jim Noble came uncomfortably close to marrying Trisha Craggs. It was not only Trisha who was uncomfortable. It was the thought of marriage. I still felt too young for I was only twenty. Anyway, any thought of marriage was completely blown out of my mind when Liz announced that she, along with Jennifer, Muriel, and Trisha, were leaving the parochial valley to work in America. The news of their departure was met with a mixture of emotions. I was

My twenty-first birthday. Left to right: Frank Wade (Winnie's husband), Frank Copsey, Tubby Darnbrook and me.

upset because Liz and I had grown fond of each other, and not only was I losing her but also half my friends.

Freddy's entrepreneurial flair blossomed with the advent of the new business. He had established good connections with a hay and straw buyer from Selby called Horace Lamb. He also had contacts in Lancashire with a company called W. & J. Pie, fondly known as 'Wet and Juicy Pie'. The hay and straw business at this time was a lucrative occupation, and we had a good first year. Our policy was to purchase from areas where there was an abundance of hay and straw and then sell it on to areas where there was a scarcity.

Agricultural contracting also went well. The early 1960s was an exciting time in the contracting business as new equipment was being developed. Baling was revolutionised with the arrival of the New Holland baler, which was to take over from the Massey Harris 701. Instead of being able to bale only 1,200 bales per day, the New Holland enabled us to bale 3,000 a day at 6 old pence a bale.

That first summer in business was a good one. Freddy obtained some grassland at Briscoe Rig near Beckwithshaw, about 200 acres; God must have been on our side for the sun shone from the moment we started cutting the grass until the last bale was safely carried away. We were in profit. The money generated was used to fund another Ford Thames Trader 8-tonne wagon. And the winter told the same story. It was a good straw winter and again we made money. The lime- and slag-spreading business also gathered momentum. The Brown brothers had the makings of a successful business but sadly our success seemed to infuriate my father. He had expected us to come a cropper. In his fury he accused us of rigging the valuation, claiming that we owed him more for the business. Harry Walker, of the solicitors Newstead and Walker, became involved. He was on our side but the battle continued. We would have frequent meetings with Harry and after each would feel more dejected. He warned us that all the money we were making may have to go to my father. We wanted to spend it on new machinery, investment, expanding the business, not funding my father's petty and unfounded accusations.

The business really was a bit of a hotchpotch in those early years. We did not plan ahead; we just calculated each day's work according to the weather. In 1964 and 1965 there was little expansion for our priority was to pay our father back. During this period we concentrated on contracting work, expanding our slag-spreading activities up into Lancashire. Here we worked for our old friends 'Wet and Juicy Pie'. Again we made enough money to buy more machinery. We purchased a new 4-wheel-drive Ford 5000. This was a revolutionary tractor in its time. We also bought a new Atkinson lime-spreader. Our lime- and slag-spreading in Lancashire really was ridiculous, for the costs in time and effort outweighed the returns. In the first place it was a long way to go. Every morning Tim Grange, my slag-spreading companion, and I would reluctantly get up and set off at 4.30 a.m. with the aim of spreading 30–40 tonnes of slag a day and were never home before 10 p.m. Our team of four tippers would run in relay from Scunthorpe to Lancashire delivering the slag. We started the contract during the first week in October and by the third week, I was absolutely exhausted. Even Tim, who had excess energy and never stopped talking, was beginning to feel a little drained. We decided to look for lodgings which proved a difficult task. Slag is ground-up steel, rather like black dust. We were covered from head to foot in the stuff and looked like the Black and White Minstrels. If we had been allowed over the threshold to look around the lodgings we would have been making progress, but no one would let us in, let alone offer us a room. Eventually we found a caravan to rent at the back of a transport café in Ingleton, and were there for eight weeks. By the time we left, the towels were black, the carpet was black, our clothes were black and the sheets were black. If the caravan had been a field we would have congratulated ourselves on a job well done.

At this time, our business was really just a collection of seasonal activities. We worked long hours, planning only by the day. There was no structure.

The brothers – Freddy, Gordon, Tony and Ron in mid-1967, just after we had taken on the Zetor dealership.

It was not unusual for Freddy, who was the ultimate organiser, to see wagons back into the yard every night. The drivers would arrive at about 7.30 p.m. and give Freddy a resumé of their day, telling him what they had achieved and what they could have achieved. By 9 p.m. Freddy would be writing out his notes on the Kalamazoo machine. Winding the handle he would produce the copies, one for the file, situated underneath the Kalamazoo machine, one for the driver and one for the customer. Often we did not leave 40 Bondgate before 10 o'clock at night.

Our so-called board meetings took place late at night. We would convene in Freddy's small office above the shop at 40 Bondgate. Freddy thought we were making a good living on what he called our fire-engine work, called out at the last moment to do rush jobs, everything done on spec, that sort of thing. However, we were beginning to think that there must be some better way of running our business.

On the other side of Otley, a new business was starting up, also run by four brothers, the Ogdens. We had started to take a keen interest in their operation and discussed their business during our meetings. Their core activity was demolition. They had bulldozers and tippers, that sort of equipment. Though still in its infancy, their whole company had a much more structured and organised air about it. We thought that we too needed clear objectives: we needed to know where we were going, and what we would be doing in six months' time (even to have been told what we would be doing the day after tomorrow would have been a good start). After a number of meetings, Freddy, who thought there was nothing intrinsically wrong with Wharfedale Agricultural Services Ltd, reluctantly agreed that we should allow a gentleman to come up from London and make an assessment of our business.

Early one Monday morning, our adviser arrived; Captain 'something or other'. I forget his name. His distinguishing features were his large upturned moustache and overly wide girth. For four days he lived and breathed Wharfedale Agricultural Services Ltd. He stayed at some local hotel and every morning he arrived at 6 a.m. to survey all aspects of our operation. He considered our business plan, our accounts, our strategy, our machinery, our shop, our rates – everything. There was a lot of shaking of the head and tut-tutting but we thought little of it. Eventually he drew up his report.

I will never forget the day we were summoned to be subjected to the results of that report. We convened in Freddy's small office and waited nervously for his prognosis. Freddy folded his arms and leant back in his chair. I think he was getting ready to bask in glory, preparing himself to receive the praise, adulation and compliments he truly expected. We were more dubious. Our gut feeling was well founded. The Captain did not break it to us gently or spare our feelings. Slowly and laboriously he dissected the whole business, ridiculing most aspects of it. He couldn't find one good thing to say about it and concluded his onslaught by suggesting that the best course of action would be for us to quit and to find a proper job.

Freddy, taken completely aback by this torrent of abuse, grew redder and redder. He had allowed this man into his company to praise his operation, not to ridicule it. We all felt a little hurt by the Captain's comments, but did not have the temper to prove it. Freddy did. Like Mount Etna he erupted, hurling abuse at the outsider. He was never one to hide his feelings, especially if they were feelings of rage. His concluding shot was unprintable but, summing up, he told the Captain never to come back again. Anyone who has ever experienced one of Freddy's rages will be able to appreciate the rapidity of the Captain's exit. Grabbing his cheque, coat and hat, he scurried from the office, never to be seen again. The poor chap had obviously never experienced such raw temper, nor had he mixed before with such parochial northerners. After he had gone we huffed and puffed. I can only cringe at our comments: 'What did he know . . .', 'What a load of crap . . .', and so on. Looking back, his criticism was constructive. Wherever he is now I would like to apologise for our unruly behaviour. On reflection it was probably the best £150 we had ever spent.

In some ways we did heed his words, but we were slow to make changes then for the business was steeped in tradition and it was the product of a bygone era. Freddy was sixteen years older than me and was from another generation. For all his working life, he had been beholden to my father and to the working practices of that generation. Freddy was the boss, and as a result our objective now was to expand and improve on the traditional farming activities started by Fred Brown senior. I was sixteen years younger, and had been subjected to my father's ways for only five working years. I had not been influenced by his methods and techniques. I was full of enthusiasm and had grandiose ideas regarding the future of Wharfedale Agricultural Services Ltd. It was now 1965 and we definitely wanted our business to go in a different direction, but had not quite decided which. Like many other people, I believed that the 'grass was always greener ...' I would look with envy at the machinery dealers: Tates of Otley, for example, were the Ford tractor, JCB and New Holland dealers. They had an organised set-up: they started work at 8 a.m. and finished at 6 p.m. We were disorganised: we started at 6 a.m. and finished at 8 p.m. We knew there had to be a better way of doing things.

PART 2

Building The Business

CHAPTER 4

Zetor

At around this time, 1965–66, two significant events were to reshape the business. After a late-night meeting in Freddy's small office, it was agreed that we would make our first tentative step into the construction-plant-hire business. Then, after much debate, it was agreed that we should buy a JCB3 from a company in Leeds. This was no ordinary excavator for it had been designed and manufactured by the great Joe Bamford. At twenty-three years of age, I aspired to emulate this 'captain of industry' who started in 1945 building a farm cart and progressed to producing excavators called JCBs. His career is one of the finest examples of British engineering. His picture adorned the construction press practically every week and I had read somewhere that he was in the process of building a new factory, landscaped into the hillside at Rocester, near Uttoxeter. I hoped that one day I might qualify for a tour.

The new machine was, in fact, second hand and we paid about £2,500 to take it on. We were to charge an hourly rate of 22*s*. 6*d*. (£1.12) for its services and I looked upon this new acquisition as my passport to wealth. Having taken delivery of the machine we proceeded to make our first mistake. We took our nice yellow JCB3 and painted it red. Why red? To match our trucks of course; and in doing so, we immediately reduced its value by £500. But in making our first mistake, we learned our first lesson: always leave a machine in its colour of manufacture. The JCB was prepared by Ron. As it stood in the shed waiting to go to its first contract we all waited to find out who was to drive it. It was rather like waiting to hear who had won the Olympic bid; the atmosphere was tense, for naturally all of us wanted to drive our new JCB. I was the chosen one. On the first wet day when there was no lime or slag to spread, I was sent to J. B. Liddle at Stainburn, seven miles from Otley. There I was to practise straightening out a beck. I drove through Otley with pride, grinning from ear to ear. We were now competing with the Ingelby brothers from Arkendale, Les Seed of Summerbridge and the Hesseldon brothers of Pateley Bridge. We were no longer common or garden agricultural contractors; we were competing with the big boys, established in the plant-hire business.

For a country yokel like me, being on his way to do a job for a well-respected man like J. B. Liddle was quite an honour. When I arrived at Stainburn, J. B. himself set me to work. My task was to widen and straighten a stream that ran down the middle of his field. Within hours, Freddy and his entourage had arrived 'for a laugh' as he put it. It is true to say that I had not quite got the knack of the machine or of the job to be done. Rather than straightening the stream, I had cut huge chunks out of the banks and made it meander more than ever. 'The fish'll hurt 'umselves swimmin' down that,' was Freddy's comment. 'A long 'un'll get stuck on bends,' said another. I had to tolerate such banter for three days after which time I had practised enough. On the third day, we got our first serious rehire from Frank Suttill of Burnt Yates. At that time he dominated the plant-hire scene. He got all the work and new entrants like us, who were willing to work for next to nothing to get a name for themselves, had to rely on Frank rehiring them.

In 1966, our plant-hire business expanded 100 per cent with the purchase of an International Drott Trackloader. We put this machine to work for a company called Cubitts on Thruscross dam, about seven miles from Otley. The hire rate was 42*s.* 6*d.* (or £2.12 in today's currency) an hour.

An average working day would begin early and we would work through until 9 p.m., but the machines were unreliable, and to ensure that we had

Our first tracked machine. The operator is Tiggy Drury.

a productive eight-hour working day we had to put aside two hours each evening to make our repairs. Everyone seemed to be putting in long shifts just then. At around 6 o'clock we were ready to eat. Tony, Ron and I would descend on Tommy's café, just down from the Otley Civic Centre. When we arrived, Bill McBay of McBay's Transport would be tucking into his steak pie, chips and mushy peas and within five minutes he would be joined by his team of drivers returning from a cattle-feed delivery to Liverpool. By 6.15 p.m., Victor Ogden and his crew would have arrived and placed their order. The café was soon overrun with demolition men, lorry drivers and contractors.

It was at Tommy's café that I met a man who was later to become a great friend of myself and my family – an Irishman by the name of Jim Kierans, or JPK. No one seemed to know where Jim spent his days or where he went after his pie and chips. To us country boys he was a mystery man who appeared each day at around 6 p.m. He would arrive driving his Bedford van with Sheaf Plant on the side and JPK Plant Hire on the back. Our meetings got to be quite a habit. On getting to know him better it appeared that he was based in Sheffield. Every night we would meet and talk: Freddy, Ron, Tony and myself were fascinated by him. At this point we had little contact with the construction world. We were armed with two earth-moving machines and an inexhaustible amount of enthusiasm but we did not have the contacts to ensure back-to-back work. Jim was the answer to our prayers; he was well established in the construction world and knew where to find the jobs. It became a case of 'you scratch my back and I'll scratch yours', though Jim did most of the scratching. He found work for our small diggers and in turn we found work at Thruscross for Jim's Cat 951 Loader. Not only did our business lives become interlinked but we began to see Jim on a social basis as well. I was an ambitious young man, impatient to find work and obsessive about getting the most out of my machines. Jim with his soothing Irish lilt was a good listener. He understood my impatience and we would discuss the business over our hamburgers and chips. Jim also introduced me to a new circle of people.

In the evening he would sometimes take me to the Chevin End pub in Otley. Moving up a gear I would rub shoulders with the Ogdens and their friends. Here I was introduced to a dapper young chap called John Swale. John was the entrepreneur everyone was talking about. He was a prosperous contractor; he openly embraced prosperity; and he enjoyed the trappings of his success. A flamboyant character, he could often be spotted cruising around the district in his obscenely large American car. People like the Ogdens, John Swale and Jim Kierans enthralled me. I was eager to do better for myself, to achieve something: I had an almost compulsive desire to succeed.

To me, these people were magnetic, and I wanted to capitalise on their wealth of wisdom and draw from their knowledge.

Our business was growing and strengthening. We were working extremely hard but I still found a little time to further my romance with the young Liz Holliday. Our courting was restricted to the weekends, as on weekdays I was always too busy and unsure of what time I would be finished to be able to arrange any firm appointments. In fact, the only evening on which I could be reasonably certain to see Liz was a Sunday. Sundays were reserved for going to the pictures or going out for a Chinese meal. However, depending on the weather, we were sometimes lucky enough to be able to meet on a Friday and Saturday as well. If it was wet, the machines would be parked up early. Then, like Ayrton Senna, I would tear out of the yard, race home to Knaresborough, pit-stop to re-fuel and hose down. Within minutes, I would be back in the car, careering over the back roads to Pateley Bridge. If it was dry (and Liz was a quick learner) she would make alternative arrangements. Eventually, we decided to get married, not just for the normal romantic reasons, but also to guarantee that I lived beyond the age of twenty-four. My hair-raising journeys to Pateley Bridge had put that seriously in doubt.

While we were saving up to get married, we decided to forgo our expensive visits to the cinema, the Chinese meals and the dances. Instead we took up the less expensive pursuit of baby-sitting. We certainly had no shortage of babies to 'sit' for. By this time I was an uncle many times over. Freddy was father to three fine children, Winnie was a mother to five, Nona too had produced five, Ron was a father of two, Dot and Tony also had two each.

It was while baby-sitting that I discovered the Zetor tractor. One night, while looking after Winnie and Frank's children at Highfield Farm at Timble, I was thumbing through Frank's *Farmer's Weekly*. I noticed a small advertisement in the classified section which read 'Agents required for a foreign tractor'. It emerged that it was a Czechoslovakian company called Zetor who were offering the opportunity to sell a unique 35-hp, 4-wheel-drive tractor. I was immediately interested. There was no such thing as a 4-wheel-drive tractor in Britain and I felt that it was a niche waiting to be filled. However, there was an inevitable down side. Foreign tractors were ridiculed and discussed with scorn at that time. The traditionalists were only interested in the tried and tested machines such as Ford, Massey Ferguson, Nuffield International and David Brown. It was going to be like trying to convince a Mercedes driver to buy a Lexus. These people would be hard to convince.

On the Monday morning, I met Ron and Tony at work and showed them the advertisement. They too thought it was a good idea. We all agreed that we needed to expand the business and that we should be open to new opportunities. However, Ron pointed out that Freddy, who was from another era, and a traditionalist through and through, would not be receptive to such a product. To our surprise, however, our fears were unfounded. Freddy was very receptive, in fact he was positively in favour of the new tractor, saying that it would have tremendous appeal to the grassland farmers. That day, Freddy wrote to Skoda (GB) Ltd, Goswell Road, London applying for the dealership. Within four days we had received a reply. The news was good. Skoda informed us that 'the Yorkshire area had *not* been allocated a dealership although they had received a number of applications. We would be considered if we could meet their demanding criteria . . .' Our hearts sank. Only Freddy at this point had had any selling experience. Tony and I had not progressed beyond being drivers and labourers and Ron was still involved with repairs and mechanising. However, we felt that we had nothing to lose.

Ron and Freddy kept the dialogue going and at last, in April 1967, we learned that we had been appointed the Zetor Tractor dealers for Yorkshire. We were really excited. This was another important move forward. However, there were certain conditions to be met. Zetor noticed immediately that our experience fell short of our enthusiasm. They suggested that we should talk to other Zetor dealers, so that we might learn more about the market.

We chose to visit Much Wenlock in Shropshire, first of all, where we were greeted by a quiet chap called Morris Caulfield. Morris was honest with us. We were told both the good points about the tractor and the not-so-good points. Morris said he had sold quite a number of the tractors in the area, mainly to the grassland farmers. This cheered us up as the Shropshire landscape was very like the landscape of Yorkshire and if the Zetor had proved successful in the west, it had real potential up north. Morris boosted us further by saying that the price was good. We would be able to sell the Zetor simply because it cost less than all the other more popular tractors on the market.

However, Morris then proceeded to depress us by saying that the liftarms and drawbars were not really suitable for UK application and that the tractors had a bad habit of sticking in gear. However, he concluded by saying that the engine was first-class. We left, semi-happy and semi-depressed, agreeing not to tell Freddy about the down side as he was already beginning to regret our decision. He had totted up the cost of the new investment and was beginning to ask, 'What if there are no sales?' There was no denying that our new venture cost a great deal. It required investment. For the first time we had to do some planning.

The shop at 40 Bondgate was converted into a showroom which could accommodate two tractors as well as the existing animal products that we already sold. Ron immediately moved to become head of Zetor Tractors. Not only did we have to invest in the redevelopment of the showroom but also in product training, a development which Freddy frowned on. Freddy saw it as 'brass goin' out and nowt comin' in'. He was right, but it was still essential if we were to make a success of our new dealership. Product training involved sending Ron and Colin Smith down to London on a five-day course to learn about the new machinery. Tony, myself and the rest of the men had to work extra hard to cover the money lost through Ron and Colin's absence. At last the showroom and Wharfedale Agricultural Services were ready. All we needed now was our first delivery of Zetors. The tractors arrived: one Zetor 3045 and one Zetor 4011, both E registration. The 3045 was soon sold to a farmer at Thorne near Doncaster, and the 4011 went into our demonstration contracting fleet. It was while demonstrating the Zetor 4011 that I met another successful man and again I was magnetised.

Our first contact came by telephone; the voice at the other end was hoarse and rasping, telling us he was interested in our tractors and asking for a demonstration. It belonged to John Dobson from Carlton near Wakefield, whom I arranged to meet in a couple of weeks' time. In the meantime Ron and Colin Smith loaded up the tractor on the Thames Trader and set off to Wakefield. They came back pleased with their demonstration and full of admiration for the man they had just met. They told me that he was enthusiastic, that he had done well for himself, that he was an achiever and that he believed work could be fun. They liked his outlook and so did I. I couldn't wait to meet him. Two weeks later, he appeared at 40 Bondgate. As flamboyant as I had expected, he sauntered in, greeting Ron and Colin like old school friends and introducing himself to Freddy. 'Now where's these bloody tractors, if they're any good I'll take ten!' he roared.

Freddy immediately took a dislike to this overwhelming character. That first meeting seethed with animosity. John would bellow some witticism and Freddy would respond with hostility. They were like chalk and cheese. Freddy told John that he was 'nowt but a bag of wind', and said 'We've met buggers like you afore, all hot air, you're not gonna buy owt off us'. John laughed at such remarks. By the end of the meeting he had bought a tractor. I'm sure he only bought it to prove to Freddy that he had brass and that he was a man of means. After he had left, Freddy warned us to be wary of such 'noisy buggers'. 'Nowt but piss and wind – that's all he is.' I was not convinced. While I heeded Freddy's words, there was something about John Dobson that I couldn't help but like.

As I have already said, I was itching to get on with things, to move forward, to be a success. I was a labourer with no education, all I had was a driving ambition to succeed and the only way I knew how was to learn from those who had already succeeded. I was drawn to such characters. John was clearly a success, he had achieved. He had an impressive car and a character to match, and was an enthusiast. I was to learn a lot from Dobby.

In the December of 1967, we organised a trip to the Smithfield Show in London. We had had a successful first six months with the Zetor tractors and thought it would be beneficial to take a few of our clients to London for a few days. On the first day we planned a pleasant dinner and a look round the show. We especially wanted to meet the managing director of Skoda (GB) Ltd. Our new tractor rep, Dick Wilcox, a chap who was later to become our Zetor selling whizz-kid, came with us. Ron and I were very excited, not only about going to the show, but about our first public relations exercise. Ron and Dick set off on the Sunday night in Ron's Ford Cortina and it was planned that John, another customer called Harold Barlow and I would follow the next morning. John asked, 'Which car are we goin' in, lad?' I had planned that we should go in my Ford Anglia. 'No bloody way,' was the response, 'Nay lad, we'll go in style, we'll take my Merc.' It soon became apparent that I was not taking John to London, John was taking me.

On the way to London, I became more and more impressed by this worldly man. He had visited the United States and travelled all over the world. He noticed immediately that I had rarely been out of the foothills and decided to take me under his wing. On arriving in London we checked in at the £3 per night Mount Pleasant Hotel and met up with Ron and Dick. Ron had organised the itinerary and had arranged that we would go to Earl's Court the next morning. As an example of how green I was, Ron turned to me and said, 'Now, Albert, if you get split from the rest of us, get a taxi to bring you back to the Mount Pleasant Sorting Office; the hotel is just opposite'. I was twenty-four, going on ten. Once the itinerary had been sorted out, we organised some food and drink; the atmosphere was good.

Harold, our other customer, had lost a finger in some accident or other. When the waiter came to take our order Harold was sitting with the stub of his finger pushed into his base of his nostril. We snorted with laughter at the look on the waiter's face. He could not believe what he saw – a man with his entire finger shoved up his proboscis – it looked like he was picking his brains, never mind his nose. After the meal, John suggested that he would take me to see the bright lights of London. Not quite sure what he meant, I hesitated. I had heard all about places like London. My father had brought me up to be wary of the bright lights, had told me of the evils and warned me to steer clear. Now here was John, my new-found hero, tempting me. I felt as torn as Eve in the Garden of Eden and like Eve I followed the man Freddy believed to be the serpent. Of course London was not evil, town pubs were not 'sinful' places and Dobby was not the 'serpent'. In fact we enjoyed our stay so much that when the Smithfield Show was over, we decided to stay one more night. By now Lizzy had returned from America and we had been married in 1965.

By 1967, Lizzy and I were well settled in our semi-detached house in Otley. It was ideal for me because I was only half a mile from work. Then, in November 1967, Simon was born. I don't know whether it was just us country lads, but our outlook on pregnancy and births was very different to that of the average human being. To us it was not a major occurrence; we had dealt with the miracle of birth, in some shape or form, from a very early age. Every day without exception we had witnessed the birth of a lamb, a piglet, a calf or some other creature. You become quite blasé about the whole thing. I had no desire to attend the birth and have never been able to understand the few who do. Nowadays, more and more husbands and partners seem to want to 'share the moment', some even want to capture the whole excruciating event on film and then replay it to their friends and relatives. Fortunately for me, Liz and I were of the same opinion; she would have the baby and I would go to work. I selfishly expected Lizzy just to get on with it and give me a call at the yard when it was all over. Nowadays such a point of view is considered politically incorrect, but where I had come from this was the norm. On the day of the birth, I stayed at the yard all day and was in close contact with the hospital. Being the considerate father and husband that I was, I visited my wife and new-born son at the second possible opportunity. The first possible opportunity was taken up celebrating at the pub.

By 1968, Freddy, Ron, Tony and myself had begun to settle into our distinct and separate roles in the business. Freddy was still the overall boss, Ron was having a successful time as boss of the Zetor tractor and machinery division, I was becoming increasingly involved in the plant-hire and land drainage division and Tony had become a proficient all-rounder; in particular, he had now added welding and engineering skills to his other attainments. However, despite the appearance of unity, deep rifts had begun to appear in our relationship. There was a time when Tony and I had been inseparable. Now, sadly, that close relationship had begun to flounder. After getting married he had moved twelve miles away to Birstwith. I had moved to Otley, and we saw less and less of each other. He was surrounded with a new set of friends, worked shorter hours, and seemed to become less and less interested in the business. At first we did not know what the problem was and complained to each other, 'Our Tony's not pulling his weight'.

In the November of 1968 there were dreadful scenes. The shit really hit the fan. Freddy would spend long hours trying to talk rationally to Tony, to see what the problem was and to point out that whatever was wrong with his personal life, he could not let it affect the business; he had to pull his weight. Still his unreliability continued. He was arriving late and leaving early, presumably to go home. However, it emerged that he was not leaving early to go home but to go elsewhere. Tony had fallen in love with another woman. The drama intensified. Christmas was miserable for everyone, and things came to a head on Boxing Day 1968, when Tony finally walked out on his wife and family.

Freddy, Ron and I met at 40 Bondgate to discuss the situation, to decide what we should do and of course we came up with nothing except to work even harder and, with luck, to carry Tony through this rough patch. To take our minds off the problem we set to work immediately. So on Boxing Day, 1968, we were working our backsides off, when we should have been at home with our families. We desperately wanted to operate as a harmonious quartet once again but our future as a united force was being thrown seriously into doubt. We continued to give the business everything, while Tony continued to leave at 5 p.m. I think he was really just making up for lost time, enjoying the social life that he felt he had missed out on.

In retrospect it is always easier to understand, forgive and forget. But at the time we were dreadfully disillusioned. To us the business always came first; to Tony it was now a long way down his list of priorities. He had found a new and influential circle of friends and I will never forget the sad day when he announced that he wanted 'out' – he was going to make his own way in life. It was in the middle of 1969. Looking back, I think Tony was forced into the situation. The atmosphere at work had become tense. His days were filled with digging jibes – 'What time do you call this then? Managed to drag yourself in?'; and at about 3 o'clock in the afternoon 'Isn't it about time you were getting yourself off?' These were the more light-hearted comments. There were rows and arguments all the time: it was not a pleasant period. Some of his new friends persuaded Tony that he could do better without us and led him to re-evaluate his future. I think Tony felt that to leave was the most honourable thing he could do.

Throughtout that year, 1969, the business continued to expand as we purchased more plant-hire machinery. Ron became more and more influential. His tractor division was expanding and generating a considerable amount of income. Never the ideal base, 40 Bondgate had become totally inadequate. I am sure residents of Otley will remember those early days when tractors, manure-spreaders, diggers, loads of hay and straw and our low-loader were dotted all over town. When the yard was full we had to find alternative parking spots. Some nights this meant leaving our vehicles in the bus station. Our drivers, expert in the art of vehicle contortion, would zigzag the vehicles in and out of the narrow passage which was and still is the entrance to the yard. On one side there was an off-licence and on the other Curlew pottery. Every Christmas Eve I would call in to buy Lizzy's present and we became the proud owners of the largest collection of Curlew pottery ever. However, one day, much to my inconvenience and Lizzy's profound relief, the pottery turned into a café.

CHAPTER 5

Trials and Tribulations of North Sea Oil

IN THOSE EARLY DAYS, new premises were difficult to come by, especially premises with a yard. However, the proprietor of O'Brian and Richmonds, a Mr Wood, a much respected businessman in Otley, died unexpectedly and his premises in Cambridge Street became available. Fortunately for us, they had broad planning permission which would give us a licence to occupy and carry out our business there. We acquired it without a second thought. But there was to be one major disadvantage. Like 40 Bondgate, in time the premises were to become totally unsuitable. It was a two-acre site bordered on all four sides by terraced houses. The residents were none too happy about our arrival. O'Brian and Richmonds had been a respectable business, starting at 9 a.m. and finishing at 5 p.m. They were horrified to be descended upon by a company participating with gusto in the advancement of the industrial revolution. In those early years the heavy machinery was minimal, perhaps three or four JCBs and the odd Drott. However, as time passed, the construction and transport division continued to expand. Machinery was constantly on the move, arriving and leaving the yard. Repairs would go on well into the night, and the noise was really quite intolerable. However, we reacted badly to the adverse reactions of the residents. When they complained about the noise and pollution, instead of apologising as we should have done, we would tell them to stop complaining. They found us difficult to get on with and now, a few years older and wiser, I cannot say I blame them.

Cambridge Street became the home of the Construction and Zetor divisions. I was the only one to take up residence there. Ron and Freddy chose to stay at 40 Bondgate and so I had my first sweet taste of independence. By this time, the Agricultural division had really taken off. Business was booming and Ron, despite being the overall manager of the tractor department, could no longer adequately supervise sales, repairs and stores all at the same time. Not only was the tractor department growing, the entire business was expanding and becoming more and more diversified; indeed, it was rapidly becoming too much for the three us to manage alone. It was decided that we would have to strengthen the management team and delegate some of the decision-making. This was to be a big transition – a new experience for my brothers and myself. The management framework became more formal. Chris Powell was one of the first recruits, brought in to assist Ron as head of Agricultural Services. We also recruited a stores manager, Gordon Williamson. Uncle Arthur came down from his truck to assist Freddy with hay and straw, and Alan Watson, who had joined us in February 1966 to keep order in the offices, was to take on his new responsibility as office manager. So we were beginning to see the development of a structured business – at last.

In late 1969 or early 1970, the go-ahead was given to construct the Allerton Bypass near Knaresborough. While I had my Drotts and JCBs, I was itching to get into the same business as the Ogden brothers, earning big money with Caterpillars. The Allerton Park project gave me the opportunity. Initially, one of my Drotts was employed on the project but then Fred Parker, a wily old plant man, in charge of the quarry, tipped me off that he would be wanting a Cat 977 for the summer. 'I'll pay you £4 15 shillings [£4.75] an hour, lad.'

This was the big league. With my JCB I got only *22s. 6d.* an hour. We scoured the country looking for the correct machine and eventually came across one located at a company called Seamour Plant at Markyate. As usual we arranged to inspect it on our day off. Ron, Chris Powell and myself set off in Ron's new Toyota. On arrival we met John Dobson the second – a chap called Bill Seamour. He was another suave character, an entrepreneur who came highly recommended by our friend Jim Kierans. He showed us round his workshop but seemed a little unwilling to show us the machine. After a time we asked to see it, only to discover that we had arrived early and the machine was standing, covered in dirt, in the yard. 'When I've finished with it, lads, it'll look like that one over there', he said, pointing proudly to a fine machine to its right.

'How much?'

'£4,000 – I'll recondition it, paint it and deliver it to site – it'll be like new', he added, noting our look of despondency.

We needed a machine for the following Monday, and there was no way he could have the machine ready by then. Suddenly I saw Bill Seamour, the salesman, at work. Bill had built his reputation on nothing being a problem. When we told him that we needed the machine for the following Monday, the inevitable response came,

'No problem, I'll lend you a machine for Monday and I'll have this one ready in three weeks' time.' On that note, he held out his hand, a firm handshake and the deal was done.

On the way back, we worried: was he genuine or would we be disappointed? JPK assured us that Bill Seamour was a man of his word; he was 'no messer'. Bill loaned us a machine the following Monday morning; four weeks later the Cat 977L was reconditioned, bought as seen, no warranty given or implied. The deal had been done for £4,000. It arrived on the Sunday night, ready to take over on the Monday morning from the loan machine. Four hours into Monday morning we received an unexpected telephone call from Tiggy Drury, our operator at that time. He told us that there was 'a hell of a banging in the engine'. On the way to Allerton Bypass, Ron and I filed through our minds trying to pinpoint the problem. When we arrived we saw the trucks piling up behind the Cat; if we didn't sort the problem out quick and smart we would be off the contract. It was soon obvious that either the crankshaft or the conrod had broken.

We had been done. We discussed our options. To repair it would take ten days and this would certainly mean that we would lose the contract. With our farming upbringing we were aware that we had to live with 'the pig in the poke' that we had bought. We had bought it 'as is'; there was no going back on the deal. In despair I went to the nearest phone box in Allerton village and got through to Bill in the hope that he might have a little compassion. I explained the problem: we had had an expensive breakdown within four hours of taking the machine. Bill apologised and told me:

'I'm sorry, I do not deal in machines like that. Get it on a low-loader and have it here for midnight. We'll change it with the one you have brought back so that you can continue with the contract. I'll change the engine in your CAT 977 – and don't worry, I will stand the cost.'

I felt so relieved. Bill Seamour was exactly as JPK had told us he would be. He was a man of integrity and I learned a lesson then which I have tried to follow from that day on. In fact, the lesson continued because Bill still benefited from his course of action. Every time we needed a new machine in the years to come we never considered going anywhere else but Bill Seamour's. A man you can trust is the only sort to deal with. It was such a comfort to hear Bill's reassuring voice in that hour of need that I have tried to follow his example in my business life.

The early 1970s injected fresh enthusiasm. Natural gas had been discovered off the coast of Norfolk and Suffolk. It was a new, cheap and seemingly abundant form of energy and the country was confident that exciting money could be made from this lucrative business. As I remember it, gas needed to be transported from its source in the North Sea to Teesside, to be used to power ICI and other such industries. Pipelines were required and to lay those pipelines they needed construction workers and plant. I would visit the sites often and talk to the construction workers and contractors. The pipeline was being laid by William Press Ltd, who were the main contractors. I was interested in the job and eager to get into it. However, our JCBs and

Drott were inadequate, and if we were to be in the running it was clear that we needed some new machinery.

It was at this site that I first met the man with the answer to our problem: a chap called Bernard Lone. Bernard was the managing director of Akerman UK Ltd and had four machines working on the project. The Akerman, pronounced 'Okerman', was a new type of excavator, developed on rough Swedish terrain. Blessed with such rigorous testing grounds, the Swedes had managed to design a multi-faceted piece of machinery capable of digging in rock-bearing ground. The Swedes had also been the first excavator manufacturers to realise that machine operators are human beings and not robots, that they have the same faculties as the rest of us, and that they actually have the ability to feel discomfort. Until then, the excavator market had been dominated by a firm called Hymac. Hymac had not quite grasped the fact that operators were living beings. The Hymac cab environment was minimalistic to say the least: the operator was just given the barest necessities – a stool and a couple of joysticks about summed it up. Akerman realised that men work better if they don't have sore backsides, so their machines were provided with padded seating. Indeed, Sweden was one of the first countries in the world to think about and provide better conditions for their workers in the equipment they manufactured. For example, they introduced better cabs, a proper heating system for the machine, and also soundproofing, a feature that was non-existent in other machines produced at that time. Mechanically, too, the Akerman was far more robust than anything we had experienced before.

Unfortunately, the Akerman had a price to match this superiority, and at the time I could not see how we could ever afford one. We couldn't afford a Hymac let alone an Akerman. Our JCBs cost £2,000 each. Hymacs were an extravagant £5,000 and Akermans were an astronomical £12,000 a piece.

Akermans were absolutely out of our price range and to have even considered such an investment would have been interpreted as 'reckless, unnecessary and just our Gordon showing off again'. Despite the fundamental problem of price, I did not lose faith but continued to follow the progress of the pipelines. After the main pipeline to Teesside had been completed, the next step was to construct the lateral pipelines which would take the gas to places such as Swindon Limeworks near Skipton and other similar locations. I desperately wanted to get involved in this secondary project and continued to visit the site and talk to the men involved.

CJB (Construction John Brown) were the designated contractors. They employed the same chaps who had worked on the William Press pipeline, the main pipeline, and were now employed by CJB. Again this was all new to me. In the country, working on the farm, we were brought up to believe that people remained loyal to one company for the whole of or at least the greater part of their working life. It came as a shock to see men who only a year earlier had been working for William Press now changing loyalties and working for CJB. These men worked 100-hour weeks, earning really big money during the summer months. Once their contracts had ended they would rest and wait for the next pipeline job. This was a new way of doing business to me.

The secondary pipelines were to be laid from Swindon Limeworks near Skipton to just south of Skipton, a distance of little more than ten miles. But the contractors were going to have to cut through rock-bearing ground before the pipes could be laid. CJB Contractors had two alternatives. They could tackle the terrain by blasting and then scratching out a trench using a traditional Hymac excavator or they could pay an extra hire rate for one of the new heavy-duty excavators capable of tackling all hard excavation – the Akerman came into this category. Finally the go-ahead was given to hire an Akerman and we were to be the sub-contractors. However, there was one slight snag: we didn't actually possess an Akerman. I thought to myself that I would first get the contract and then think about how I was going to get the machine.

The job demanded an Akerman H12, worth about £13,000, but I knew that that was out of the question. There was no way that Freddy and Ron would agree to that sort of finance. The only compromise I could think of was to purchase an Akerman H9 which CJB might accept on the basis that there was no alternative. And an H9 might be slightly more acceptable to my brothers as it was £2,400 cheaper than the H12; that was to be my selling point. Night after night we would sit on the meal bags at the back of the 40 Bondgate works. Freddy would be arguing his corner, saying that any cash we had was needed to acquire more vehicles. I certainly could not argue against that: the transport division was prospering and bringing in much of the income. Ron, too, was against me; he argued that the tractor division needed all the cash we had. I could not argue with that either; Zetor really was 'bringing the corn home', as it were. I didn't really have a leg to stand on. My argument was feeble. We were getting nowhere when I suddenly thought it might be a good idea for Bernard Lone to come along and throw in his two penn'orth: maybe he could convince them. Not surprisingly, Bernard received a sub-zero reception from Freddy and Ron. Our first tactic was to see if Bernard would perhaps be kind enough to lend us the machine, just to see if the Akerman was all it was cracked up to be. Lo and behold, Bernard refused. At this point, Freddy and Ron made it quite obvious that Bernard's intrusion with his 'bloody fancy excavator' was most unwelcome and unless he could come up with a smart idea pretty damn quick, we would not be buying. Bernard could also be described as an ever-so-slightly awkward chap. Ron was allocated the job of 'negotiator' but negotiating with Bernard was a contradiction in terms.

At this point in our business career, everything we owned we had paid for in cash. We were brought up by my father first of all to earn the money and then to buy something with it. Bernard introduced us to the concept of hire purchase. He kept pointing out that the only way you could finance specialised machinery was to buy it on HP and let the machine make its own repayments. This sounded like a bloody marvellous idea to me, and once I had a grasp of the concept I put the idea to Ron. By this point I was getting a little hot under the collar. I had had the contract from CJB in my hand for a week and I still had no machine.

Ron was surprisingly receptive to this new idea. I don't know whether it was his progressive outlook or just his relief that we could find a compromise that would go some way towards keeping cash intact for other activities while satisfying what was becoming known as young Gordon's ego trip. Anyway it was decided that we would buy the Akerman H9 on hire purchase. Bernard brought along a finance company and the negotiations continued. Unfortunately Ron and Bernard continued to misunderstand the meaning of the word. Ron would be saying '£10,600 – that's a bloody joke, Hymacs are only £6,000'. Bernard would retort, 'Well, this isn't a bloody Hymac is it?', and so the 'negotiating' continued. Fortunately for Ron he'd met some awkward buggers before. Through the Zetor business, he had been subjected to that most rare species of 'awkward bugger', the farmer.

As both Ron and Bernard had had to fight their corner before in life, they felt at home with each other. I have a vivid recollection of the day when the deal was supposed to have been completed. I arrived at 40 Bondgate to find John Knipe still sitting in his low-loader in the back yard, waiting for the go-ahead to pick up the new machine. Entering the building I was met by the sound of raised voices: Bernard and Ron were still deep in 'negotiations'. The HP man sat uncomfortably examining the wallpaper. I can't remember the exact words but the general threat being conveyed from Bernard to Ron and vice versa was for one to shove the excavator up the other's arse. Stalemate had been reached. Ron was abiding by the saying 'You never miss tomorrow what you didn't have yesterday'. Bernard was still singing the praises of the Akerman: 'This is a superior specialised machine and you've got to pay a superior price for it – it's as simple as that'. Bernard would not be budged. Ron retorted, 'We'll bloody well manage without it then'. This was getting us nowhere. I decided to step in as peacemaker. Bernard was taken over to my office at Cambridge Street and a compromise was eventually worked out. Bernard gave us four spare Bofors teeth: they were worth very little but enough to oil the wheels of the negotiations.

The contract was put in place and the hire purchase agreement signed. Breathing an almighty sigh of relief, John and I, like Batman and Robin, left at once and hopped into our waiting low-loader. Quickly negotiating the narrow exit out of the yard at Bondgate, we set off to Bradshaws at Wandsford, near Peterborough, to collect the Akerman H9. Time was running out: we needed to have the machine on site by 8 a.m. the following morning. It was going to be a close shave but we managed it.

The pipeline business was to become more and more attractive as our other activities went off the boil. Our tried and tested method of land-drainage was becoming outdated and the Dutch Barth and Van Den Enden machines were taking over. They were capable of simultaneously digging the trench and laying the land-drainage pipe. This was a massive leap forward in drainage technology: these machines could do as much in one day as the old-fashioned method could do in fourteen days. And as the drainage methods improved so the competition intensified and the price plunged. It didn't take me long to become totally disillusioned with the drainage business and I turned my attention more and more towards contracts for laying pipelines for gas- and water-mains. We were also becoming more involved with landscaping. All these new activities needed a new management hand and this time it was to be a professional. So in April 1972, Kevin Murphy, a civil engineer, joined our ranks.

The early 1970s were a busy time in Ted Heath's Great Britain. Business was progressing well under the Conservative government, but they were still trying to come to terms with the effects of the socialist period that had preceded them, when Labour had said 'yes' to anything if it provided jobs. In 1973 came the exciting news that oil had been discovered off the coast of Aberdeen, promising to bring a new wave of prosperity to the country. When the oil was first discovered I remember there was a great need for drilling platforms. The platforms would be constructed in huge dry docks, they would then be floated out to sea and upturned to form the familiar rigs we see today. The problem was that at that time Britain didn't have the facilities for building the platforms: the dry docks we had were simply too small. Holland, France and Germany had the facilities and were duly offered the necessary contracts. By now it was 1974 and we were back under Labour's control. However, and this is the part that has been a constant puzzle to me, at the same time as Anthony Wedgewood (Wedgy) Benn offered contracts to builders abroad he also gave the go-ahead for dry docks to be built in Scotland. What was the point of building dry docks if we were not going to use them? As I remember it, Holland, France and Germany had completed their contracts before Britain had even finished the dry docks. This seemed to me, an ill-educated country boy, a ridiculous investment on the part of the Labour government. The concept of 'employment at any cost' quite evidently had its flaws; so far as I could see, the only gain from such an illogical decision was a reduction in the unemployment figures.

Our gas pipeline work had gone well and by now we had acquired another two Akermans. However, the pipeline contracts were short and in the winter months our Akermans had to stand idle. The discovery of North Sea oil, therefore, opened up new horizons for our earth-moving division. I had heard talk of plans to place a number of oil pipelines ashore at Peterhead and Sullam Voe in Shetland. These would run the length of the country and open up a new era of prosperity for my specialised Akermans. However, to be able to appreciate the benefits later on I would have to survive the period from 1973 to 1974. In 1975 the pipeline laying would be completed and on stream but until then we would not receive a penny. The result was a serious cashflow problem and our first brush with receivership.

In the meantime, in order to keep our trucks and excavators busy we decided to take our first shot at bulk excavation work. Our initial small contracts went well and our success injected us with the enthusiasm to carry on. We were keen to find more work and before long found ourselves involved in a joint venture scheme with some Pakistani contractors from Manchester. The project was to work on the M62 out of Goole. Working as subcontractors, we were again successful and this project led us on to the next. The Manchester company and our team were to be sub-contracted on the Renfrew Bypass outside Glasgow. For one reason or another the Manchester company was dismissed from the site. Balfour Beatty, who were the main contractors, then invited Wharfedale's earth-moving division to undertake the main earth-moving contract. After much discussion and negotiation with the site manager, Don Monroe, Kevin Murphy and I decided to take on the main contract. I can only thank God that the bypass was not one yard longer for that extra yard would almost certainly have taken us to bankruptcy.

The whole project was a shambles for us. It rained every other day that summer and as a consequence our earth-moving was hopelessly inefficient. We lost a tremendous amount of money. I would retire to bed at night almost in tears. Initially, Balfour Beatty were unsympathetic to what they took to be our incompetence: However, as the summer progressed and the bad weather continued, Alistair Chalmers and Bob Rankin became more sympathetic to the plight of the agricultural simpletons from Yorkshire. If they had not taken pity on us, we would have never survived the lousiest summer of my business life. Balfour Beatty ended up owing us £50,000 in delayed payment and we finally settled for £25,000, but at that time it meant survival. Thank goodness that Freddy had had a good summer with the hay, straw and lime business and Ron had continued to sell tractors at a furious rate. Without the profits generated by their side of the business, we would have sunk without trace. My one saving grace that summer was a contract on the M62. We were given a grass-cutting contract on the section between the M1 and A1 with the proviso that we had to get the job done within one week. The contract was to be carried out in time for the grand opening of the new motorway. We managed the job well and picked up our reward of £6,000 – which went a little way towards tiding us over. However, as the winter wore on our need for cash became more and more desperate. The bills were piling up and our overdraft was stuck at £70,000. During the course of that year we had been advised by our auditor/accountant to recruit an in-house finance director to assist Alan Watson. We selected a man for the job and for the first time we received sophisticated financial reports on a monthly basis. The reports were promising and showed that we were actually making money. However, our carefully selected financial 'expert' was getting it wrong! His form of 'creative accounting' was in a league of its own – optimistic was not the word. And when it was discovered by our new auditors Brown Butler & Co. that his £70,000 profit was in fact jsut better than break-even he had to go.

The October of that year was a dreadful month. We had many meetings with Trevor Gurney, the much respected young accountant who had been appointed by Brown Butler to look after our accounts. Trevor had examined every aspect of our financial statements but could not improve our results. Finally, he assembled Freddy, Ron and myself to deliver the bad news. Despite working harder than we had ever worked before the results were poor, and the bank wanted to see us the following morning. However, Trevor told us that while our trading result was lacklustre, our net asset position had not been eroded. 'If you can convince the bank that the Renfrew Bypass contract is behind you and make a solemn vow to return to a stable financial position and restore your twelve-year good business record the bank should be willing to back you.'

The next morning we arrived early at the bank. Mr Bygate, the bank manager, arrived promptly at 10 o'clock. He then proceeded to talk about the weather, his garden, and so on. At this point I thought he was quite a nice fellow. However, once he had got the pleasantries out of the way, Mr Nice Guy became Mr Nasty.

'R.O. [the regional office] has instructed me to call in the overdraft. You'll receive a letter within the next twenty-four hours telling you of this action and in the meantime I'd be grateful if you could hand over your cheque books.' We were effectively out of business.

Freddy was absolutely devastated and so he should have been. He had proudly led our little business without a hiccup for twelve years and here we were with our first setback and all the bank wanted to do was close us down. When he heard the news, Trevor reached for the telephone and rang his senior partner, a chap called Roy Garthwaite. I shall always remember Roy for his sandwich-box. It was one of those compartmentalised sandwich-boxes, the type where you can put an apple in one compartment and your sandwiches in another; such organisation filled me with confidence. An organised sandwich-box represented an organised mind, which in turn told me that Mr Garthwaite would be a thorough and meticulous accountant. Trevor was ashen-faced as he delivered the bank's sentence to Mr Garthwaite. Roy asked to speak to Freddy: he had a wonderful, unruffled, steadying approach to everything he did and immediately calmed Freddy down, telling him to go home for an hour or so and leave everything to him.

Roy then had a word with us. He told us to go and have some lunch and by the time we returned he would have rung the Midland Bank's regional office and sorted things out. Trevor, Ron and I kept a stiff upper lip as we walked out through the back shed of 40 Bondgate, but it was obvious to the group of workers in there that something was wrong. Over lunch with Trevor we discussed what could be done. Trevor kept flicking through our debtors' list. He pointed out that we were owed about £50,000 which was overdue. In those early days, it was considered impolite to go and ask for cash or collect debts; that would have indicated that we were in financial trouble and we didn't want that. For twelve years we had adopted a policy whereby our debtors paid us when they were good and ready, within reason of course. However, Trevor said that it was our only chance of survival and that we could have the money collected within seven days if we really 'put our backs into it'. We decided that our options were limited and that we would take Trevor's advice. We also decided to break another of our golden rules: we would share our serious problem with the rest of our managers. In previous years we had played our cards very close to our chests, but if we were going to survive we would need their help in the debt-collection process.

On the way back to the yard, Trevor rang Roy who told him that Mr Goodison, from regional office, was out playing golf. Roy added that he had left a message with the golf club that Mr Goodison was to ring him as soon as he had finished. In the meantime we summoned Kevin, Alan, and Andrea Crossland, our office manager, to Freddy's office to give them the bad news. Trevor had established that the £50,000 he had estimated was correct, due and available for collection. The atmosphere was incredibly tense as we waited for Roy to ring back. To while away the endless minutes we started to talk about a programme we had all seen the night before. The programme was about an ancient marriage custom in Papua New Guinea whereby the father of the bride reared pigs which were then gathered up to be given as gifts and eaten at the marriage feast, a custom called a 'Grand Mocca'. While we talked, Trevor rang Roy again saying, 'When you speak to Goodison, buy us seven days. We have a £70,000 OD and you can guarantee him that we can reduce it by £40,000.' He finished in typically prudent accountancy terms, such as 'unless I'm being misled'. Within ten minutes, Roy had telephoned us back. Goodison had won his round of golf and was in a charitable mood. He would give us seven more days. We had to collect a minimum of £40,000 in that time to ensure that the bank reversed its decision. Andrea, with her smoker's rasp, exclaimed, 'Let's have our own Grand Mocca'. Now Andrea was and still is a 'one off', a born organiser and optimist. She was the office leader; and we all had a healthy respect for her ability to see the bright side of any situation. Fortunately Andrea realised that time was of the essence. Organisation being her strength, she set about making lists of who was to go where to collect what. We were all filled with a mixture of relief and guarded excitement. It was great to be able to share our financial problems with the rest of the management and to see Wharfedale Agricultural Services working as a unified force. We were all pulling together to save the company.

At Andrea's command we collected our lists. Andrea had written the name of the debtor, their phone number and the amount owed on each. Like ants we scurried from office to office, relishing the new challenge; we knew that we were working against the clock. It was well after 9 p.m. by the time I got home that night. Liz and I discussed the dilemma and I retired after dinner exhausted – more in mind than body. In bed I mulled the situation over: for the first time in my life, I was face to face with the possibility of failure. We had built up a business from very little using our own cash and bank borrowings and here we were facing the fact that it could all collapse at the drop of a hat. We were powerless, subject to the authority of the almighty Mr Bygate and the dominion of the bank. I remember thinking, 'How can this one man bring our livelihoods to an end? How can he rule the fate of fifty or more people?' We had been in business for eleven years. We had paid his interest bill every year. Good old Mr Bygate had made money out of us; Mr Goodison had probably paid his golf membership because of us; and here we were, with our first setback – a short-term setback at that – and they could barely wait to pull the rug from under our feet. I remember thinking how ridiculous it was that one person should have such power to determine the fate of fifty others. I was young, and perhaps could be forgiven then for not knowing the existence of a bank's 'old boys' network'. Naivety prevented me from realising that they might quite relish our downfall, that our loss would be someone else's gain.

There was a plus side though; at least we had another seven days. I lay there thanking my lucky stars. Thanks to Roy Garthwaite and Trevor Gurney, I would not have to suffer the humiliation of watching the Midland Bank close our business, or at least not for another week. I fell asleep with new fire burning in my belly, thinking, 'We'll show them'.

The next morning I arrived at work to find Freddy gloomy and despondent; his pride had taken an unnecessary bashing. He was worrying about how he was going to pay the farmers in the Selby area for the hay we had collected only a week before. It was a justifiable worry because the hay and straw business was an essential part of our company and we did not want to upset the farmers or give them any inkling of our current financial problems. If the secret got out, he feared that our forage business would be finished.

Freddy and Ron quite obviously wanted to wring my 'bloody neck'. 'If it hadn't been for your bloody Scottish job, we wouldn't be in this mess. We should have stuck with lime and slag – you and your wretched fancy ideas.' What they forgot was that although I was the first to bring the Renfrew Bypass job to their attention, the decision to go ahead with the contract was a democratic one; we were all responsible for it. The plant-hire business had earned us good money in 1972 and 1973 but between 1973 and 1975 work had been in short supply. The problem was created by the gas pipeline work finishing two years before the oil pipeline work started. This vacuum had really knocked the wind out of our sails.

At 9 a.m. Andrea arrived. She gave us a scolding and put a stop to our nonsense. 'Stop blaming each other and get on with collecting the cash', she exclaimed. Under her command, we were marshalled like troops. Kevin Murphy was dispatched to Rotherham Borough Council. I can remember us saying, 'How the hell can you ask a council for a cheque?' In those days, it just was not the done thing. Anyway, Kevin did and we got our money.

By the end of the first day, we were pleased with our offering. Kevin was the star. He had collected a long-awaited cheque from Rotherham for the construction of the Herringthorne playing-fields and the rest of us had bits and bobs which added up to a first-day total of about £11,000.

I can't remember who it was, Andrea, Trevor or Alan Watson, who spotted what was to be our saving grace. It was a detail that had been overlooked by the bank, and it was to preserve our credibility and keep the vultures at bay. When Mr Bygate had visited us and called in the overdraft of Wharfedale Agricultural Services Ltd, he had not mentioned our small transport company, Fred Brown (Norwood) Ltd. We still had the cheque books and we were in credit. To us Wharfedale and Fred Brown (Norwood) Ltd were all one company, though legally they were not. However, we decided that if we did get pressure from those demanding money, we saw no reason why we could not pass cheques from this company. Sure enough the telephone started ringing, the farmers were wanting payment for the loads of hay and they had heard rumours that we were 'as good as knackered'. 'I don't know where you've heard that . . . cheques are in the post' was Freddy's casual reply. Rumours were quashed and our credibility remained intact.

While all this activity was going on, I still couldn't believe what was happening to our little business. The removal of our cheque books, even though we were doing all in our power to draw in our debts, brought us perilously close to destruction. Fred Brown Ltd provided us with a lucky escape route but I still couldn't accept that one person had the right to destroy our livelihood in this way. By the end of the week, we felt we had experienced life on death row. On day seven, the date of the proposed execution, we learned that our appeal had been heard and accepted: we were pardoned. Mr Bygate was given a sum in excess of £50,000 and our overdraft was down into the bottom half of the facility, with Fred Brown Ltd actually in credit. Wharfedale Agricultural Services Ltd had survived to see another day.

During that decisive week, Trevor had finalised the accounts and hastily arranged a meeting with Mr Bygate and Roy Garthwaite, the aim being to discuss what could be done for Wharfedale. Our rapid expansion over the previous few years had meant that we were permanently scratching the top of our overdraft limit and the bank had clearly got the wrong impression, jumping to the conclusion that we had run out of our own working capital and that we were hiding losses far greater than we were admitting to.

Trevor assured the bank that in future he would vet all our accounts. Moreover, we assured them that we would return to profitability and that the loss-making contract was well and truly behind us. And Roy assured them that he would oversee the whole process. His calming influence clinched it. We were allowed to carry on business with a severe reprimand and a reduced overdraft. I saw it as a bridge to cross, a milestone in the maturing of our business: one day a small blacksmith's shop, the next a factory. To cope with the growth you have to adopt new systems. From this bad experience we learned a very important lesson; a business is not just about finding the work and making the sales, it is also about fund management, knowing exactly what is being received and what is going out. Alan Watson was again in control of the day-to-day accounts. Brown Butler ensured on a monthly basis that the figures were meaningful and correct. We were determined never again to go through that appalling experience which had brought the company to the very edge of ruin.

Business proceeded cautiously. As my department was to blame for our near-downfall it was decided that to save cash, the hire purchase on one of my machines would not be paid for three months. Freddy felt strongly about the whole issue, saying, 'If they don't bloody well like it, they can take the bugger away'. Fortunately Declan Wyer at Allied Irish Finance had a sympathetic ear and left the machine with us during this difficult period.

By 1975 the bells of prosperity rang out in the construction sector. The oil boom had lifted the country and while at first there was no pipeline work to be done, Shetland needed airfields, and the local infrastructure had to be changed. The supply of machinery for available hire was soon exhausted in Scotland and contractors were looking further afield to meet their sub-contracting needs. A new Cat 977L, which we had had on order for over a year (the usual waiting period in those days), was at last ready for collection. This news would have been met with excitement had it not been for the other news that the bank would not allow me to take charge of the machine and that I would have to find another buyer for it immediately.

In fact, this was not a problem for there was a ready market for Cat equipment in Saudi Arabia. I arranged to pick the Cat up from Glasgow and have it taken to my friend Bill Seamour at Markyate, who would relieve me of my problem for a small profit. However, such easy solutions rarely go according to plan. The Cat was ready but the export to Saudi was not so my plan had to be shelved. Despite this setback, I popped up to Glasgow to have a look at the machine. I then decided to put an alternative plan into action, travelling north to Aberdeen and Peterhead in search of work on the Scottish oil pipelines. It was through sheer luck that, while looking for a hotel that night, I met a man called Alec Morton. He had just returned from the Shetland Islands where he had received a contract to supply machinery for constructing Sumburgh airport. This work was to keep him busy night and day throughout the winter months. Alec needed another machine and offered me £9 an hour for my Cat 977L. The machine would work twenty-four hours a day, seven days a week. In bed that night I worked out that within six months it would be paid for. I was convinced that we should grasp the opportunity but what would Freddy and Ron say? On returning to Yorkshire, I broached the subject carefully and received a surprisingly good reception. I worked out that the machine would cost £21,000 new and with Wedgy Benn's grant of 20 per cent, only available in Scotland, this initial price would be reduced to £16,000. I pointed out to Freddy and Ron that by putting the machine on hire purchase we could actually start off with more liquid cash in the bank than we would have without it. Freddy and Ron were all for it; the Saudi order had not come through and we simply had to do something. So the machine was duly shuttled from Aberdeen to Shetland and so began one of our company's most prosperous periods.

CHAPTER 6

Back to Socialism

THE FOLLOWING YEAR the national economy was flat, the Saudis, or more precisely the OPEC nations, had got their heads together in what seemed at the time a bid to crucify the rest of the 'oil supping' world. Overnight they doubled the price of oil, and petrol was rationed as prices shot skywards. The result was upwardly spiralling inflation: Britain was apparently bleeding to death.

Under Harold Wilson's Labour government, oil had to be brought ashore as fast as possible regardless of cost. We couldn't afford the Saudi oil so we had to get our own. As inflation gathered pace, the construction companies carrying out their 'bread and butter' work got into desperate straits. Motorway and bridge construction was carried out on fixed-price contracts. Unfortunately, while the price of materials escalated, the price of the contracts did not. Contractors were carrying out jobs at a massive loss and there was nothing they could do about it: they simply could not survive. Two of Britain's largest road-building companies were teetering on the edge of bankruptcy, and it was predicaments like this, coupled with the arrival in Britain of the International Monetary Fund demanding to know what the Chancellor intended to do about the overheating economy, that made the government department dealing with future works pull its socks up. Politicians brought in what was called the Baxter Formula. This allowed contractors to calculate their accelerating material costs on a monthly basis and then pass them on to the government through their contract prices. But unfortunately this led to further inflationary pressures.

At the time, I was convinced that the Labour government of 1974 had got it all wrong. It seemed to me that Harold Wilson, through his grant system, was simply making the rich richer and the poor poorer – at least in the short term. Of course under a true socialist system, any wealth created is taxed back two years later. Equipment companies moved from areas where there were no development grants to areas where there were. The net effect was that twenty jobs were created in Newcastle while twenty people lost their jobs in Birmingham. To move to development areas was only common sense. Companies that didn't take advantage of the situation went bust. They could not compete with the artificially low equipment costs of their competitors in Newcastle and Scotland.

There were plenty of capitalists only too willing to exploit the grant system and I too learnt how to play the game. By 1975–76 the whole system was completely out of hand. Every day imported Swedish, German, French and, to a much lesser extent, Japanese machines arrived at Britain's docks. Wheeled on to low-loaders, they headed for the far north up the A1 in order to continue laying the never-ending oil pipelines from the North Sea. Initially a machine could be bought for, let us say, £25,000. At that time, finance companies were bursting to lend money, as they always do in the middle of the sort of boom/bust cycle that we are all now familiar with. You could buy these machines for, say, two months' hire purchase payments in advance and thirty-six instalments, with, let us say, a £1,500 deposit. All you had to do then was to fill in the famous Department of Trade and Industry grant form claiming that your machine was working in a development area and hey presto – two weeks later you received a cheque for 20 per cent of the overall cost, which in this case would be £5,000. The net result, after having put down a £1,500 deposit, was a bank balance that was £3,500 better off. By the spring of 1976, the sharks really began to move in. Both equipment suppliers and buyers had cottoned on to the fact that nobody was controlling this wave of machinery buying so why not 'up' the price of the machine and 'net' a bigger grant. Why not book a machine costing £25,000 for £50,000 and pick up a grant cheque for £10,000. Before the end of the summer of 1976, every Tom, Dick and Harry rolled up in Scotland with his £25,000 excavator booked in at £75,000 and contributed still further to the escalating inflation. I remember one of my first Akerman H11s, which I had bought for £11,000 in 1973, second-hand from John Bradshaw, actually appreciating in value. I sold it back to Sweden for £15,000. The country boys from Norwood had never made money like this before. Despite the problems in the rest of the economy, we were experiencing 'boom time'. The little Brown empire was having a fresh flush of prosperity, and I was attracting a small fan club again. Even Trevor Gurney had offered me his vote of confidence.

Every three months or so I would go on my rounds up to Shetland and into Aberdeen to convene a five-minute meeting to put up the hire rates of my ten or so machines. In two years we had gone from near bankruptcy to being quite wealthy individuals. We could have expanded at a much greater rate. But our expansion was cautious, unlike the growth of companies such as the Ogden brothers, Road Plant of Rawdon, Bace from Middlesbrough, and Hughes of Doncaster. These companies had taken real advantage of the gas and oil boom period, financing huge fleets of equipment to work on the Shetland Islands and Orkney as well as throughout Scotland. Unfortunately for many it was to end in tears.

By the late 1970s, the economy was sliding into the dip of the eight-year cycle and the downturn was once more upon us. Hughes, Road Plant and many others fell into the open jaws of the receivers. One of the few exceptions were the Ogden brothers. Theirs was a well-run outfit, led by the eldest brother Robert. We used to say that once a pound note got into Robert's hand it was there for good; every pound became a prisoner in the Ogdens' account. Once the downturn came, and it did with a crash in 1978, the Ogden brothers were able to get rid of their redundant fleet of equipment by distributing it around the world. We had a bit of a rocky ride but were able to find work here in England on water contracts or by doing jobbing work on the post-boom contracts in Scotland. The work was steady and we were still in business. While my department was only jogging along, Freddy's was doing well, his transport division had begun to move away from the drudge and sheer hard work that went with the hay and straw business into the more lucrative world of heavy low-loader transport. This proved a popular move forward – it was easier to plan for and more financially rewarding. Ron's tractor division was also doing well. The Zetor that had been the butt of so many jokes in the late 1960s and early 1970s had stood the test of time; by the late 1970s, sales were at boom proportions. For the first time ever, the small Brown brothers empire was beginning to give us all a good standard of living. We each had a Mercedes car. So as not to be too 'over the top' we had manuals, rather than automatics; we said we'd get an automatic next time. Our next objective was to maintain, if not improve on, this standard of living, the standard that had been provided by North Sea oil.

By 1977, we knew that it was time for change again. At 40 Bondgate we were bursting at the seams with Freddy's ever-expanding transport fleet and Cambridge Street looking like Liverpool docks, with excavator jibs stuck up all over the yard. The neighbours at both 40 Bondgate and Cambridge Street were growing increasingly intolerant; day in day out our 70-tonne low-loaders would rattle their way through the housing estate.

Looking back, the 1970s were an exciting time. We went from prosperity to near bankruptcy and back to prosperity all in the space of ten years. Like my business life, my personal life also had its inevitable ups and downs. We lived on a housing estate full of normal people working normal hours and living normal lives. Lizzy grew increasingly sick of my long hours. By 1970 Tina had been born. She brought up the children singlehandedly with the support of Tony and Doreen, our extremely kind neighbours. I kept promising Lizzy that these long hours would pay off in time. The harder I worked the sooner we could afford to buy a house in the countryside where we both belonged. We were both restless to get away from the town but at that time the natural environment, open fields and rural life, was available only to the very rich. As farmers or farm labourers, which is really what we were, we fitted neither in the town nor with the landed rich.

However, to our surprise, a country house came up for sale on the Chevin, a large hill to the south of Otley. The house was not exactly in the country but nor was it in the town; it would have been a good stepping stone. After looking round the place, Liz and I decided that we would buy it. We bargained with the owner and got the price down from £10,000 to £9,750, way beyond our means. But we decided that by cutting out non-essentials, we could manage. Besides, the sheer pleasure we would gain from being 'sort of' in the country would more than outweigh the fact that we were going to have to cut back. It was decided that Liz would take care of the 'move' and I would carry on putting in my long hours to make sure we could afford our new abode. Unfortunately our house buying coincided with the onset of the much publicised trend of 'gazumping'. About four days before we were due to move, I began to suspect something was wrong and called in to see the seller, whereupon he announced that someone had offered him £10,000. If I was willing to give him more than that, I could have it. There was one element of my strict upbringing that I treasure to this day. My father always taught me that if you shake hands on a deal, you must without question, while it is within your power to do so, honour that deal. Our man was going against this principle and I did not respect nor like him for it. I was angered and torn. I did not want to give this man the satisfaction of offering him more money and yet I knew that Liz would be heartbroken by the news that we had lost the house. I couldn't believe that this man would do this to us, a young couple, for the sake of £250.

In a fit of rage I told him where he could stick his house and hoped that, one day, someone would do to him what he had done to us. I went home and told Liz; she took it well and we decided to carry on with our search for a country house. With that, we packed our bags and took off for a weekend to Blackpool. Having well and truly drowned our sorrows we settled back into 23 The Whartons, next to Tony and Doreen, where we were to stay for another three years. House hunting was put on hold not only because we could not find the affordable place of our dreams but also because by 1974 we were in the middle of our gas and oil pipeline vacuum and decided that it was not such a good time to be spending so much money. However, we were eager to take advantage of the price escalation, and as a short-term measure we moved out of 23 and into 31 The Whartons. The new house cost us £14,000 and we sold our old one for £9,500. The idea of the move was to keep in touch with house prices inflation so that we could eventually afford the house that we really wanted. Unfortunately

1975 put paid to a lot of our plans. It was a traumatic year for both my business and personal life. We planned another child but the house move, the near bankruptcy of the business and the death of Lizzy's mother meant that our third child never arrived.

After we had got settled into number 31, I became very restless. I desperately wanted to participate in some sort of sport. A team sport was out of the question, because with my irregular working pattern I could never guarantee that I would be able to turn up. I needed a sport that would involve predominantly me. It was at this time that I first discovered that most dirty but exhilarating of sports, stock-car racing. John Hillam, a business friend of Ron's, was a keen follower of the sport. The more I spoke to him the more I got a taste for the racing. On the face of it, it would fit my lifestyle perfectly. We already had the truck to carry the stock car around and the engineers in the agricultural department could see to the repairs. That would not be a problem because they were all keen enthusiasts.

At this time, Formula One stock-car racing was very popular among the working class of Yorkshire and Lancashire. What had been a poor man's sport in the 1960s had developed into a big crowd puller by the 1970s. The races were held at stadiums such as Belle Vue at Manchester, Odsal Top at Bradford and stadiums at Leicester and Northampton. As the sport took off, the crowds grew and with the added interest came more sophisticated machines. When I started racing, there were some real stars pushing the sport along. Stuart Smith was one of the major pioneers. With the encouragement and backing of his father he had developed a new concept of car. Instead of driving a converted car with bumper bars, he and others introduced the first specially made vehicle. The new-style stock-car had an American V8 engine, a truck gearbox and a 3-tonne-van back-axle. The new beast could race round Belle Vue stadium twice as fast as the old cars.

The sport was run by BRISCA – the British Stock Car Association – which ran a league table listing drivers under five grades. Novice drivers started out as white tops. Once you were no longer a danger to yourself or to others and had finished a few races you became a yellow top, followed by blue tops. At the higher end of the scale there were red tops and then there was the reigning champion, the gold top. The roof of the car was painted with the colour depicting your grading. After watching a few races I decided that this was the sport for me and after a tip-off from John Hillam I bought my first car.

I bought the car from a chap at Wakefield called Nigel Mellor. My hastily recruited 'racing team', featuring Martin Greenwood as chief mechanic and Stuart Fozzard as tyre and petrol man, 'did up' the car and painted the top white to denote my novice status. In the mid-1970s the sport was at its

Stock-car racing days.

height. Otley had its own stock-car fan club which met monthly and followed the drivers to every event. I remember my first race – it was at Rochdale and I was jittery with nerves. The gold and red tops were treated like royalty as usual while the poor unfortunate white tops had to queue up outside on the street. At the first race I went to I had not entered, so along with all the other novice hopefuls I had to wait for Mr Parker of Parker Promotions, the promoter at the stadium, to come down the street and inspect the car. If it was in a bad state or dirty he would send you home; after all, he was paying us to attend.

Once accepted and safely assembled in the pits there was still one more hurdle to overcome before I was allowed on to the track. Queuing up outside the start gate I had to wait for the gate man to give me permission to enter the race. He was not obliged to let me race as I was not entered in the programme. However, after a good deal of foot-kissing and grovelling, I was allowed on to the grid to take part in my first race. Quaking on the back row I revved my engine, waiting for the flag to be dropped. I posed little threat to anyone other than myself on that first race. Out of sixteen cars, at least one third were casualties, with two cars finishing the wrong side up and one on fire. It was a pretty sensible sport really. By some miracle, I made it through to the consolation race and survived to see another day.

On the way home, I recounted every detail of every lap to anyone within earshot, embellishing the story every time. Ten renderings later, as we drew into Cambridge Street, I had successfully managed to brainwash everyone into believing I was Alain Prost the second. I had developed my own little fan club and managed two more races that season to the chant of 'round the bend and up the straight Gordon Brown in 338'.

CHAPTER 7

One More Hour at Heathrow

By 1977, I was thirty-five years old and becoming increasingly restless with my working life. The Scottish oil pipeline boom had introduced us to a larger world, an intoxicating world full of opportunities, a world outside the Washburn Valley. We had developed a taste for the finer things in life and had no intention of regressing. I wanted to expand, move forward, take calculated risks. After the cashflow problems of the early 1970s, we had progressed slowly and carefully. We had been wise to do so, as we had protected ourselves, unlike many others, from the inevitable slump. Despite this security, my division had reached a plateau, caused by a slowdown in the pipeline business. As a result, I was finding it increasingly difficult to get work for my specialist Akerman excavators. I realised that my division was in need of a change of direction, a new focus, and that I would have to start looking for a different and more lucrative form of work. What exactly that would be I was not quite sure.

Sitting in my office, in the early summer of that year, I pondered on the future of Browns, thinking particularly of my division. I could go deeper into the earth-moving business but that was not a prospect I relished. After all, as a sub-contractor, I would have given myself an earth-moving life expectancy of three years, followed by a quick but painful demise at the hands of a major contractor, and I certainly was not prepared to fall into that trap. While considering my alternatives, I was disturbed by the phone. At first, I dismissed the call as unimportant – just another dealer out to find cheap equipment. I had no way of knowing how the man at the other end of the line had the capacity to reshape my life. He announced himself as Arndt Jacobsen, a Norwegian from a place I had never heard of before:

'Good morning, Gwardon Brown?', he enquired.

'Speaking.'

'Just the man I want to speak to. I heard you had some Akerman excavators for sale. I might be interested. What can you tell me about them?'

By late afternoon he was seated in my office. I learnt that he was a small contractor from Roadburg, a little town north of Oslo. He was travelling around England to see if he could find some good machines and heard that I had some excavators for sale. On arriving, he handed me his business card and glancing down I noticed an illegible logo embossed at the bottom.

'What's this then?' I said, pointing to the logo.

'Moxy.'

'What the hell's a Moxy?' I joked.

This seemingly insignificant conversation was to mark the beginning of the best and worst years of my life.

We discussed the machine and I learned that it was manufactured in a small town called Molde, on a fjord on the coast of Norway. Arndt told me that the factory was newly built using government money. Molde was a redevelopment area and the Norwegian government was trying to bring work and jobs to the region.

I was intrigued by this apparently unknown product, and was eager to know more. Perhaps I could buy two for my plant-hire fleet. Much to my surprise, I found myself asking Arndt about the UK dealership arrangements; cogs were beginning to turn. Arndt finally left my office several hours later promising to post some information on to me.

Ten days passed before I received the promised brochure. Before examining it I read a note from Arndt which he had attached to the front: 'Gordon, here is the information as promised. I hope it is of interest. I've been in touch with the factory and you should get yourself over to Norway to see these machines. Look forward to hearing from you – Arndt Jacobsen.'

I mulled over the brochure and got used to the idea that this dumptruck should be taken seriously despite its 'Mickey Mouse' name. The more I looked and the more I read, the more impressed I became. A Moxy would be a sensible addition to my fleet. I was impressed by the fact that it had a 6-wheel drive. The competition produced only 4-wheel-drive dumptrucks, except for one with a patchy reputation called Nordverk. The Moxy was innovative and worth my attention. I would visit the factory.

I went round to see Ron at the tractor showroom straight away. He was receptive; Freddy was less so and was not impressed by my rather impulsive decision to visit the factory in Molde. His negative reaction was understandable. In the family business cash was now carefully controlled and distributed, especially after our relatively recent cashflow scare. Freddy could not justify my 'whimsical' desire to blow £500 on what he thought would be a 'bloody jolly': it was a luxury that we could certainly do without. Despite my eldest brother's negative reaction, I decided to go ahead with the trip and rang Arndt.

September was chosen as the ideal month for both of us, since work would be levelling off after the summer madness. After the initial excitement generated by meeting Arndt, getting the brochure and deciding to take the plunge to visit the factory, Wharfedale got back to business as normal. But September arrived and I embarked on what was to be one of the most important journeys of my life. I caught the 7 a.m. plane out of Leeds-Bradford Airport down to London Heathrow. We landed on time but were in for a long wait. It was the era of the 'strike', an era when barely a week would pass without some disruption to one's plans. Business in Great Britain had ground to a standstill, held to ransom by the Unions.

As I waited and waited to hear when we would be boarding or if we would be boarding at all, I spotted the newspaper stand, and saw the bloated face and body of my adolescent hero staring back at me. Elvis Presley was dead.

As I waited, my trip was beginning to lose its initial sparkle. Tarnished by a catalogue of bad omens, I had left under a cloud of disapproval from Freddy, the air traffic controllers were messing me about and now, to cap it all, my ultimate hero, the king of rock and roll, was no more. Perhaps I should go home?

I sat for hour after hour, reflecting on the significance of these omens. Maybe Freddy was right after all. Maybe it was an unnecessary holiday, a waste of money, a whim, and 'bloody typical of our Gordon'. By 3 p.m. I decided to give it one more hour and if, after that, there was still no indication that we might be boarding shortly I would head home, defeated. My trip to Norway was so nearly the trip that was not. I was so close to throwing in the towel that afternoon, turning tail and heading back north. I sat patiently for one more half hour. I had convinced myself that Freddy had been right and that it was a bloody stupid idea. Who did I think I was, with my fancy ideas? My one-hour deadline was rapidly approaching and I was ready to catch the plane home when my thoughts were interrupted.

'Would all those awaiting the British Airways flight to Oslo, please proceed to gate number so and so.'

I was six hours late but better late than never. I amended my negative thinking and decided that this was fate, my visit to Norway was simply meant to be. All of us boarded the plane only to find that we were to be grounded for another hour and a half. Perhaps the staff felt that we needed a change of scenery. Perhaps they felt that it would please us to move out of the departure lounge and on to the plane; at least it was a tactic for giving us fresh hope of take-off.

At last, at 4.30 p.m., we received permission to leave. Looking back, I can only ask the question, 'Why did we stand for this disruption?' The strikes were never ending; one after another they came. One day the car workers were holding the country to ransom, the next day it was the air traffic controllers, and so it went on.

Arriving in Oslo at last, I was taken by taxi to the Viking Hotel, where the topic of conversation was Arthur Scargill and the 'great British strike'. I struggled to defend my country: scraping the barrel a bit. In reply to their jibes about how I could possibly live in a country that had Arthur Scargill, I pointed out how nice it was to live in a country where men like him could exist and be tolerated. I then swung the conversation towards football. My one saving grace was that I lived just outside Leeds, so I said that I supported the local team, an impressive first-division side called Leeds United. The Norwegians were suitably impressed. They knew Leeds United well because every Saturday afternoon they could watch football live on television, ironically a luxury not available in England at that time. Later, Arndt picked me up from the hotel and took me from Oslo to Roadburg, his home town, where I inspected a Moxy dumptruck for the first time.

The first thing that impressed me about the Moxy was the 6-wheel-drive concept with its unique rear-axle system, plus the ruggedness of the unit. It had been designed for Scandinavian countries and it was clear that this ruggedness would go down well with the earth-moving contractors in the UK.

The following morning I was up bright and early, ready to sample another new experience. To get from Roadburg to Molde we were to travel in a tiny 4-seater float plane. Despite the fact that I was well into my thirties, I was still a farmer's son at heart. I had not travelled much and this trip to Norway, meeting the locals, flying across fjords and so on, was an eye-opener for me. The journey seemed to take an age. At least there were no air traffic control problems; we simply took off when we were ready. To gain altitude, we had to turn and turn the plane, up through the mountains; it was like a Biggles adventure. The journey was slow but the scenery was breathtaking. By the time we reached Molde it was dark and Arndt flew up and down the water shining his spotlight below to make sure that the water was free of boats. When he was confident that we could land safely, the plane dropped on to the water. However, we were to receive a pretty cold reception from the local constabulary. Arriving at the jetty, we were greeted by grim-faced policemen who took great pleasure in scolding Arndt and fining him for an unsafe landing.

Having paid up, we booked in at the Alexandra Hotel. The following day I was taken to see the factory, considered by those in the know to be a monument built by the Norwegian taxpayer with little regard to market developments. I couldn't believe they were using only a quarter of this enormous factory to produce trucks: it just couldn't be economical.

The following day I returned to the UK, feeling somewhat more buoyant than when I had left. I had liked what I had seen and was eager to get up to Yorkshire to report to Ron and Freddy; I was sure that I could convince Freddy of the worth of the Moxy. I sat on the plane, submerged in a world of my own. My mind was working overtime. One minute I was thinking, 'Perhaps we could afford two, maybe even three units; that would really make something of the plant-hire fleet'; the next, I was dreaming of grander, seemingly unobtainable goals, 'Perhaps we could become the UK dealer for the Moxy dumptruck'. It was barely worth thinking about. How could we possibly expect to land such a dealership? How could Brown's, a small, insignificant firm, operating out of two scruffy and totally inadequate yards, possibly become the UK dealers? How could we compete against the Cripps, the Levertons, the Anglo-Swedish Engineering Co. and the JCBs of this world? I juggled with these thoughts until I was jolted from my reverie by the unmistakable roar of the reverse thrust. We were home.

On my trip to Norway I had indicated to Moxy that I would be interested in the UK dealership, and they had seemed keen on the idea at the time. However, October and November passed without a word. By December 1977, I still had heard nothing. My optimism was beginning to fade and I began to doubt their interest. Christmas came and went and the New Year began in earnest. It was mid-January 1978 before I received the long awaited call. The receptionist popped her head round my office door at Cambridge Street: 'Excuse me, Mr Gordon, but there's a funny sounding gentleman on the phone. I can't understand a word he's saying. I think he's called something like Sven Yellow; sounds like a joker to me but he says he wants to speak to you. What shall I do?'

Bemused I asked her to put him through. The call was transferred and my eardrums came in for a whole new sound sensation. I was subjected to the effervescent voice of Mr Svein Hjelle (Yella), an experience never to be forgotten.

'Hi, is that Gwardon Brown?'

'Hello,' I replied, somewhat taken aback by this forthright individual.

'I am the new sales manager at Moxy. The man you met in September – you remember him, Terje Vargil? He has left now. I'm the guy that you'll be dealing with from now on. I'll be over on 20 February, so get your cheque book ready. I'm gonna sell you some Moxys, the best dumptruck in the world . . .' Out flowed the sales talk in Svein's confident American/Norwegian twang. This bloke had all the jargon of an American ice-cream salesman, he was on a roll and I couldn't get him off the phone. 'This truck doesn't get stuck in the mud . . .' and so on and so on, he went.

Despite the fact that I couldn't get a word in edgeways, I found this Norwegian jack-in-the-box endearing. He was not someone you could feel indifferent towards. You either liked him or you didn't and I found myself amused by him. The appointment was made and our conversation ended. When I replaced the receiver, I found myself looking forward to meeting him for he had put forward some pretty important suggestions: 'I can see no reasons why you guys should not be the Moxy dealer', he had said.

PART 3

The Moxy Era

CHAPTER 8

Meeting a Super Salesman

I SIMPLY COULD NOT UNDERSTAND why Moxy should be interested in using the Brown brothers from Yorkshire as their UK dealer. I also knew that when Svein came over, we would have to make sure that our operation appealed to him, and that was easier said than done. I thought seriously about how to impress my Norwegian friend, but my options were limited. I could have met him at 40 Bondgate, which despite its reasonable offices was nothing more than an unimpressive old tin shed. Alternatively, I could have met him at Cambridge Street, premises with a reasonable yard but with the disadvantage of being in the middle of a housing estate. Neither yard conjured up the desired image of a successful international dumptruck dealer. However, all was not lost. I thought I knew how I could impress this effervescent Norwegian.

At the same time as my introduction to Moxy, Freddy was well advanced in negotiations to buy a storage depot just outside Otley. The Riffa depot, situated on the Harrogate Road in Pool-in-Wharfedale had been a wartime storage base; after the war it had had various uses. At the time when we became interested in it, it was owned by West Cumberland farmers and was used mainly for storing animal feed. Riffa was ideal for us – out of town, with easy access for our transport fleet, and adequate warehouse space for servicing our machinery. To be able to afford the premises at the agreed price of £75,000 we needed to sell our existing yards. This was the only thing holding up the sale, and to my way of thinking, a mere hiccup. Riffa was, to all intents and purposes, ours. I decided to use Riffa as my trump card.

On 20 February 1978 I parked my car outside the arrivals terminal at Leeds-Brighton Airport and waited for the legendary Svein Hjelle, sales manager of Moxy A/S, Molde, Norway. There was no difficulty in recognising him. I spotted him at 100 metres – a larger than life hell-raiser, stormtrooping his way through customs, an extravagant being to whom no one could be indifferent. I quickly escorted him out of the terminal and bundled him into the car, thinking, 'This bloke's worse than John Dobson – what on earth is Freddy going to think!' Here I was again in the company of another Mr Super Salesman. Svein, like John, was someone I took an immediate liking to; but there was an aspect of his personality that took a bit of getting used to – a cultural difference. Svein insisted on calling everyone by their second name. This form of address was not really acceptable in the UK and went down extremely badly with Freddy, who took exception to being called 'Brown'. It also proved to be a confusing form of address when Ron, Freddy and I were assembled in the same room.

I drove Svein straight to 40 Bondgate. Fortunately for me, he had had a couple of drinks on the plane up from London and was quite oblivious to the tin shed as I escorted him through it at a record pace. I introduced him to Ron, Freddy, Andrea, Alan and the others and he slowly repeated their names, using his customary 'Brown, Crossland, Watson' and so on. I then took him to his hotel. We had decided that Ron and I would take him out that evening, and settled on the Queen's Head at Kettlesing, a pub with a reputation for an excellent steak. On leaving Svein I told him that I would pick him up after work, at about half past six.

When I arrived to collect him, I found him as overwhelming as ever. He was like a clockwork toy. I had left him for a few hours and here he was, fully rewound and harassing the staff. He had helped himself to a few more drinks in my absence and was even more boisterous than before. I cringed every time he drew breath. Now I found him arguing with the receptionist: first he complained about his key, and then about his room. He even blamed her for the 'bloody awful weather'. I hustled him out as fast as I could and into the security of the car.

On our way to the pub, Svein amused himself by talking incessantly. In between listening I was beginning to regret my decision to take Svein to a pub where we were known, and to which we might want to return after he had gone back to Norway. Svein first filled me in on his background. He was thirty-two years old and had been everywhere and done everything. He had lived in Germany and America, sold fish, flown planes, you name it and Svein had done it. By the time we arrived at the pub I was feeling totally inadequate. Entering the pub was like being thrown to the lions. 'How on earth are we going to control this bloke?', I asked myself. Once inside, Svein did not disappoint me. True to form, he began to haggle about the beer. He was joking, of course, but unless you shared his sense of humour, you could easily have been offended. He then moved onto the whisky, 'Only the best whisky for Svein Hjelle'.

Ron and I asked the landlord if he could do us three of his best steaks. We wanted to impress our guest and a good steak would put him in the right frame of mind. The landlord, Doug Kendall, was proud of his culinary reputation and only too happy to oblige. We knew he would not let us down. The steaks arrived and were excellent. We could not have asked for better food or better service. He really did us proud. The landlord, pleased with his work, came over to ask if everything had been to our satisfaction.

Before I had time to draw breath and praise his expertise, Svein steamrollered ahead, 'Well, it wasn't the best steak I have ever tasted, but it was okay, I suppose.' Ron and I squirmed in our seats.

Svein did not only succeed in annoying the landlord and all his staff, he also succeeded in dominating the conversations of those seated within a three-table radius of ours. Wherever Svein went he could guarantee centre stage. He told everyone in the pub that he was a Norwegian, pronounced 'Norwigean', stating that Norway was the land of fish and the prettiest girls in the world. By the end of the evening, the landlord, his staff and all those who were unfortunate enough to have dropped in had grown accustomed to this overbearing foreigner who had appeared suddenly in their midst.

The following morning I went to work early and got the day-to-day tasks out of the way – the usual phone calls, mail to sort out and so on. Then I headed off in the direction of Svein's hotel for another dose of Svein. After he had handed over the room keys, paid the bill, invited everybody over to Norway and made a generally rowdy exit, I bundled him into my car and set off back to Otley. On the way I made a diversion passed the Riffa depot, pointing it out to Svein.

'Well, of course, the Cambridge Street and Bondgate depots are only temporary until we get this place sorted out.'

I could tell Svein was suitably impressed.

'I thought the sites in Otley were permanent?', he questioned.

'Oh no, no not at all, we just moved in there until we get this place to our liking.'

We carried on along the Pool road, past the paper-mill and down into Otley. Turning into the Bondgate yard we were greeted by Ron who took us upstairs and into my office; Andrea brought us three mugs of coffee and we sat down at the table, Svein on one side, Ron and I on the other, ready for business. However, ready for what sort of business I did not know. We had no cash and yet we were faced with this man who wanted to sell us two machines at £40,000 each. We were reluctant to accept that to enter into this type of business we would need some type of credit. We knew only cash. You earned it, you saved it, then you bought something with it. My father's motto had been, 'If you can't afford it, don't buy it'. First of all, Svein tried to sell us the machines for cash – we spluttered into our coffee before regaining composure and casually indicating that cash was not quite feasible at this point in time. Svein got the gist and moved on to option B. 'Come on, boys, I can spare you only two machines off my March production line; if you can't pay cash how about a letter of credit?' We hummed and hahhed long and hard. I scratched my head and cleared the wax out of my ears thoughtfully before writing several dummy calculations on a piece of paper, giving the distinct impression that a letter of credit was a far more feasible option than the first.

The morning rolled on as Svein tried desperately to think of some way that he could sell us two machines and we tried desperately to look as though we knew what he was talking about. Doing business with two lads from the country was proving stressful. By midday we were no nearer to finding a solution than we had been at 10 o'clock. Rubbing his eyes Svein declared it was lunchtime; 'Come on, boys, I need a beer.'

At the Hare & Hounds at Bramhope we ordered steaks and beer, and settled down to some lunch. Svein's mind was still buzzing: 'There must be some way we can sort this out. When we get back to the office, I'll ring a banker mate of mine back in Bergen and have a word with my Moxy boss, Hatlebakk.'

Once back at 40 Bondgate, Svein excused himself to telephone the banker from Bergen and Hatlebakk in Molde. He gesticulated wildly but Norwegian was a riddle to us and we had to just sit and wait. Some time later he returned to my office, flushed and enthusiastic. 'I spoke to the old man and he says cash or letter of credit, but I'm gonna take a chance on you two – don't let me down – if it goes wrong, Hatlebakk will string me up – my banker says he'll do the two dumpers on ninety days' credit. Sign me two bills of exchange. I can then discount them and whilst I'm doing all this you get out there and sell those two machines.'

Ron and I were more than reluctant. Before we could even consider agreeing, Svein had a bit of explaining to do. It was time to come clean. I casually asked the question: 'Do you really think we can sell these two units and meet the bill of exchange in ninety days?' There was more to-ing and fro-ing, but eventually Svein won us over. The deal was done and we would soon become the proud, if somewhat ill-at-ease, owners of two 6-wheel drive, 25-tonne Moxy dumptrucks.

Reluctantly excited at the prospect of our new acquisitions, I drove Svein up to the airport to catch his connecting flight to London. 'Don't look so worried, Gwardon, you've bought a good machine. This will be the first of many, many deals. I will make you a rich man,' he joked. He was right. It was to be the first of many, many deals.

When I arrived back at home, Lizzy was waiting anxiously in the kitchen.

'Had you forgotten?'

'What?' I asked dismissively.

'The auction at the Civic Centre.'

'Bloody hell, yes, I'd forgotten all about it – what time is it?

'It starts at 8 p.m.'

I just had time to get changed into my suit. There was no way that I was going to turn up in my work gear as the Yorkshire saying goes: It is no good being nowt and looking nowt.

In my excitement at buying the trucks I had completely forgotten that a cottage a couple of miles out of Otley had come up for sale. It was a cold, bleak-looking place, plonked in the middle of a field with no lane, no water, no electricity, set right on the edge of the Blubberhouses Moor. It was not a cottage to everyone's taste, but Lizzy and I liked the look of it. It was up for auction and the auction was that night. I had already had a word with my bank manager who had said that I could go up to £24,000 but no higher.

After grabbing a bite to eat I set off from The Whartons estate and down to Otley to find that the Civic Centre was packed. When the bidding started, it was pretty soon up to my threshold and I knew that my instructions were to stop, but I decided that I could afford to go just a bit higher. Unfortunately for my bank manager I carried on bidding until the hammer dropped at £28,000. Gordon and Elizabeth Brown were the proud owners of Weston Moor Cottage. I could hear murmurs all around: 'Must be crackers.' 'Nowt but a pile o' rock covered in whitewash' muttered another. All I could think was, 'Bloody hell, I've spent a lot of money we don't have today'.

Liz was worried by the price but excited that we were moving at last. We'd had an eventful day, bought our first two Moxys, bought a new house and to top it all Liz had booked a skiing holiday. Two days later we set off for Austria – a break would do us good. Having experienced our first fondue, our first taste of Glüwein, our first schnapps and our first encounter with third-degree bruising, we returned home ready for the new challenge ahead.

I was really excited about the future. Until now I had made a slow natural progression from farm labourer to agricultural contractor, drifting into plant-hire and North Sea oil; but the Moxy was to be our first big challenge. It was a project that I had sought out myself and wanted to develop.

Arriving back at work, Alan Watson told me that the two Moxys had arrived at Grimsby on the *Sote Jaal.* Straight away I headed for Grimsby to see for myself. I found them perched on a mountain of Norwegian timber on the top of the boat and supervised their unloading before following them back to Otley on the back of our low-loader.

Word had got around that the Brown brothers of Otley were going to import the Moxy from Norway. The managing director of Anglo-Swedish UK, the Volvo distributor and the company that was to be our greatest competitor, was the first to call: 'Too expensive for the UK market . . . No one wants 6-wheel-drive dumptrucks . . . and . . . by the way, did you know Moxy of Norway are broke?' were among a few of the comments that I could remember from that first meeting.

Another Volvo rep contacted me, wanting to know what on earth he would be up against. So off I went to his house in Doncaster armed with my reel of 8 mm film. We closed the curtains and set up the projector before sitting down to the three-and-a-half-minutes promotional film, and thus my Moxy marketing campaign had started. Before the day was out the Volvo rep had telephoned all the other Volvo reps and within the week everybody who needed to know that there was an alternative dumptruck to the Volvo was in the picture.

The trucks were unloaded at Cambridge Street, pre-delivered, greased round and made ready for their first demonstration. Dave Ashbrook, a long-serving employee of the Wharfedale and Brown operations and a man never renowned for his abundance of enthusiasm, was appointed as our demonstration driver. I met him at Cambridge Street and showed him around the machines. I was as enthusiastic as ever: 'So what do you think?' 'We'll see,' came the non-committal reply.

We decided to have our first demonstration in private. Baystons of Aberford were to be our guinea-pigs and our experiment was to clean out their pond. David and the trucks went off ahead while I stayed back at the office to plan the day's work with the intention of catching up with Dave

Weston Moor Cottage on the day of the auction.

at about midday. However, before I had the chance to leave, I received a telephone call: 'They're bloody useless, Gordon, both of them are stuck . . .'

I felt catastrophe looming, if Dave was right. I had £80,000 worth of explaining to do – the trip to Norway, shipping, entertaining Svein . . the reception with Freddy would not be pleasant. I told Ron of the problems and we set off to Baystons. By the time we arrived, Dave, who had sensed my disappointment on the phone, was having a little more success with the trucks but was still totally unenthusiastic about the project. The pond was completed and the trucks taken off the job. A few more jobs were completed but the level of enthusiasm was certainly not high enough to recommend people to pay £10,000 more than Volvo were asking for what seemed like a worse product.

Every night I would sit alone in the Cambridge Street offices and discuss the problems with Svein in Norway. He was not to be defeated. 'I tell you, Gwardon, there is no problem; Moxy is the best dumptruck in the world. Perhaps you are using it wrong. We have trucks in Africa, Norway, Denmark, and we have no problem – no problem at all, no complaints. It is you English boys, you must be doing something wrong . . . I think you need a third truck!' Night after night he would try to convince me that I needed a third truck – but no way could I approach Ron and Freddy. 'Now then Freddy, you know these two trucks we've got – the ones that cost £10,000 more than the closest competitor but which are completely useless, yes, well how about we have another one?' Yes, I can imagine how well my suggestion would go down.

I was beginning to lose hope; I felt a buffoon, I had saddled us with a dreadful, expensive mistake. Then, in the depths of my gloom, I received a phone call from Balfour Beatty who needed trucks to work on a project for the Kielder Dam in Northumbria. I duly sent the two Moxys and to my absolute amazement and relief they were suddenly competitive with Volvo. There was no superiority but at least they were making money, which was pretty essential given our cash resistance at that time. The explanation for their improved performance seemed to be down to the hard stony ground they were working on. Again I spoke to Svein. 'Look, Gwardon, I will send you another truck with different tyres – what do you think?' 'Ok – it's worth a try.'

Ten days later, the third truck arrived. With trepidation, I made my supervisory visit to the docks to oversee the unloading procedure. With churning stomachs we returned to Cambridge Street, pre-delivered, greased round and prepared for yet another doomed demo. Nervously I watched Dave get in the truck and start to do his stuff. True to his word, Svein had put different tyres on – Michelin radials – and the difference was astonishing.

Even pessimistic Dave was excited, I was excited, Ron was excited and Freddy was relieved. Here was a truck that could go places the competition could not possibly reach: it could run rings around the opposition. It really had been a case of the blind leading the blind. Svein, an out-and-out salesman, who knew nothing about the truck business, had sold us two trucks in Norwegian spec, complete with Norwegian rock tyres, absolutely useless on UK wet ground conditions. With our new Michelin radials we had a truck we could do business with; we were ecstatic.

Bursting with our new-found optimism, Ron and I decided to really push the boat out. We gambled on a no-expense-spared day. A reception at the Devonshire Arms at Bolton Abbey was to be followed by a site demonstration at Grimwith reservoir near Grassington. Ron took care of the on-site arrangements while I, with the help of a publicity agent, put out a launch package for the construction trade press.

On launch day we carried a full-page advertisement which compared the Moxy to its Volvo rival:

We have a third more traction,
a third more power
and a third more load-carrying capacity
than YOU KNOW WHO.

The launch campaign was cheeky but its success meant that almost every major contractor turned up at the Devonshire Arms on demonstration day. Serious enquiries were received from all over the country but the first order was placed by Don Swindale of Cleveland County Motec. However, as my father taught us, 'The order's not an order 'till cash is in t'bank'. Seven days later we delivered the truck to a water-treatment site at Green Hammerton near York; we banked the cash and then we celebrated.

John Harwood was our second customer, an eccentric entrepreneur from Norfolk. 'If your truck's as good as they say it is, bring one down here and I'll 'ave three,' he said. Ron and Dave set out, accompanied by our new rep, 'Carrot Cruncher,' a nickname coined because of his East Anglian accent. They demonstrated on a sea-defence project and returned with an order for three. A week later we delivered, and received a cheque for £137,000. I think this put us in credit at the bank for the first time since we had started. After Harwood came JPK from Leeds, then D. C. Lunnan from Ongar, Chris Moore from Haslemere and Buckingham Plant from Silverstone. By the end of the year we had sold twenty units.

At about the same time as I received that first call from Svein Hjelle, I received an equally interesting one from a man called Colin Gibson of Land and Marine. The lucrative pipeline work in Scotland had dried up some years earlier. However, as a result of the prosperous years we had spent up there, we had met a few people, done a few favours and had a few done in return. While working on the pipelines we had got to know a number of international pipeline engineering specialists and other construction and plant-hire companies from around the world. Once the jobs were over, we all loaded up our excavators and dispersed to find new work for our machines. However, work had proved difficult to find in recent years and the market had gone flat. Colin's phone call was a godsend.

After initial pleasantries, Colin began to tell me about the new job he was involved with. He was out in Argentina, working on the Tierra del Fuego project. It was a job that involved piping gas from Tierra del Fuego across the Magellan Straits and on to the industrial parts of Argentina. Colin told me that the equipment out there was totally inadequate for the job. He knew we had done good work in Scotland and wondered if we could send out a few of our excavators to Argentina. Before he could get the phone down I had them on a low-loader to Liverpool docks, closely followed by Gerry Duffy and Jeff Phillis. These two innovative drivers saved us a lot of money in the long run. Part of the contract was that if a fitter were needed we would send one out. However, as it was, Gerry and Jeff never wanted one. If anything went wrong with the machines, they would use their initiative and fix it themselves. During the whole of that two-year contract we never once had to send out a fitter. We had won a low-cost high-revenue job that was to help us through the problems of the late 1970s.

Inflation was now rapidly approaching 'out of control' proportions, though within the Brown Group its effects were diminished by the success of our business as a whole. Freddy's transport business had grown to thirty-five trucks, he was doing well with the agricultural division and Ron and I were succeeding with Moxy and the Tonstad road planers. Another cushioning effect was the implementation of the Baxter Formula which helped to adjust our monthly revenue in line with inflation. However, economically the country generally was in a mess. It was in the those last years of the 1970s that 'my man of wisdom' joined the company. We had known Len Baxter for many years; he had worked as farm manager for Farnley estates before leaving Otley to go to Totteridge to work as farm manager for Express Dairies. However, by 1974 he had decided to retire and return to his Yorkshire roots. It was quite by chance one day that Freddy bumped into him at the local garden centre and Len asked if there was any work going, just light work to occupy him until he retired. Len started immediately as odd job man at Cambridge Street before assuming an even more important role as 'Gordon's man of wisdom'. Every lunchtime, Len and I would spend valuable time putting the world to rights and saying how the country should be run. Len was a real socialist who lived by the word of Maynard Keynes, despite the fact that his entire life had been spent enjoying the trappings of capitalism, or certainly alongside the trappings of capitalism, working for the landed gentry. Len believed that we should run the country as they did in the 1920s.

Despite his state of partial retirement, Len quickly proved that his qualities were a good deal greater than those of a yard sweeper. He could often be seen with a sweeping brush in one hand and a telephone in the other, solving queries, taking messages and sorting out unruly drivers. Soon after we had taken him on, he was promoted to the job of plant manager. Friday night was wages night. Every Friday the operators and drivers would ring up poor old Len to give him his weekly blasting: 'What about me greasing money, Len, and me lodge, and you've underpaid me by three hours and it should have been eight hours at double time not four, and what about this travel time you've paid me? I need more than that. You've paid me short. I can go to Ogdens and get 5p an hour more and what you gonna do about it?'

Once more we were held to ransom by the employees who at that time could demand exactly what they wanted. Wages were spiralling and it seemed that we were powerless to do anything about it. However, Len was not. He stood his ground despite the torrent of abuse that he received from the dissatisfied drivers who wanted more. Every week someone would leave to go to work for Ogdens and every week someone from Ogdens would come to us and replace our deserter. Over the years Len became part of the fixtures and fittings. He often threatened to retire and occasionally he actually did retire. In 1982, for example, we closed down the workshop one afternoon to celebrate his years of working for us. However, despite our various attempts to retire him and despite his various attempts to retire himself, he never got to grips with the fact that retirement meant that he didn't have to turn up for work the following Monday morning. We would give him a big send-off on a Friday and by Monday he would be back again ready for work. After a number of years of this things had reached a point where we had given up trying to retire him. He would still come in twice a week at the grand old age of eighty to tidy up, sweep the workshop and to express his views on the state of the economy, still insisting that John Major needed to be educated in Keynesian theory.

Having got our company's finances straight, I decided, much to my bank manager's relief, to set about putting my own finances in order. Weston Moor Cottage had cost us £28,000 in the form of a bank bridging loan. However, to make the place habitable we needed to spend a further £15,000 on it. I had a problem. I could not raise a mortgage on a house that would not stand up to an inspection for valuation by a building society. I could not borrow any more money from the bank to do the necessary alterations to ensure that a mortgage could be raised. I was in a Catch–22 situation. I suppose I could have borrowed from the company. However, at this time the company needed every penny it had to support its own working capital. One possible solution was to sell our house in The Whartons as quickly as possible and give myself a small pay rise to cover the eventual mortgage. However, this option would leave us without a roof over our heads until Weston Moor Cottage was fit to live in. Fortunately for us our problems were solved by big sister Winnie and my childhood hero Frank. Winnie and Frank had decided to expand their farm, moving out of their old farmhouse and into a new one about a mile further up the road. They agreed to let their old cottage, Ridge Top, to us until Weston Moor Cottage was ready. Within no time at all, we had sold 31 The Whartons and moved into our rented cottage. With the money we received from the sale of our house we were able to do the alterations to our new abode. Whenever I got the chance I would visit our whitewashed shack and watch it being transformed into a cosy cottage. The transformation was subject to several setbacks because of the heavy winter snowfall of 1978. However, by March 1979, the job was complete and we were ready for the move.

Looking back, our six months at Ridge Top was one of the happiest times of our married life. After twelve years of self-imposed exile it was our first taste of living in the countryside. Ridge Top was a picturesque place, smothered in creeping roses with low-slung sash windows, uneven walls, low ceilings and a narrow spiral staircase. Outside there were numerous farm buildings, a hay loft and some huts. Much to the delight of Tina, our daughter, then aged ten, Frank had pigs. Tina would spend hour after hour, perched on tiptoe, straining to watch the antics of the piglets. She gave them all names, always falling for the runt of the litter, who was bullied and shunted, often going to an early grave. Occasionally, much to Tina's horror, one would be killed in the night, the poor unsuspecting little thing squashed by its mother while asleep or bullied to death by the other piglets. Tina would always notice if one was missing and naively ask Uncle Frank where it was. Unfortunately Frank, who was not as sensitive as he might have been to the feelings of an animal-doting ten-year-old, would blast her with the truth. None of this 'Piggy's gone to heaven' twaddle. He would just give it to her straight. 'Runt got crushed by t'old sow.' Tina would be inconsolable for several days, while Lizzy would try to soften the blow, explaining that Uncle Frank had not meant it was dead, it had just been taken down to the other farm. Within a couple of days another runt would be born and off we would go again. With Ridge Top there came an old farm dog called Jill – a border collie who had never quite got the hang of rounding up sheep and cows. She was hard of hearing, a little short sighted and, due to her occupational and physical inadequacies, she was up for adoption. When we moved to Weston Moor Cottage, Jill came too.

Gordon Brown and family, 1992.

CHAPTER 9

The Transition

By MARCH 1979 we had moved. The house was exactly what we wanted: a country cottage, away from the rigours of the town, out in the open. In summer, the garden and marsh below the house became a hive of activity. The moors would come alive with the perpetual sound of the skylarks hovering high above, the distinctive 'pee-wit' of the diving lapwings, and the sedate strut of the curlew. Occasionally, if we were awake early enough, we watched our resident fox returning from a night of destruction to the safe haven of the nearby rhododendron bushes. On other occasions, our garden became infested with dozens of pheasants, pecking their way through the rockeries and shrubs, one eye on their business, the other warily surveying the house. If they were to catch sight of us at the window, they would utter their distinctive warning cluck and leg it down the garden, building up speed until, eventually, in their own peculiar ungainly fashion, they would lift off and glide back to the security of the rhododendrons.

Back at work, changes were taking place. Freddy had undertaken the job of adapting Riffa to suit our requirements. Stan Hawkins was appointed foreman of operations. Hundreds of square yards of concrete were laid and the buildings were divided into three units. The reason for these divisions was not only to divide up the business into its agricultural sector, transport sector and plant sector but also to maintain a division of the salary structures. In the agricultural business, the engineers were operating on a local salary structure. Then we had the transport workers who were commanding a higher rate of pay, and the plant operators commanded even more money.

The division of the salaries caused much arguing amongst Freddy, Ron and myself. I used to justify the high wages for my lads by arguing with Ron that his agricultural workers had the luxury of sleeping in their own beds each night, while we had to live like gypsies, travelling from one major contract to another, living in caravans. Freddy would shout me down, pointing out that his men were professionals with class 1 licences – they needed 'looking after'. Each felt that his division was more important, that his men justified the highest wage and in the end we simply went round in circles.

Towards the end of 1979 the Riffa premises were almost ready, with Freddy's transport operation being the first to move in. The luxury was completely new to his men. For the first time ever they could service four trucks side by side with the door shut and the heating on, instead of operating out of the cramped and damp conditions they had had to do previously. At last Freddy had a truly professional transport organisation. Ron and I were soon to follow with our plant and agricultural divisions. Our new premises were a dream come true. At last we had the premises to suit our operation, for we had long since grown out of Cambridge Street and Bondgate. Riffa was perfect.

Unfortunately, the good dreams were tainted by the occasional nightmare. That year was good for Moxy sales; sold units were high and demand was still strong, but service problems were beginning to raise their ugly head. I began to dread the night-time phone calls from Willie Dalrymple, our manager in Scotland, repeating time after time the weaknesses of the Moxy. The problems were always the same. The market in Denmark had already collapsed, having experienced the same problems as us. 'It's the same problem again, Gordon. The bolts around the edge of the axle housing on both sides of the driveline at the back of the truck – well, they are just not strong enough', Willie used to complain.

As if this wasn't bad enough, we had recurring problems with the pinion gears which drove the bull gears within the Moxy's unique driving-system on the rear axle; they were all made out of poor, unhardened material, and, in addition, the axle castings, which were of local Norwegian fabrication, were all beginning to crack at the bottom. We were heading down the same rocky path which the Danes had already trodden. However, we had already decided to claw our way back up. We had no intention of suffering the same fate. The first action we took was to utilise our young, energetic and enthusiastic service team to their optimum potential. If a Moxy was showing signs of weakness or had broken down, our field service team was there in a trice – distance was no object, day or night irrelevant – we made optimum service our objective. Our opinion was that the least we could do was provide a top-notch after-sales service until the problems were solved.

In the short term, repairing the machines was the answer. However, in the long term more radical action needed to be taken. Ron and I would bombard Moxy with phone calls. At first, Svein made light of the problem, but we persevered, pointing out that the owners bought the machines on hire purchase, basing their purchase on at least 95 per cent utilisation if they were to stand a chance of meeting their repayments. Bodging could only be a short-term measure. Besides, we could not maintain such a gung-ho 'never mind the cost' after-sales service. We were ploughing so much of our generated profits back into the units and we couldn't stand it for ever. I often felt that if Moxy had been manufactured in a country with an engineering background we would not have had these problems. Norway's traditions were firmly rooted in fishing and shipping, not manufacturing dumptrucks for wet conditions.

Finally, Birger Hatlebakk, Serge Burkow, the designer of the Moxy, and Svein boarded a plane to England to see the problems at first hand. They finally conceded that we were experiencing the same design weaknesses as had been experienced in Denmark and comforted us with the knowledge that the factory were working on a more robust design. At last there was light at the end of the tunnel; if we could assure our customers that the design was being improved, and were able to keep the machines working until the improvements were on the market, we knew we could go on from strength to strength.

I really believe that, in those early days, the most important factor in our success was our outstanding after-sales service. When I think about it the core of our customer base was made up of budding entrepreneurs, Chris Moore, Buckingham Plant, Peter Stevens, Geddis Brothers and Jimmy Fenton to name but a few. All these people seemed to be willing us on; they seemed to want to identify with and help our fledgling construction equipment sales group to find its feet. They seemed to like the fact that we were always accessible, and could always contact us day or night. Our business cards always carried our home telephone numbers for we knew how frustrating it was to be told at 5 o'clock in the afternoon: 'Sorry, lad, that's it 'till tomorrow – give us a ring at 8 in the morning, and we'll see what we can do.'

In the construction industry, time is money: our aim was to minimise the frustrating breakdown time for our customers and make them more profitable. They were only too aware of the aloof 'them and us' attitude of 'the big boys', the blue chip companies which lost no sleep over upsetting a few of the smaller operators. Such companies as Levertons, Caledonian, Cripps and Blackwood Hodge had grown fat on socialism throughout the 1960s and '70s. They made safe money out of the nationalised industries such as the National Coal Board, the Central Electricity Generating Board and British Steel, as well as from local authorities. They belonged to a sort of 'gentlemen's club', the emphasis being on how many lunches they could consume, and how many golf tournaments they could play in. The champagne sunk in the big company expense sheets was ultimately recharged to their customers via the product they were selling. Those organisations had grown rich on the security of nationalised industry. They were up there on the top of the pedestal, kings of the castle and rulers of the roost. However, if they had bothered to look over their shoulders they would have seen a new breed of construction-equipment sales companies snapping at their heels.

By late 1979, a new mood of optimism had gripped the construction industry. Contractors such as Balfour Beatty, Tarmac and William Press were sub-contracting work to local privateers. They wanted small companies who operated one or two 6-wheel-drive articulated trucks, and who would be able to provide them with the personal and comprehensive service they required. Blackwood Hodge and Levertons were not equipped to deal with these small entrepreneurs. They did not need to. The small truck operators at this time were more trouble than they were worth. This is where we stepped in. We sold these small contractors trucks and then looked after them well. Sales began to gather pace and by the end of the year we had sold seventy units. It gave me much pleasure to deal with these up and coming entrepreneurs, but none more so than the deal I forged with Norman Cleave. Norman is a contractor living in Port Isaac in Cornwall, and I had an enquiry from him in late 1978. I drave 350 miles from our depot down to see him prior to Christmas, and after asking the way several times I finally arrived outside his house at 7 o'clock inthe evening. I was greeted with good old Cornish hospitality with scones, home-made jam and clotted cream.

I sat round the fire with the Cleave family explaining the virtues of buying Moxy over Volvo until midnight. By this time it was too late to look for a hotel and Mrs Cleave invited me to stay for the night.

Imagine my surprise when I sat down for breakfast next morning and Morman said: 'We have had a family discussion and here is an order for a Moxy D16B. Mrs Cleave will make you a cheque out before you leave. Deliver it the first week in the new year, and it had better be as good as you say.' With that I left, and sang to Radio 1 all the way back to Yorkshire. A salesman's life revolves around ten disappointments to every one order obtained, and I still think that the Cleave order ranks as one of the most pleasant I have received in my selling career.

It was not long before our customers began to hint that they wanted a factory visit. They had spent a lot of money with us: some had bought as many as three or four trucks and thought it was time to see where the Moxy was made.

Ron and I had been the recipients of such hospitality ourselves, visiting Deutz Tractors in Germany and Zetor in Czechoslovakia; both trips had gone well and were obviously important, from a sales point of view, to both Deutz and Zetor. However, we were well aware of the fact that if they went badly they could be damaging. Anyway, we finally agreed to lay on a visit to Norway. Svein would organise the entertainment from the Norwegian end and Ron and I would make sure that transportation was sorted out from England. We selected our customers from all over the country. Willie selected his from Scotland and Ron and I sorted out ours from the rest of Britain. To ensure that things went with a bang we decided to recruit a well-known character who could add a sparkle to the dullest of occasions.

He was called Phil Sharp, better known as 'Sharpy', who was approached and accepted the prestigious position of 'social manager'.

On the day of our departure, Ron and I set off to the airport armed with our list of names. Our 'social manager' was one of the first to arrive. Never one to hide his success, he roared up to the entrance in his Rolls-Royce, parked in the 'no parking' section and bounced out before completely taking over proceedings. Sharpy was closely followed by another 'shrinking violet', D. C. Lunnan, also never one to hide his wealth. He too roared up in his Rolls-Royce, vying with Sharpy for pole position in front of the departure terminal. Sharpy grabbed a copy of the itinerary. Air UK was the operator. First, the plane had to pick some of our customers up in Norwich before landing at Leeds-Bradford Airport. Then it was to head up to Edinburgh to pick up another ten passengers, and on to Aberdeen for the rest of the Scottish contingent, before finally leaving the country to land in Bergen. From Bergen we were to fly to Molde.

It was not the easiest itinerary in the world, nor was it the best transport operation, but it was the best available at the time. Once aboard, Sharpy continued to carry out his role of social manager. Once we had taken off, he decided to assist the air hostesses with their drinks distribution, thus ensuring that we all received ample measures. Putting on his pinny, he started to serve everyone with drinks and totally dominated the flight. He then took £5 from everyone, explaining that Norwegian alcohol was extremely expensive and that he felt that in his capacity as social manager he should be in charge of purchasing alcoholic beverages from duty free at Aberdeen airport. We all marched out of duty free and through customs with our cardboard boxes of alcohol. The customs officers tried to exert some sort of control but with our high spirits and Sharpy's silk tongue we were soon waved through.

When we arrived in Bergen, Svein and Sharpy joined ranks. Knowing that everything was taken care of, Ron and I were able to enjoy ourselves thoroughly. That evening we had a first-class dinner in Bergen and the duty free came in handy for revelry afterwards. The following morning we transferred to Molde, landing on the tiny airstrip by the sea. We transferred to the Molde factory and Hatlebakk proudly showed off what his entrepreneurial flair and Norwegian development money had achieved. In the afternoon we visited a hydro-electric plant in the nearby mountains and the day was rounded off with an excellent meal at the Alexandra Hotel in Molde. It had been a successful trip, everyone had enjoyed themselves and we had received an order for two more trucks from D. C. Lunnan. Ron and I returned home satisfied that it had been a first-class public relations exercise and should be repeated.

Then the next decade began with disturbing news from Norway. It was well known that Hatlebakk had received a lot of government aid with money generated by the oil boom. These grants had enabled him to build this immensely large factory which would probably take another ten years for the company to grow into. And it was obvious that Moxy alone could not do this for him. For every truck sold he was probably losing £10,000. As with many other such projects around the world, Hatlebakk had come up with the idea, the government had come up with the money and soon they were growing impatient. They wanted to see results. Hatlebakk tried to persuade them to be patient and insisted that the sales achieved in England would soon be realised across the rest of Europe. However, despite his optimism, the markets in Denmark, Norway, Sweden and France, for example, were floundering because there were real problems with some of the components and there was a lack of funds to put them right.

Svein called a dealers' meeting on 20 August 1980. All dealers and potential dealers were invited to go to the factory at Molde to discuss how a general market, less dependent on the UK, could be established. All the delegates arrived at the Alexandra Hotel in Molde; unusually there was no one there to meet us. It later transpired that the factory was locked in a series of crisis meetings with its bankers and government officials. When we arrived we were told by reception to have dinner and that Svein would arrive later. Looking around over dinner I tried to identify who was who. I kept glancing across at a fair-haired man who, I was convinced, was the German dealer. After dinner, he came over and introduced himself.

'Hello, I presume you are with Moxy, too?' he inquired in broken English.

'Yes,' I confirmed, 'and which dealer are you?'

'I am Thomas Strasser from Austria.'

Immediately we struck up a friendship. Gradually, one by one, the visiting dealers introduced themselves to each other and then made their way to the bar. I soon realised that this was a lesson on how not to have a sales-dealer conference. By the time everyone had got to know each other, and had had a few drinks, they had also conceded that the Moxy dumptruck was perhaps the worst product ever made. Our meeting drastically needed some Moxy personnel to break up the party and stick up for their product. By the time Svein turned up, he and his company were not quite the flavour of the month. He apologised for his absence and told everyone that a coach would collect us from the hotel at 9.30 the next morning.

As instructed, we boarded the coach in the morning and set off for the Bamsekroa, a restaurant on the way to the factory. While the other dealers had coffee, Thomas Strasser and I stood off to the side and surveyed the tense situation. As far as we understood, the meeting was to be led by

Hatlebakk himself, flanked by Svein, the sales manager, Serge Burkow, the chief designer, and Ingolf Sollid, the head of service. Hatlebakk eventually arrived, accompanied by one or two other people who, I believe, were his finance directors from a sister company called Glamox. However, he didn't stay long, making only a short welcoming address, apologising for his imminent departure and finally handing the whole thing over to Svein, who was then verbally attacked from all sides.

The dealers from Denmark, Holland, Belgium and Sweden all but lynched the defenceless Svein. However, the French dealer, Henri Celton, who was

Receiving an award from Birger Hatlebakk on behalf of Brown Anglo-Scan Equipment – Svein Hjelle, the larger-than-life salesman, is just behind me.

not only a gentleman but also too old a hand to participate in such a slanging match, decided to speak in his defence. Henri stated that his problems with the product's weaknesses were not as acute in France as they evidently were in other countries. When Henri sat down, I decided to speak. By this time we were all well aware of the problems and the weaknesses of the product. To a great extent, I felt that the Benelux dealers had a valid argument but, like Henri, I also thought I had to point out the positive side, which I hoped would lead to a more balanced discussion.

'We became the UK dealer for the Moxy in 1978, when we sold seventeen units. By 1979 we had raised our sales to seventy units, and we hope to sell one hundred units this year.' I then went on to explain how we had increased our market share while theirs had declined. 'We ploughed back much of our generated profit into giving a better after-sales service and by doing this we could support the product and increase our market share. One way to solve this problem in the short term is to take a little more profit in the sale of the unit and then use that money to provide after-sales support.'

That day I learned the lesson that you should never bring all your dealers together under one roof on the same day. Meet them individually on their own soil, listen to their grumbles one by one and then take action. By bringing everyone together, little problems experienced by all dealers suddenly grow ugly heads and before long they consume all the good points of the product. I learned that such epidemic grumbles can be kept at bay if what had marred the discussions at the Bamsekroa was never repeated.

That evening we had a meal at the hotel. Rumours were circulating about the reason for Hatlebakk's hasty departure. Most people seemed to think that a number of influential people, including Hatlebakk and the government officials, had gone to a meeting in Oslo in order to put together a deal by which Volvo would take over the Moxy plant.

The Swedish dealer expanded on this theory, pointing out that a collaboration between the two countries could be mutually beneficial. The money generated by Norway's new-found oil wealth together with the industrial expertise of Sweden could form a formidable industrial force. The evening rolled on to the sound of rumour and counter-rumour, conjecture and counter-conjecture, and we all retired to bed feeling somewhat uncertain about the future of Moxy.

Over the following months it became more and more obvious that Hatlebakk and his factory were in serious financial difficulties. Svein was no longer his old vivacious self. He began to lose his sparkle and it was obvious that the knife was beginning to turn. Our telephone conversations were no longer light or jovial. Now Svein had no time for small talk: 'Gwardon, how many trucks can you take to the UK and when can you let me have the money?'

Svein's only concern was to get the trucks out of the factory and turn them back into cash. Fortunately for us, the news of the problems did not reach our customers. Moxy's financial difficulties were mainly confined to the Norwegian press, and only a small low-circulation construction magazine had tagged on to the story in England. During the rest of 1980 we managed to sell every truck we could get our hands on, and we also had a tremendous year selling the Tonstad road planers. Such was the success of the road planer that we received enquiries from South Africa, and, after a number of telephone calls, we established that the interest was certainly worth a demonstration down there. It was while I was on my way to Johannesburg that I received the news that Svein needed an urgent word with me. When I called him, I learned that he had been fired. For as long as I had been involved with Moxy, I had always known that his presence at the factory had never really been accepted. Those closest to him admired what he did, but to everyone else he was like salt in a wound. They thought he was aggressive, loud and totally lacking in diplomacy. But he had the interests of the factory at heart, he had guts, and he was one of the few who dared to go where angels feared to tread. He had no qualms about going back and telling Hatlebakk and the chief designer, Serge Burkow what was wrong with their product. In my opinion he was exactly what the factory needed. However, diplomacy was not his strong point, and the bosses, instead of listening to Svein, who was after all the man who breathed enthusiasm into the dealers and gave feedback to the factory, had fired him. I had not only lost a good workmate, but also a man from whom I had learned much in such a short space of time.

Like most of the other dealers, I telephoned Hatlebakk to offer support to Svein. In his broken English, Hatlebakk explained to me that while Svein had done a lot of good for the factory, matters were moving out of his hands and he had to be removed. Svein tried to rally support from his fellow workers but, with the exception of his own sales department, the support that he so desperately needed was not forthcoming. In fact, they were glad to be rid of this effervescent character and glad to fall back into the sleepy world that had existed before his flamboyant arrival. I had lost my new-found friend and the factory had lost its driving force.

When I arrived back in the office a few days later, I found waiting for me the telex that confirmed Svein's dismissal. Beneath it lay another telex summoning me to Norway to meet 'Superman', the guy who was going to sort out this dreadful mess. Moxy had become occupied territory, the upstart had been done away with. Hatlebakk was no longer in control and the aggressors, the government officials and bankers, had appointed a dreaded consultant.

Hatlebakk met me at the airport in his 1935 Fiat car, a vehicle which he only brought out for special guests. I felt honoured and took up my position next to him in the front seat. The consultant was relegated to the back. Hatlebakk was no longer in charge; indeed he was now a mere puppet with the government and bankers pulling the strings. While we both resented the presence of this man we had to appease him. If we wanted a product at all we had to accept the wishes of the government and not pull against them. On the way to the factory Hatlebakk started to outline his plans for the future. He believed that the marketing department needed to be a good deal more sophisticated and that Moxy needed a much more professional approach. The consultant had been brought in to study the market. My role was to convey market prospects to this miracle worker and, once his study was completed, Hatlebakk would implement his magical suggestions and everything would then be perfect. If only it were that simple.

I must admit that, before I met this self-employed wizard, I was somewhat sceptical about his formidable powers of resurrection. Having met and worked with him for three months I realised that I had been more than right. He cost the earth and achieved nothing. I am afraid that I have never had reason to reverse my cynical opinion of these people. If you delve into their backgrounds, you usually find that they have either been fired or have never been able to hold down a position in the field in which they are supposed to be an expert. They speak with such authority on their specialist subject, spouting theories and regurgitating formulae, while taking direct responsibility for nothing. To emphasise their incompetence they usually ask that you sign a disclaimer, before adding insult to injury and demanding payment in advance, aware that three months down the line you are going to say, 'Hang on a minute, what have you achieved?' And the answer more likely than not is 'Absolutely nothing'. I am yet to find the elusive consultant who is willing to put his own money where his mouth is.

We finished 1980 on a pretty poor note, which meant that Ron and I had an unhappy New Year. By this time the construction and transport-related industries had started to move away from holidays only on Christmas Day and New Year's Day to a full eight-day shutdown. There was much time to mull over our problems and Ron and I met frequently to discuss what we were going to do. For over seventeen years we had been aware of the need to seize opportunities when they arose and the need to change when the situation demanded it. In the early years, we had moved from agriculture into construction; when the plant-hire work dried up around us we had moved north. When that had dried up we had gained the Argentina contract and from there we had expanded from plant-hire into plant-sales, gaining the Moxy dealership in the UK. Ron and I were aware that circumstances were about to dictate further change and in order to survive we knew that we were going to have to be ready for it.

With our expanding business we recognised the need for us to change direction in one department or another every year. We had matured greatly during the last seventeen years and we knew that the problems at Moxy would not go away without some sort of restructuring there. The more we discussed the matter and spoke to Svein, the more it unfolded that Moxy would either run out of cash, be taken over, or go through some form of major restructure. One way or another we had to be mindful of the fact that we had created a structure in the UK which we did not want to break down. It was a structure which involved Willie Dalrymple in Scotland and Roger Jay looking after the south, a structure which served an ever increasing number of customers who were becoming part of our 'family'. They were both loyal to us and loyal to the product. That loyalty was so strong that neither Ron nor I could bear to contemplate letting them down.

There were now over 200 trucks operating within the UK. People had made substantial financial commitments. These commitments could only be afforded if the trucks were able to earn at a consistent level. Our customers also relied on their trucks having a strong residual value. Moxy had to be kept going if we were to maintain our credibility. We had been able to offset the downturn in the agricultural industry by the upturn in our construction-related dumptruck business. (Agricultural tractor sales throughout the UK dived from a starting point in 1963 of 35,000 units to 30,000 units in 1979 and dropped still further in 1980 to 21,000, and there was no sign of recovery.) Elsewhere in our group, matters were not all plain sailing. Our machines were now back from Argentina. There was no North Sea oil boom left and we were scratching around for work. However, transport was enjoying stable times, as new regulations introduced throughout the 1970s were making it possible for us to run a professional organisation and still receive the rewards.

By now Freddy had become very much involved in his show-jumping activities. His daughter Gillian had started her riding career at the age of eight in 1966 and by 1981 she was taking part in all the large show-jumping events throughout the country, including such prestigious events as the Horse of the Year Show. Freddy himself spent most of his time on the farm and with his horses, while his son Ian, with John Hinchcliffe, now looked after the transport business. There was no longer the earlier closeness of the brothers. The larger business demanded that Ron and I travelled more and more and attended more and more meetings and discussed policies whenever possible, mainly in Ron's smoke-filled office late at night.

Over the Christmas period, we discussed our problems and mulled over our alternatives. We knew that any changes would lead to criticism from the more traditionalist members of our company but we realised that we would have to cope with that as best we could. Tentative talks had already taken place with Willie Dalrymple about the future of the business in Scotland and it was generally agreed that sooner or later this would have to be absorbed into the main group.

Running alongside these talks were our discussions with Frank Weldon of Fiatallis who was trying to persuade us to take on the dealership for Fiatallis construction equipment in Scotland. It was a difficult time because on the one hand we had what appeared to be a good family business that was generating reasonable profits, but on the other hand we did not have sufficient working capital to take the major steps that would be necessary to protect our future prosperity. Looking over our shoulders and across the sea to Norway we were well aware that if Moxy sold out to Volvo or another corporation we would automatically lose 50 per cent of our turnover. As responsible directors and custodians of the family fortune, Ron and I knew that we would have to protect the down side. Freddy was not deeply involved in the day-to-day operations and as a result he was not really aware of the effect that the potential demise of Moxy would have on the group. We had to be realistic. We had to recognise that in one way or another the last two years' profits for our group had all probably originated from the Moxy bandwagon.

On the Fiatallis front the major problem which Ron and I had to wrestle with was that as engineers and entrepreneurs we knew that the real future lay in handling quality equipment, such as Caterpillar, Akerman, O. & K., Volvo, or Liebherr, equipment which dominated the construction business at that time. Fiatallis in truth was a second rater. While the equipment was basically good, the support offered by certain dealers was weak. As a result Fiatallis had to make do with a small following of dedicated customers who liked the equipment sufficiently to put up with the poor service. It probably lost them nine customers out of every ten it had gained over the previous twenty years. To offset this major down side there were two important positive factors to build on. Fiatallis was the only nationwide distribution available to us and Willie, Ron and I were in the prime of our careers and bristling with the relish of a challenge. In addition, we were still riding on the wave of Moxy's success.

When the day of decision came in April or May that year, we chose to start by taking on Fiatallis in Scotland and the border areas. We absorbed the assets of the former Fieldtrack organisation and Willie moved into their premises. In addition to this, we knew there was the possibility of our gaining the territory of the Selwood dealership. A St Helens-based company, they looked after the territory from the Scottish border south to Birmingham and even on to the home counties. If this happened it would give us a market area covering nearly two-thirds of the UK. This would certainly be enough for us to cut our teeth on and would go some way towards protecting us from the potential demise of Moxy.

Back at Moxy the consultant heading up on the sales side in place of Svein was surviving well; he was still in place and trucks were piling up round his neck. Hatlebakk was totally involved, tearing round Scandinavia trying to convince civil servants and bankers to continue their support as well as doing his best to keep his anti-Volvo lobby going. By this time I was getting dragged further and further into Moxy's internal squabbles. On the one hand Moxy was being destroyed, both from within by its consultants, and from the outside, by its dealers – with the exception of the UK, which had become a complete anomaly. Moxy had died in every other country because of poor engineering support as well as poor quality components. In Britain, Willie Dalrymple, Phil Townson, who was service manager at Riffa, and Roger Jay, who was in charge of our London depot as well as being sales manager for the south of England, ensured that the shortcomings of the truck were taken care of.

The customers were happy because the machines were up and running. If there was a problem, it would be ironed out and the machine would be working again within a very short time. Instead of declining sales, we were experiencing growth in our market share. Indeed, by 1980 we were taking out 80 per cent of the factory's annual production. It was this statistic which alerted a number of Norwegian dignitaries in high places to make contact and it was this contact and the subsequent meetings which would ultimately dictate our direction for the next decade. Securing the Fiatallis dealership became priority for the Brown Group. The Moxy situation in Norway was looking increasingly precarious, and if the winds of change were to blow in the wrong direction, something solid would be needed to counterbalance the damaging effects. Ron, Willie and I all agreed that we had to get moving with the Fiatallis dealership negotiations. While I was busy scampering backwards and forwards to Norway, keeping abreast of the situation over there, Ron and Willie were pushing ahead with negotiations in Turin.

As the weeks passed, I found myself either visiting Hatlebakk or speaking to him almost every day. Gradually the Swedish plan unfolded. Hatlebakk explained that the Swedish and Norwegian authorities were considering some sort of technology transfer: financial aid generated from the oil boom would be the basis of the Norwegian contribution, while Sweden would offer its industrial expertise. In effect, the Swedes wanted to transfer grader production to Norway and transfer dumptruck production to Sweden. Hatlebakk was vehemently against such a deal. He knew that were he to win the first round and ensure that the Swedish option did not go ahead, he would still have a long slog ahead of him convincing the 'funders' that they should continue to back the factory and put up the money to stabilize its precarious position.

As far as I was concerned, first and foremost the Swedish solution needed to be tackled. If it were allowed to proceed it would have been to our detriment. All the work we had put into promoting the Moxy product, emphasising its advantages over Volvo, would have gone to waste. All our successful marketing would have been for the benefit of our main competitor. We would have looked absolute fools having put in so much effort only to be beaten by factors outside our control. An invitation to meet with the Norwegian civil servants and bankers gave us a much needed boost. At last we were being given a chance to fight the Moxy corner.

That summer of 1981 I attended a succession of meetings at which more and more was revealed to me. Norwegian and Swedish politics were knocking sideways Moxy's future success. A certain lobby in Oslo, which wanted Norway to increase its economic involvement with Sweden, was pushing hard for Moxy to be handed over to Stockholm. It was only when Ron and I were called upon to appraise the advantages of this transfer that we were able to assert, along with others, that this would be a futile exchange, an exchange that would certainly not benefit Norway. The Swedish 'Greeks bearing gifts' proposal would simply take Moxy dumptruck production to Sweden and in exchange Sweden would transfer grader production to the Norwegian factory, along with the manufacture of some components. This would once again enable Sweden to dominate the articulated dumptruck market and, as a compromise, supposedly would give some work to the people of Molde. We quickly pointed out that the grader market had been in decline for over ten years and the annual sale was dropping rapidly.

After a number of meetings, culminating in a full-scale discussion involving Ron and me, we were able to point out that grader production offered no long-term future for the Molde plant and that the growth market was definitely in articulated dumptrucks. We were turning the main proposal on its head. We were fighting a dumptruck war, Moxy versus Volvo, and at that point Volvo were losing in the UK.

To our relief, Hatlebakk telephoned us soon after the meeting, thanking us for our assistance. The first round had been won. Moxy would retain its independence. However, there was still the problem of the ongoing financial instabilities. The bankers and government officials had had high hopes of the Swedish solution succeeding, but here they were once again back at square one with economic reality staring them in the face. With the Swedish solution out of the way at least everyone could face the real problem, the long-term future of the Moxy factory. The government development fund in Oslo was saying, 'No more funds will be available to the Moxy regime so long as Hatlebakk is there'. Paul Hallan, the bank manager at Forretsningsbank in Trondheim, appointed to sort out the tangle, was also saying that no more cash was going to be made available from his bank to support the operation. On the other side of the fence were a handful of local politicians in Molde who were factory-based, and campaigning vigorously for more jobs to be filled locally.

Everyone, including Hatlebakk, the bankers, the authorities, and the people of Molde, had had such high hopes for the factory. They had been convinced that it would bring jobs and wealth to the area and yet here we were, only a few years down the road, and all those hopes and dreams were being dashed. The funders just could not wait any longer. Hatlebakk believed he needed only a little more time but time was no longer on his side: the backers were about to kick the stool from under him. Fortunately for Moxy, its demise was postponed. Nothing was going to interfere with Norway's annual July shutdown, their three-week summer holiday. I found it intriguing that everything was put in abeyance and the pieces were not to be picked up until August.

My trips backwards and forwards had gathered momentum to the point where I was going to Norway sometimes twice a week. The journey time was unacceptable. The only way to get to the Molde plant was to leave Leeds-Bradford Airport early in the morning, travel to London, then wait to catch the London-Oslo flight, and then wait again to catch the evening Oslo-Molde plane. The whole process took a day out of my working week. The only possible advantage was that at least I had time to think. I came to the conclusion that somehow, somewhere, this extremely dark cloud must have at least a glimmer of a silver lining.

My mind would work overtime on my frequent lonely visits to Norway. I would find myself dreaming of owning the factory. I knew that, at that time, such a dream could be nothing more than that. However, in the long term it was not such a ridiculous idea. The Brown brothers in England were being considered more and more as an authority within the dumptruck industry and I began to believe quite seriously that the final outcome could be one of full or shared ownership.

During my long journeys I could take comfort from the fact that Moxy sales in the UK were continuing unabated and good profits were being accumulated, and at the same time Ron and Willie were making good progress with the Fiatallis dealership. Although we had only just taken over, already a number of machines had been sold at good margins. On one of my fleeting visits back to the UK I had been able to sell four large Fiatallis machines to Land & Marine for an overseas contract, so while I was dreaming of the future in my long flying hours to Molde I could bask comfortably in the knowledge that our own UK operation was very profitable and continuing to expand. I also became increasingly aware that my twice-weekly visits to Molde were costing a fortune. But I knew that my frequent sorties were essential if I was to keep abreast of developments.

By now we were right in the middle of the July period. Most of the dealers in other countries had given up on the Moxy dream, leaving the UK as virtually the only outlet through which Moxy could distribute its ever-mounting stockpile of dumptrucks. I had to put maximum effort into the future of Moxy, trying to ensure that the product and the factory itself would succeed. But to do this I would need to be much more mobile. I could not continue spending one day getting to the factory and another day getting back again. It was essential that I cut down on my travelling time.

After yet another twelve-hour journey back to England I decided to look into the possibility of buying a small private aircraft. First of all I approached Ron on the subject, who sympathised with the time consumption, but like me found it difficult to believe that our new-found prosperity could really support a small private aircraft of our own. Ron listened to my thoughts through a halo of smoke; he always thought better with a cigarette in his mouth. 'Look at it this way, Ron, look at it optimistically. If Moxy does collapse, and let's hope it doesn't, but if it does – well, it could offer a real opportunity to us. The bankers have said that for the factory to have even a short-term future, they must get rid of the stock of trucks, turn them back into cash, and how do you think they can do that? Who could sell them all? Why, us, of course, their best outlet could be in the UK. If we were mobile enough to grasp the opportunity we could more than cover the cost of the aircraft.'

One thing I will say about Ron; he was always a good listener. By the time I had said my piece, he thought it was not such a daft idea after all. He too was sick to death of wasting time running backwards and forwards to Fiatallis in Turin and visiting Willie Dalrymple in Glasgow. We decided that the expense of our own six-seater plane could be justified and immediately turned our thoughts to acquiring one. We had both heard of a larger-than-life character, who was based just a few miles from our Riffa depot, and we knew that the place to look for a small aircraft in Yorkshire was in his organisation called Northair Aviation. Our larger-than-life friend was Ernest Crabtree.

I asked the switchboard to get me Northair Aviation. Having been put through to the Northair switchboard I found myself at the start of what was to become a unique experience. I announced myself to the switchboard operator, Janet, who questioned me in depth: Who was I? Where was I from? What was the nature of my business? Not just anyone got put through to Mr Crabtree, but she would see what she could do. Initially, I had been very excited at the prospect of buying an aeroplane. I had certainly not bargained on an interrogation of this sort. It was presumptuous of me to assume that Mr Crabtree would actually want to sell me a plane. But, oh no, here I was battling to speak to this well-known character. Finally, I was put through but in the midst of outlining my requirements, he interrupted me, 'I'm busy at the moment, lad, but get yourself up here on Saturday morning and we'll talk about it then.'

During the next days I made a number of enquiries about the Mr Crabtree I was about to meet, and after averaging out the comments I received, I came to the conclusion that I was about to meet a man with strong principles. Saturday morning came and I arrived at Northair for my 11 o'clock appointment. Unfortunately I was five minutes late; to most people who know me, this would have been considered astonishingly punctual. However, Mr Crabtree was not impressed. This large figure met me in reception, bellowing 'If you are going to do business with me, lad, the first thing you had better get used to, is arriving on time. Is that clear? I haven't time to mess about waiting for you to arrive late.' Softening a little, he said, 'Come in, lad, and let us talk about this aeroplane.' I outlined our basic requirements, based on the aircraft owned by the Ogdens', only to get the reply, 'I don't look after Ogdens' aircraft. It's in the next hangar. I drink with the Ogden's but I don't maintain their aircraft for them.'

Before long I felt more at ease with this large bellowing character. He came across as an absolute bully but I soon realised that this was really to give me some sound advice, and that was, 'Do you think you can really afford to run an aircraft?' He told me that the initial purchase was the cheap bit. Keeping it in the air is where the real cost comes in. He finished by saying, 'Go away and think about it. Tell your brothers what I have said. If you are sure you can afford it, I've got just the plane for you.' Just as I was going out of the door he boomed after me '. . . and I don't want to mess about with you any more until you can show me you've got some brass'.

During the year leading up to the troubles at Moxy, we had set about separating all our activities so that we could identify which were the profit generators and which were the drainers. We knew in our own minds that much of our profit was generated from sales of Moxy and Tonstad but we wanted to have the detail at our finger-tips. So during 1980 the construction-equipment sales were separated into a new company, Brown Anglo-Scan Equipment Ltd and we named the importing company Moxy Dumptrucks

UK Ltd. This had the effect of leaving all our traditional business, such as tractor sales, plant-hire, agricultural contracting and hay and straw merchanting, all back inside the old Wharfedale Agricultural Services. Fred Brown Limited, the transport company, had always been a separate company and had jogged along making between £10,000 loss and £30,000 profit each year. Dal Plant Services Ltd, which had been a plant-repair company, had now joined the Brown Group and were the Fiatallis and Moxy distributors in Scotland.

By July 1981 we were already nine months into our new financial year, and the true facts were unfolding. Moxy Dumptrucks and Brown Anglo-Scan Equipment were already making £500,000 profit while our traditional company, Wharfedale Agricultural Services, was losing £90,000. Our smaller companies, Brown Brothers Construction and Fred Brown (Norwood) Ltd, were making a contribution at this time of only £30,000. Ron and I had suspected all along that this was the case, and now we felt vindicated. While our sales of high-value capital goods had stretched our financial resources, they had been the sole contributor to our wealth generation.

Between 1978–81 our net worth had climbed from £500,000 to £1.5 million. I had listened to all the doubting Thomases and tolerated their jibes; I had often been accused of flying my kite too high and of overstretching our bank resources; but now at last the statistics were beginning to reflect the truth. Trevor and Roy at Brown Butler were beginning to support our approach to the construction-equipment sales business. In the past Roy had been strongly in favour of Freddy's traditional methods of earning a living. By the time August arrived, the facts proved beyond doubt that if we had continued with the traditional activities we would have been on our way to bankruptcy.

CHAPTER 10

The Buyer for Moxy

RON AND I NOW FELT that we should have more say in the day-to-day running of the group. At last we had proved that the construction-equipment sales department was earning the lion's share of the profit. We felt that our success over the last few years would go some way towards convincing the traditionalists within our company that we knew what we were talking about. We also hoped that they would at least hear us out on the subject of the proposed purchase of an aircraft and understand that such an investment would enable us to have more time for selling machines. By this time Trevor Gurney was beginning to assert more authority in his organisation and supported us in our bid to buy an aircraft. The three of us presented the idea to Roy and Freddy and to our astonishment, Freddy was most receptive to the idea. He realised that we could no longer live in the past. If there was an opportunity to grasp we had to be in a position to grasp it.

In fact Freddy was quite sympathetic towards my lifestyle. He was very much a man who liked to sleep in his own bed at night and he had no difficulty in understanding the fact that I did not like spending three nights out of every seven in a hotel room. My constant travelling back and forth had not gone unnoticed by my eldest brother. After one of our usual late evening discussions all three of us decided that if we were to progress, and provided we could find a small aircraft which was economical and comparatively cheap to buy, the matter should be seriously considered. I was given the go-ahead to return to Ernest Crabtree for some ideas. Finally, Ron, Freddy and I reached agreement. A small plane would be an investment – a workhorse rather than a luxury – a mode of transport that would overcome the time-consuming problem of getting to and from Molde. However, before we went ahead, we thought it prudent to check carefully the feasibility of it all. None of us had any idea about buying or running an aircraft; we were entering unknown territory and before we did so, we wanted to be armed with all the facts.

It was decided that our main priority was to find a good utility aircraft, one that we could dispose of if our master plan, the saving of Moxy, did not succeed. The more I sat and chatted with Ernest Crabtree the more comfortable I felt. Ernest was certainly not going to push a plane at us just for the sake of it. His main objective was to spell out to us exactly what we were letting ourselves in for; he did not want to be responsible for selling us something we could not afford. I told him that we wanted a working plane, not a luxury item, and Ernest came up with a plane that fitted the bill exactly – a cheap hull with two fairly long-life engines on board. It was down at Gamston Airfield, about ten miles from Doncaster, so Ron and I went down for an inspection. Golden Eagle 421 Bravo Charlie Sierra Victor was, on paper, just the ticket. Ernest reassured us that he could put it in the air for not a penny over £80,000.

Having decided upon the aircraft, the next problem was to locate a safe pilot. A gas-conversion-kit salesman turned pilot came highly recommended. Ray Hughes was a character we had known years before; since those early days he had worked overtime on his studies and had become a pilot for Ernest. Even then people were recommending that we should only consider a two-pilot operation, but quite foolishly as it turned out, we never really considered employing two pilots. Our attitude was, if one pilot was legal then that was safe enough for us. I put it to Ernest again and again that I would be the one predominantly flying with Ray and he asserted, 'I have no problem with Ray's safety. I even let him fly my wife and I think the world of her.'

Golden Eagle BCSV could not be got ready quite as quickly as we wanted. 'Right, lad, I'll tell you what I'll do. You can borrow one of my planes to get your show on the road. Borrow Hughsie for now and in the meantime I'll get your plane ready', suggested Ernest. When the first long-awaited telephone call arrived from Norway in the first week in August, we were ready and airborne with Hughsie at the helm.

By August, the Moxy saga had progressed. As with all these situations, the consensus of opinion and loyalty was being divided. There were two camps emerging. The first telephone call I received was from Mr Hals, the local bank manager in Molde, asking me to attend a meeting. He told me that the bank was planning certain moves and asked if my interest extended to going over the action involved. I outlined that the major part of our business in the UK had now been committed to the Moxy and I had no alternative but to be involved. The next telephone calls were from Hatlebakk asking me to meet him in Oslo with his finance director and his son; once again he was trying to piece together a last-ditch rescue plan. Again we went through the usual line of enquiry: 'Can you give us a firm order for 250 trucks in 1982?'; 'Is there any chance that you can pay for some of them in advance?', and other such desperate questions.

In amongst all this we had our own business to look after. By this time I was blessed with the luxury of having Freddy, Ron and now Willie back at the base camp all agreeing that whatever could be done in Norway should be done to try to keep the goose laying the golden eggs. August was crammed full of to-ing and fro-ing, constantly phoning Trevor for advice, with the cause looking more and more lost for Hatlebakk. Leif Owner's development fund had now firmly made up its mind that there was to be no more assistance. This left only the bank or an external funder. Hatlebakk asked once again if there was any possibility that we could come up with funding but when one looked at the balance sheet of the operation, it was just impossible. The whole thing was totally lopsided.

In our many meetings the factory was variously described as the GMC of northern Norway, a Rolls-Royce in the middle of a desert with no petrol. Somehow it was all out of balance. The enormous factory was far too big for Moxy's immediate production requirements and there was nothing else in the area to occupy the space. There was no alternative apart from funding. Finally, all the to-ing and fro-ing culminated in a number of meetings which took place between 5 and 7 September 1981. I was first of all ferried down to Oslo, then back to Molde where we were joined by lawyers. We were then taken by car to Trondheim by the local bank manager and the lawyer to consult with Paul Hallan. All the time I was being probed as to how much assistance from the Brown Group could be relied upon and how much help from me personally might be available.

After finishing our deliberations at 2 o'clock on 7 September I certainly did not think that anything disastrous was about to happen to Moxy. I was asked to leave the meeting and was taken back to my hotel in Molde where to my surprise the hotel foyer was humming with the local press. When I reached my room and turned on the television I saw Paul Hallan on the evening news being interviewed and he finally declared that it was 'konkeus for Moxy'. I had learned sufficient Norwegian during that month to know what that meant: Moxy was in bankruptcy.

I sat in my room that night and kept the whole thing to myself. There was no time for sleep. Time and time again I went through the facts, mulling over in my head what could be done – what would the future hold? The embarrassment that Ron and I would suffer, for the private contractors whom we had persuaded to invest in Moxy dumptrucks in the UK would feel totally let down. Moreover, this scandal would destroy the residual value of the Moxy equipment, an aspect so important in this type of business. Income generated on a daily basis is one thing, but all contractors rely on the ultimate profit to be made when they sell the unit on disposal. I tried to spell this out to the bankers in Trondheim that day in order to convince them that one setback like this would put Moxy back two years, but it was to no avail. They had taken their decision to grab what they could by withdrawing their loans. They would get what they wanted and it was now time to bring the matter to an end.

The following morning I had to be awake early. Fortunately, the time difference between Norway and England secured me a precious hour, an hour to think further before I had to make the unpleasant phone call to my brothers and break the news that Moxy was bust. Added to this the working day in Norway started at 7 a.m., so this at least gave me a further hour of thinking time. Then the telephone calls started . . . Svein Haga, the office operations manager, enquired whether I would be going to the factory. I went down early to breakfast only to be called to reception. A rushed telephone call from Per Overbo, the bank's lawyer, told me that I was needed at a meeting at 9 a.m. at the Forretningsbank just along from the hotel. Also there would be Mr Hals, the bank manager in Molde, and Paul Hallan, who had travelled down overnight from Trondheim. Per Overbo rounded off by saying that he thought it was most important that I should attend the meeting as a proposal of great interest to me would be made. I quickly ate my breakfast and made sure that I was at the bank well before 9 o'clock.

To my amazement the press were already gathering in the hotel foyer. As a foreigner I had not realised what a terrible local disaster this had been. I was left in no doubt when I got a glimpse of the *Romsdals Budstikke* on the stand with headlines across the front page 'Moxy Konkeus'. By the time I arrived at the bank everyone was waiting and the meeting started immediately, with Paul Hallan informing me that the ideas formulated previously had not gone unheeded. They had no alternative but to put the factory into bankruptcy, but, provided I would agree to continue marketing the trucks in the UK and assist in other countries, his bank would put up a sum of money to keep the factory going while a search was made for a suitable purchaser. He would take a personal interest in the running of the factory along with Per Overbo and the unit managers. The day continued with meeting after meeting, first with the bankers and the funders, and then with Union personnel and of course the press.

It was finally decided that I would be put on the payroll. While it was not the solution I wanted, at least for the time being this was a small consolation prize. By now, of course, I had told Freddy and Ron what was happening. I was able to dress up the news by saying that although we had a bankruptcy on our hands, we were still in business. The more I walked from office to office, the more I thought the best course of action was to dress up the whole scenario as much as possible, maintaining their confidence in the future of the product. If we were to survive this disaster in the UK the best thing we could do was manipulate the press into not announcing a bankruptcy. We would say that, 'Yes, there was a problem', and 'Yes, it would be sorted out', and, above all, 'We will be actively involved in the day-to-day operation at the factory'.

Back in Molde Paul Hallan was now organising the whole affair like a military exercise. While Per Overbo was the legally appointed receiver, Paul Hallan, acting for the major creditor, the bank, seemed to be very much at the centre of things. Indeed, I soon came to have a healthy respect for him. He had a very British mentality, which was obviously due to the fact that at some point in his career he had held a banking post in Britain. During the endless whirlwind of meetings in the days that followed I soon adopted one of his many mannerisms. In a rather military style, Paul used to listen to all proposals, but if the proposal clearly stepped over the line you got a firm 'Certainly not', thus ensuring that there could be no misunderstanding.

Running along with the endless meetings the daily press was full of speculation and counter-speculation: the whole thing had become a big issue in Norway. Millions of Norwegian krone from public funds had been poured into the project. Parallels were being drawn with the De Lorean scandal in the UK. By this time Hatlebakk had been totally sidelined. You had to admire his pioneer instinct for originating this unique vehicle in the first place but sadly things had gone badly wrong for him.

Much to my delight, within a matter of days the manufacturing plant was more normalised and a small amount of funding was made available to continue production. Paul Hallan and Per Overbo were quickly finding their feet and one of the first issues Paul Hallan addressed was my personal salary. While Hals, the local bank manager, had initially promised that I would be on the payroll in some form, Paul Hallan was quick to stop any conflict of interest, pointing out that in the first instance we were a dealer in the UK and he very much wanted to use me in that role. Second, he wanted me around as a fallback, as someone to whom he could sell finished units, in case the factory had to close down completely. Third, he quickly concluded that if I was not a buyer for the factory I should be, and suggested on many occasions that I should look seriously at taking over the unit.

During September, October and November there was much coming and going and speculation, as interested parties visited the factory and the press suggested possible buyers. The local shipbuilders, who operated with the luxury of subsidies, were just some of our many would-be buyers. After being introduced, I told them, much to their surprise, that there never was or could be a possibility of producing dumptrucks to order. I explained that the truck business was an extension of the car business. You had to build against a known demand and then go out there and fight for your share of the market. I would explain to them, as I had done to the banks, the *Dagens*

Neringsliv and everybody else prior to the bankruptcy, that a business like Moxy can only thrive on stability, reputation and residual value. At that time, not being competitively priced was not a prohibitive issue as the 6-wheel drive Moxy had no real competition. The shipbuilders came and went.

By November Paul Hallan was getting restless. I had watched proposals come and go with interest. Slowly but surely I was getting quite enthusiastic about the possibility of our purchasing the factory and gestured on a number of occasions to Freddy and Ron that there were possibilities, only to be put in my place with, 'We have no manufacturing experience and besides we do not have any spare cash', two issues which I could not dispute.

It was at a chance meeting at our office one day that a person called Tony Walker showed up and indicated that he could be a potential buyer for the factory, as he had recently sold out his own trailer business. He didn't need to tell me twice that he had some loose change lying about, and within days I had all the figures presented to him. His stimulated interest dictated a weekend visit to the factory in Molde, and it was decided that Tony would submit his bid for the business in conjunction with the Brown brothers.

By the time we had concluded our assessment and indicated our bid, it was becoming clear that, because of local political pressure, a Norwegian buyer would be the favoured solution: they had no interest in Moxy being owned by a company outside of Norway. A gentleman in Oslo named Kirston Bergo was emerging as the most likely candidate.

While Tony and I had been in Molde over the weekend we had noticed that Kirston Bergo had already started playing to the press, who seemingly were able to push their noses into everything. What was even more strange to me was that their participation was encouraged by bankers, lawyers or anyone who could get their head in front of a camera. I was first introduced to Kirston Bergo in mid-November and I did not have to do much probing to discover that he appeared to have more knowledge of advertising than of manufacturing. My introduction to him was the start of a most incredible business experience.

Until then I had been limited to working within a family business, and, more to the point, to working with people among whom a good business ethic was normal and was rarely questioned. Moreover, working with three brothers meant there was total frankness between us and, above all, unquestioned trust and loyalty.

Paul Hallan and Per Overbo were finding themselves in the position of deal brokers, and were becoming convinced that Kirston Bergo was a man of means. However, while wearing their many hats, they wanted to try to strike a deal which might at least have some chance of succeeding. So when I arrived back in Molde that November, Kirston Bergo had already been introduced to potential partners with engineering expertise in the shape of two gentlemen called Ingar Pettison and a chap whose name escapes me. This trio would be available to have dinner with me that evening. It was Paul Hallan's wish that I should become the fourth member of the team in order to bring some marketing experience to what would be a new company. These two people I had seen on a number of occasions on my frequent visits to Molde. In the first instance they were near neighbours of Svein Hjelle, but I had also met them socially at the Alexandra Hotel where all business people in Molde congregated from time to time.

Right from the start I was very suspicious of my proposed partners. They just didn't come up to scratch. For example, at our first meeting I was most surprised to have dinner with Kirston Bergo with stubble on his chin. I was not too concerned about Mr Pettison, but the other local chap really did give cause for concern. I had met him socially before and knew that it would not be long before the drink would start talking. I was not to be disappointed. Within half an hour, the conversation had degenerated to ground level. Out of the window went any chance to discuss common-sense proposals and it was soon decided to defer any meaningful discussion until the following morning.

The next day our meeting from the previous evening was rescheduled with the addition of the fifth member of our newly formed organisation. To my horror, our late addition took the guise of yet another dreaded consultant. The person concerned was Alf Lau, who would become the new company chairman. I suppose we had fashioned a sort of scenario for success, but we had a strange cast: a chairman of whose background I had no knowledge, two engineers, an advertising man and a salesman. Paul Hallan was like a dog with a bone. He had done well and he felt sure that his cobbled-together rescue package would ensure that the bank would get out unscathed.

All we needed now was an accountant: this final but very necessary component was provided by Lars Petter Osa, an accounts company from Molde, and our chosen member was a fresh-faced young chap called Jan Vidar Nerland. We shook hands with a knowing smile, for Jan Vidar had been the man whom Tony Walker and I had employed during the week of our secret negotiations. Jan Vidar had worked long hard hours for us over the previous weekend and I had been impressed with the results. I did not know it at the time but that handshake would be the start of an initially rather patchy, but in the long term a very valuable, business and personal relationship.

Initially, Alf Lau was responsible for the financial projects. Jan Vidar was used as an independent bean-counter with no management role, but as he had worked previously on the account he was familiar with all aspects of the business. Having got everyone assembled the democracy started. Alf Lau was elected chairman, Martinus Forcett would become chief executive, and the remaining three would become directors. It was proposed that we would take over existing loans from various government departments. There would be an opening share capital of NKr. 6 million (£500,000) of which the Brown brothers would be called upon for a quarter-share contribution of £125,000. I continually emphasised that we did not want to be involved at all in the equity. It was quite obvious to me that the whole thing had the makings of a shambles, even at this early stage, but obviously we had to stay put in order to ensure that the factory was kept going. Ron and I flippantly referred to it as the goose that laid the golden eggs.

Right from the word go, our calculations were always made on the basis of how many trucks we could sell in the UK before the factory collapsed again. We calculated that we ought to be able to deliver 150 with a profit of £6,000–7,000 per truck; and our share capital would cost £1,000 per truck. If we found that we had to get drawn in to this shambles, we never looked upon our cash input as share capital. It was more a kind of entry fee to give the factory some sort of temporary respite in the hope that somewhere along the line a long-term solution would turn up.

By the end of December the basic structure of a theoretical company was in place. Paul Hallan continued as power broker. He and Per Overbo reassured me on several occasions that Kirston Bergo did have money. The local press were already hailing Kirston Bergo as an absolute hero: 'Wealthy man from Oslo rescues Moxy factory' read the headlines. And he responded by basking in his new-found fame.

Martinus started to rehearse his role as chief executive of Moxy Industrier A/S with Hart Makeris as the consultants, Romstals Fellas Bank as the bankers, and with lawyers, accountants and goodness knows who else. For our part we just wanted the trucks to be manufactured. Everyone there had a vested interest of some sort. I had had no previous experience of this sort of meeting, as all my previous transactions had involved only two parties, the vendor and the purchaser. On those occasions there would always be a clear indication when the transaction was over – it was when the cash was handed over. That day the discussion drifted from an idea to an intention to the detail of a project and then to its final conclusion. The power brokers who had emerged by now were Alf Lau, Paul Hallan and Per Overbo, with Hallan ensuring that all obstacles were immediately removed to make sure that the whole transaction could be completed without any real difficulty.

Throughout January, February and March it was one thing after another but by now the factory had taken on quite a normal stabilised look with Martinus in daily attendance. Trucks were going to England. We on the UK side of the water were speaking of a normal situation and indicating to everyone that our involvement was much greater than it was in reality. The reality was that we had no wish to take part in what was becoming, as was increasingly obvious, a bit of a joke.

We wanted to stay only on the fringe of things, keeping our finger in the pie but no more. We agreed that our contribution would be £125,000 and by the end of March 1982 all obstacles but one were removed. Glamox, a sister company of Moxy, were insisting that an inter-company loan of approximately £150,000 be paid or secured on some basis and had started to insist on personal guarantees from the four shareholders. This led to many arguments. Freddy, Ron and I were adamant that we were not going to offer any form of personal guarantee – we had not done so before and we were not going to start now. In the endless round of telephone calls which followed, we managed to dilute it to a company guarantee but still brokered by Paul Hallan as a joint and several guarantee given by the shareholder companies. To keep the pot boiling I argued long and hard for the joint and several part of the guarantee to be dropped, as I was aware that two partners in the gang of four would be unable to make any contribution and I also had a good idea that the third was not all he was cracked up to be. He was certainly not a man of means as had been pictured by the Norwegian popular press. I was rapidly approaching the conclusion that he was really little more than a 'bull-shitter'.

At the end of March Paul Hallan was desperate to get on with proceedings. We received a telex telling us that the other three partners had put their signatures on the personal guarantee, and all he needed now was for us to add ours. He concluded by saying, 'Please can you persuade your brothers and get this matter concluded immediately'.

I spent that day tramping back and forth across the yard, trying to persuade Ron. I soon realised that we would have to consider some other form of diluted entry fee. Freddy and Ron were aware of the importance of the truck supply to our ongoing business and gave me the go-ahead to find some sort of delayed acceptance of Paul Hallan's terms, but in no way would we have a joint and several guarantee. Telexes went backwards and forwards all morning as we searched for a combination of words to suit both parties. On Hallan's part, he needed to give words of comfort to Glamox. However, for our part, we needed to leave sufficient mud in the water to ensure that we could argue that we had been unreasonably pressurised into giving a guarantee that had been brokered by a beneficiary. Paul Hallan was insisting on a deadline of 12 noon and we finally agreed to a confused set of words which were later to cause eight years of argument.

My diary notes show that the discussions went on all day on Thursday 1 April 1982 and throughout the following morning. I was still not sure about anything until I received a telex timed at 4.10 from Alf Lau which briefly said, 'All is okay at Moxy now, start work'. On receiving the telex I sat back in my chair and reflected. I admired Paul Hallan greatly. I had never seen, before or after those meetings, a bank manager get quite so involved in ensuring that, come what may, nothing was going to stop him getting his bank out of the deep dark hole that Moxy had created. For my part I did not feel fulfilled in any way by the situation. I had achieved just about what I had, a mandate from my brothers to achieve, nothing more. I had managed to keep the goose alive and, above all, had ensured that trucks would continue to be produced and dispatched to the UK. I was annoyed with the guarantee situation because deep down I knew it was a fudge.

In a way I had overestimated Paul Hallan. I thought the whole deal had been heaven-sent for him and was convinced that when it came right down to the wire he would have picked up the responsibility for guaranteeing Glamox the last £150,000 rather than lose the deal. I am sure that, on his side, he was aware how important it was that trucks should continue to be produced and transferred to the UK and he was convinced that I would back down. The result in reality was a draw. The words used in those last three telexes were subject to extensive lawyers' interpretations on an annual basis for eight years to come.

While everything I experienced in the UK was positive, I could not say the same for Norway. Freddy, Ron and I always discussed our business on a daily basis. There were no endless, time-wasting meetings; it was a case of 'this is the problem; this is the solution', and a decision was made. On the other side of the North Sea, things were very different. My fortnightly Moxy Industrier discussions were deeply frustrating as I sat through meeting after meeting where little was decided upon.

From my point of view Moxy Industrier A/S never really existed. It was a complete and utter fudge from day one. Almost immediately unrest entered the camp. Alf Lau was not happy with the way things were being handled at the factory and it was decided that a professional chief executive would be sought to launch the company. I was a thorn in their side; at every meeting I would repeat my well-rehearsed speech about selling the Moxy product. Selling a product with a £55,000 price tag was not about smart selling, as would be used with consumer products like lemonade or baked beans. It was about confidence building, selling a product which had good after-sales service guaranteed and a proven residual value. Confidence was not something that could be gained overnight.

My enthusiastic co-directors had pitched production at 200 units for the twelve months of 1982 and Alf Lau's laptop computer had convinced everybody, including the bank, that fantastic profits would be made. However, the reality of the situation was very different. At that time, we had only two real markets. Norway had taken ten units on a special deal with Paye & Brinck, appointed the new dealer for Norway, and the rest had gone to the UK. This was not sufficient for a viable factory and I am sure that if the facts had been known on 2 April 1982, when Alf Lau confirmed that there was new life at Moxy Industrier A/S, we would have conceded that the company was already insolvent.

May was, as is normal in Norway, a most unproductive month. Traditional national holidays interfered with production. My diary notes indicate frustration at the endless meetings which took place during April and May deciding policy and I was very much an outsider with little input. It seemed that my four Norwegian co-directors were the ones making the decisions.

By the time June came and the first truly formal meetings took place, Alf Lau was beginning to despair. Neither truck building nor truck sales were on target and to cap it all the quality of what little was being produced was sub-standard.

Bothered by output and quality, my thoughts turned once more to getting some cash in for the sold units and I became perturbed at how long it was taking Paye & Brinck to pay for their ten trucks. This most credible of organisations was certainly taking its time in paying up. I was bemused. Not only was it strange that they had not paid for their goods but no one seemed too bothered about the situation. This puzzled me greatly. Here we were producing and selling below target, obviously struggling, and yet no one seemed to give a toss about whether we had been paid by Paye & Brinck. Furthermore, I was instructed to keep my nose out of it, to leave it to them.

However, while perturbed by this situation, I was pleased to hear that the other partners had at last paid up their share capital. I was also delighted to learn that the board had appointed a new chief executive, Svein Stafos, from Volvo in Sweden. He was to start on 1 July. It was ironic that the paths of Moxy and Svein Stafos should cross so soon after his involvement in the Swedish-Norwegian proposal to exchange financial aid for industrial know-how. Stafos had been the man at the centre of the grader-manufacturing department of the former Volvo company which was rumoured, as part of the Swedish-Norwegian exchange, to be transferring to Molde. However, that move was never to take place; production had ceased and so Svein Stafos was free to join Moxy.

Back in England, visits to create confidence with Moxy Industrier's major suppliers, such as Scania and ZF, had been arranged and our first exhibition in Paris was imminent. It was generally felt that this would change our fortunes, certainly in France if not in the rest of Europe, by showing that we were well and truly back on the map again. During the course of the summer, while there was no chance yet of international markets for Moxy being resurrected, we won an order for six units from Portugal and six units from Israel.

By 1982 our turnover at Brown UK had increased from £1.5 million 1979 to a projected £10 million in 1982 – our new-found fortune in Moxy and Tonstad equipment was providing us with healthy profits but with limited working capital we were being stretched financially. In the early years, visits to the bank were few and far between and the bankers were always left to Trevor Gurney of Brown Butler to sort out. As our financial inadequacies grew, Trevor's visits became more frequent and he no longer went unaccompanied. More often than not, Freddy and I would tag along, while Ron preferred to abstain.

Every morning I would consult Andrea and Alan Watson to see how many Moxys we could afford or what we could afford to pay for that day. If we had enough cash in I would set off round the corner to the bank. Grovelling profusely I would humbly ask the manager if he could advance funds so that we could transact more of our £65,000 units. However, inevitably the day arrived when the local bank could no longer cope with our lumpy cashflow and off we marched down to the big city to see if Trevor could find us someone else who would have a better understanding of our growing business. Trevor told us that the NatWest branch in Leeds had, most unusually by banking standards, appointed a young and aggressive manager. Trevor suspected that he might be sympathetic to our needs. Figures were prepared, projections calculated, best suits cleaned and off we went to Leeds. Trevor marched us from his office to the NatWest. When we arrived I fully expected to be thrown into a side room and left to sweat for twenty-five minutes. I had always been led to believe that bank managers were higher beings and far too busy to see anybody straightaway. However, to my surprise out stepped a human being, a young and highly personable individual, who shook our hands and actually expressed delight at seeing us. I was amazed. He quickly got a grasp of what we were trying to achieve. He spoke to us as equals and told us that he would come and see us at the new Riffa depot as soon as he could. His name was John Tugwell, and he was true to his word. After the usual to-ing, fro-ing and necessary probing we received our new banking facilities.

PART 4

Brown Group International

CHAPTER II

An Interesting Time

LIFE WAS EXCITING AGAIN. On the face of things, Moxy looked as if it had been rescued, though I knew deep down that the newly created Moxy Industrier A/S production unit was only a temporary solution. Paul Hallan had done a first-class job for the bank but the old financial shackles which had brought down Hatlebakk's company were still in place and without a miracle it would be terribly difficult to service those loans. For the time being we would have to make the best of what we had. That was a strange time. In the UK life was positive and everyone involved in the company had just one objective – to be the best. This was instilled in everyone from the top to the bottom of our company. But, in Norway, the mood was very different. I continued to jog along from one meeting to another, but I was really just an employee working for the factory on the days they needed me; my only contribution was that of a caretaker export sales manager until the new managing director was installed. Unfortunately, under the new regime, I did not really have the stomach for jetting around the world, drumming up export Moxy business one day and then spending the next deciding from where we could rustle up last month's wages. In England, the pressure was eased somewhat by my loyal colleague Clive Wadsworth, the sales manager, who in his gentlemanly way was doing a great job for me in clearing up all the loose ends. He was always there as a conduit through whom Ron, Freddy and I passed messages, for by now, because of our diverse activities, our meetings inevitably had become less frequent.

One other satisfying aspect of our operation was that we were still very much a family business, but now without the daily family quarrels which appear to be a feature of all family businesses. The company had become so diversified that we had created a second management tier. We brothers tended to meet now only formally at board meetings where Trevor Gurney kept order. Ron and I met in the evenings and talked for hours on the telephone about the general direction our group was taking.

As a company, we were looking forward to the annual plant-hirers' and contractors' site-equipment demonstration show at Hatfield. For the first time we would be there in all our glory with a large stand equal to those of our competitors, such as Levertons and Blackwood Hodge. We had been eagerly anticipating this all through the spring and it was decided that we would make a real impact at the show.

Willie Dalrymple was doing well in Scotland with the Fiatallis franchise and Ron was well advanced with taking over the Selwood section of this dealership which would take us down to Birmingham. To add to this we had what appeared to be a credible solution at Moxy. In all we had everything we needed to build on for the future, and to convey this fact with maximum impact we launched our own newspaper, *Earth Shattering News*. My diary shows that it was all hands on deck between 2 April and the production run on 26 April. Clive had a large input into co-ordinating this venture. Like a real newspaper, it was printed during the night of Monday 26 April and delivered fresh to our SED stand for the 9 a.m. start on Tuesday 27 April. Our staff proudly puffed out their chests and thumbed their noses at our Volvo competitors, two stands down the aisle, who had done their best to capitalise on the problems we had suffered. Our customers, too, rallied round us, always willing to support the fledgling underdogs. The British contractors seemed perfectly satisfied to watch 'David' putting up a strong fight against the arrogance and power of the 'Goliaths', such as Volvo, Terex and Caterpillar.

By the time of SED our plane had been in operation for seven months and was proving a shrewd investment. In those early days we only had a small team and no depot network, so it helped us to get around the country, doing deals at a speed which would have been impossible by road. At the SED, Cessna Golden Eagle was used to ferry potential customers backwards and forwards to see our new range of machines. Willie Dalrymple brought his hand-picked contingent of Scottish contractors; there were only six or seven of them at most. However, after a successful day at the SED, merry with a cocktail of whisky and beer, and amply stuffed with potted meat sandwiches, crisps and peanuts, the Scottish contingent had taken on a snowball effect: there were certainly more than six or seven for the homeward journey. The Golden Eagle was going to be a bit inadequate; a jumbo would have been more suitable. After weeding out the numbers as best we could, we loaded the merry Scots aboard and watched them head along the runway. Rumour has it that Willie noticed that they were rapidly running short of tarmac so he suggested to his Scottish comrades that they jump up and down to gain momentum. Fortunately, despite its excess baggage, the plane took off and the seven contractors, Willie and an unknown number of others were soon airborne and heading back north of the border.

On the political front, Margaret Thatcher was settling in and the battle lines were being drawn to take on the unions. I used to become nervous at times when strikes were discussed because I had seen the damage that strike action had inflicted on our industrial base during the 1970s. During this period we had been such a small fish that the ripples in other parts of the industrial pond had left us pretty much unaffected. However, now it was different. Our trucks were predominantly employed throughout England and Scotland hauling earth and coal on mining sites and any disruption in this area would have a serious effect on our sales generally.

Of the three brothers, Freddy was a serious supporter of Margaret Thatcher. He was as tough a disciplinarian as she was and he fully supported her confrontational approach to the situation. To my knowledge, Ron never aired his political views in public, or certainly not in the same way that Freddy did, and for my part I was still a little confused. I had voted Conservative even though we had prospered under a Labour government. I am never quite sure of the reasons why but, like others at the time, I was becoming increasingly afraid of people like Arthur Scargill and other prominent union leaders who for some unknown reason seemed to occupy more of the media's attention than our elected representatives. I think my politics were tempered by our financial situation. We had managed to keep our business private and expanded on bank borrowings. Any industrial disruption could have had a disastrous effect on our growing business and I think it was this which made me sceptical of Margaret Thatcher's approach, which would inevitably lead to a confrontation. During this period of our business life there was no room for politics.

Looking back through my diary, April, May and June saw us endlessly reorganising. First, there were all the upheavals of Moxy; then there was the changing of the bank, followed by SED in the UK and, at the end of June, Expomat in Paris, which resulted in a Portuguese dealer being appointed, an enquiry for six trucks in Israel and many other leads being processed. Throughout April and May we were either at Moxy meetings in Oslo or they were meeting us at our Riffa headquarters. We would have meeting after meeting with component suppliers, trying to encourage them back into the factory so that we could continue to manufacture the units: it was no easy task.

After Expomat, at the beginning of July, we welcomed Svein Stafos into the fold as he took up his new position as managing director of Moxy Industrier. May and June had been a honeymoon period and by July the honeymoon was officially over. With hindsight, none of us faced up to reality during May and June; we had all buried our heads in the sand and waited for the new MD to come along and 'do his stuff'. By the time Stafos slid into the driving seat, my diary notes suggest that I greeted him with my personal anxiety about the product and the financial situation at Moxy. No sooner had he arrived, however, than the dreaded July shutdown was upon us and Norway came to its customary standstill.

On the marketing front we had quite a coup in the shutdown period. The Israeli enquiry for six trucks was turning into reality and the Livnat family arrived in England on the day that I was due to go on holiday. By the evening we had a provisional order for six units. I could go on holiday with ease of mind. At this time my daily outlook was dictated by how many trucks we had sold and at what point we were on the overdraft.

July flew by and on 1 August Norway was back to normal. The first week of August was dominated by meeting after meeting. A mystery was unfolding. The Moxy operation up to this point had been dominated by the Norwegian shareholders but now the board was looking more balanced. There was a Swedish managing director, a Norwegian part-time chairman and I was from England. One of the financial mysteries which had bothered us for three months was this: someone at the factory had now decided to take an interest in the ten dumptrucks which had been sold to Paye & Brinck, the new Norwegian dealer. This business had previously been handled by Kirston Bergo and other factory personnel, and I had been instructed not to interfere as he was quite capable of handling the situation. By now the outstanding money for the payment of these trucks was well overdue. A telephone call from Paye & Brinck's factory immediately resolved the mystery. Paye & Brinck confirmed that they had paid for the ten trucks immediately on delivery and no monies were outstanding. Further hasty telephone calls between shareholders established that something very peculiar was going on.

Alf Lau called a meeting immediately and questioned the Norwegian shareholders at length to try to track down the missing cash. An obvious connection was immediately apparent between the collection of cash from Paye & Brinck and the paying up of share capital by the Norwegian shareholders. The shareholders were getting a little hot under the collar as the jigsaw was put together. Alf Lau probed deeper; but his line of questioning was abruptly interrupted by high drama when a most astonishing turn of events took place. Kirston Bergo started to pull contorted faces and groan in pain; he suddenly announced to the meeting that he was feeling very ill and that his doctor had diagnosed him as having a terminal illness. He said that his time was running out and he could not stand up to such an impertinent line of questioning. Nobody knew what to say or do; we could not continue demanding explanations from such a sick man. Obviously we wanted to get to the bottom of the mystery but we had to respect Bergo's health. Consequently, Bergo's announcement had the effect of deferring our probing questions as well as any further action we might have decided to take. Bergo was hustled from the boardroom to recover. I have never been quite sure how many were in on the conspiracy but I have my suspicions that the whole event was stage-managed to avoid embarrassing the chairman and to give the Norwegian shareholders time to put back the cash which everyone was now beginning to suspect had been misappropriated. I'm glad to say that Bergo is still fit and thriving.

I was so angry with what I had learned. All my suspicions had now been confirmed. I had found it strange that Paye & Brinck had not paid for their machines and thought it bizarre when I was told to keep my nose out of it. I had an inkling that the Norwegians were up to something, but quite what, I did not know. Suddenly, the picture became clear. I flew straight home to London on 19 August, and immediately got in touch with Trevor Gurney to give him the news. While we had gone into this with our eyes open we did not expect Moxy to be in trouble quite as soon as this, nor did we expect that it would be trouble of this sort. After all, the company had been properly constituted and had an independent non-executive chairman who was there to keep order.

I was so angry about the situation that I spoke again with Trevor on the Saturday and we decided that we would return to Molde on the Sunday night. Our own plane now gave us this flexibility. We left Leeds-Bradford at about 7 o'clock that evening only to make slow progress over the North Sea. About 9 o'clock it was obvious that we would not reach Molde that night, so we had to divert into Stavanger. After failing to find a hotel at short notice we spent the night trying to get as much sleep as possible on the airport seats. Then we set off again at 5.30 the next morning and arrived in Molde at 7 o'clock, reaching the factory by 7.30 a.m.

The old faithful were still in place and only too willing to help us in our quest to get to the root of the mystery. They too were incensed by the situation. Svein Stafos, Trevor and I set about examining the books. Soon our worst fears were confirmed. It was clear that the share capital was gone and the company was probably trading illegally. My diary notes again show 'Meeting with Alf Lau at 1.30 p.m.' and 'Emergency meetings' going on all afternoon with various interested parties. The day rounded off with Trevor and I having dinner at 7.30. It was my fortieth birthday and I had nothing to celebrate. Once again work had interfered with my private life. Trevor Gurney spelt out over dinner that he could not see any hope and I should reconsider my own position.

A board meeting was called for the following morning, 24 August 1982. Trevor and I were astonished when the finances of the company were passed over as though they were irrelevant. More importance was attached to deciding who wanted coffee and who wanted tea. It was claimed that further investigation was needed before they could even consider our findings. The meeting then moved on to more pressing matters such as the building of trucks for the NCB in the UK. I remember thinking how farcical it all was. Here we were in a financial maelstrom and yet were managing to pass it all off with about as much importance as you might attach to losing twenty pence down the back of the sofa. After discussing the NCB order, we moved on to discussing brakes, turning rings, chassis problems and so on and the meeting finally ended at 4 o'clock. Trevor and I flew back to Leeds-Bradford with no real conclusion, only that for our part something had to be done quickly.

Browns had to accept the fact that Moxy Industrier was desperately in need of more capital; without it Moxy could not survive. Alf Lau was investigating all possibilities and was quite confident that one Norwegian institution or another would come along and bale Moxy out. Only a few months earlier, I had seen the finance-raising efforts of Paul Hallan and knew it had been a struggle. I had to be realistic: the chances of finding another backer were minimal. We could console ourselves with the fact that Browns UK was doing quite well but we all agreed that we were in no position to do anything for Moxy ourselves without jeopardising further what we had already achieved in the UK.

Once again it was back to looking for a new profit generator. Once again we were going to try to widen our horizons. Freddy suggested that I should go to Egypt to explore the possibility of finding work in Cairo. I was to look for work similar to that which we had done on North Sea oil and in Argentina. We learned that the Cairo sewage schemes were getting well under way and that some of the contractors with whom I had worked on previous projects were calling for machines. I was not enthusiastic about going but I knew that real profit-generating work could now be found only overseas. Anyway, this trip would provide me with an opportunity to satisfy a nagging desire I had had for quite some while.

I have not mentioned this in my story hitherto but even at the end of the Hatlebakk era and during the Moxy Industrier period there was said to be a white knight called Mustapha Sami who would be happy to enter into Norway from Egypt – a mystery man with sufficient funds to resurrect the flagging Moxy enterprise. The Brown brothers were kept well away from this man, mainly because with Mustapha Sami on board the Norwegians would have had no further need for us; without such a white knight, our help and presence were essential to them.

Rumours circulated from credible sources within the factory that this man had visited the factory under both regimes, wearing a white gown in true Arabian fashion, and senior personnel had been seen 'licking his boots'. Rumours suggested that he would be prepared to inject money into the factory and would immediately relieve them of 200 trucks. I was intrigued by this white knight from Egypt and having obtained a description and address I decided to use my trip to Cairo to see if there was any substance to these stories.

As was always the case, I wanted an additional reason to justify this expensive trip, and so I arranged to visit the Livnat family from Tel Aviv. They had just taken six Moxy trucks to Israel to work on a newly constructed power station. The whole trip was shrouded in mystery as the contractors, inviting me to Cairo, assured me that I would be able to get to Tel Aviv even though the world at large was led to believe there was no contact or connection between the Arab countries and Israel and that you simply could not be seen to be dealing with both. You had to choose one and then form a puppet company, probably in Liechtenstein or somewhere, which could look after the other. After some hurried arrangements I left for Cairo on 22 September 1982 and stayed at the Sheraton. My first meeting took place at 11 o'clock the following morning in Cairo. I was advised to leave the hotel no later than half-past eight because of traffic problems.

Between all my meetings I decided to put aside some time to try to find the mysterious Mustapha Sami. First, I trawled the taxi rank in search of a driver who could speak a little English; having found one, I showed him the address I wanted to go to. Sitting back, I prepared myself to meet the infamous Mustapha Sami in his plush office block in the centre of Cairo. To my surprise, the taxi-driver started to head off in the direction of the less attractive part of the town. After flapping my hands around, I eventually gained his attention. He stopped the car and I asked him where we were going, surely Mr Sami's office was in the other direction towards the city centre? I told the driver that he was a very rich man with investments overseas. The driver smirked, a knowing smirk, before assuring me that this was the right way. We twisted and turned down more narrow side streets, passed beggars on the street corners and went further into the slums. Eventually I went from door to door and the passages grew darker and darker. By then I had come to the conclusion that, whoever Mustapha Sami was, he was not a man of means, and I abandoned my quest. Perhaps he was just someone who liked going to Norway for his holidays, all expenses paid. To this day I have never met the mysterious white knight and I am still curious as to who he is and what his real intentions were.

During the following Thursday and Friday, I crammed in more meetings, all the time asking my hosts how I could get from Cairo to Tel Aviv. Always the same answer came back. 'Be at the reception counter of the Hilton Hotel in Cairo at 4 a.m. on Sunday morning.' I had no reservation, no ticket, nothing to indicate how I was to get from Cairo to Tel Aviv. I was told in hushed voices that my journey would happen, but there would be no evidence that it had taken place. As directed, I arrived at the counter at 4 a.m. to be comforted by two or three other businessmen standing around rather nervously. After a short period, a man arrived with some torn-up pieces of paper, on each of which was scribbled a number. We were all given a piece and were told to make our own way to the airport. There would be no indication on the monitor boards: we must just ask for Air Sinai.

On the hotel steps, I hailed a waiting taxi, only to be pushed aside by the hotel security guard. Immediately a row broke out between the taxi-driver and the security guard and it was obvious that my choice of driver was not acceptable. The angry exchange continued until the taxi-driver fell to the ground, having being struck in the mouth by the obnoxious guard, who then proceeded to bundle me into another waiting taxi, this time one of his own choice. By now, I was becoming a little apprehensive. I must have asked the driver a dozen times, 'You are definitely taking me to the airport, aren't you?' He repeatedly assured me that there was no problem and that he would get me there.

After an unpleasant twenty minutes, I arrived safely and immediately started my quest to find Air Sinai. There weren't many people around and I went from one to the other asking for the airline. It was only when I stopped flapping around that one of the people I had previously asked came over to me and, out of the side of his mouth, said 'Follow me'. Eventually about six of us were shown through a series of passages around the airport and turned up at a small aircraft which was to take us to Tel Aviv.

CHAPTER 12

Moxy in Trouble Again

To my relief, Isaac Livnat was waiting for me. With a beaming smile and a vigorous shake of my hand, he welcomed me to Tel Aviv. As we strolled to Isaac's car I recounted the story of my 'magical mystery tour', telling him about the episode with the taxi-driver, the intrigue at the airport and so on. From the airport we went straight to his yard and met Zeevik, his son, and the rest of the day was spent looking at six Moxys and making a note of their various problems. Having examined the machinery, I really just wanted to head for home, not because I had grown tired of the Livnats' company but rather because that day marked the start of Yom Kippur. After a few quick phone calls to the airport, however, I had pretty well ruled out any chance of catching a plane back to England, and it looked as though every other non-Jew had had the same idea as me. Consequently I had no choice but to stay the night. Zeevik left me at the hotel on the sea front and handed over a small bag of essentials prepared by his mother. Poking my nose in the bag I found a loaf of bread, cheese, apples and oranges. He told me that nothing would move the following day and that I had to prepare myself for a long and uneventful twenty-four hours. As a joke, I said that I hoped the Arabs would not invade this time; Zeevik told me that the Israelis would not be falling for that trick again: from now on the military would be on guard.

After a long day I dined early and went to bed. In the morning I woke to silence, complete and utter silence, it was quite unnerving. Looking out of my bedroom window, I could see no sign of life; there was no one on the beach, no one in the town at all. The only thing I could see was an ambulance and a police car standing a distance away from my hotel but I couldn't see anyone in uniform. I wrote in my diary: 'Nothing to do for the first time in my life'. I spent the first part of the day exhausting my English newspaper which I had collected at the airport, strolling around my room and reading the hotel notices ('What to do in case of fire', 'Breakfast times', 'Laundry service' and so on) before looking through all the drawers and the cupboards. In a moment of extreme boredom, I decided to carry out a fitness programme that I had seen on television at the hotel in Egypt. The programme suggested travellers should put their toes under the end of the bed and start by doing one or two sit-ups to strengthen their stomach muscles. To my disappointment, I literally could do just that – one or two. I have gone on doing this ever since in my fight against an expanding waist-line and I am proud to say that I can now do up to 100 in any one session.

The day passed slowly and I spent much of it mulling over the problems which I knew lay ahead. While I had been away it was clear that Svein Stafos would have got the measure of his job and would have started to realise the enormity of the problems he would have to face. Anyway, the Livnat family picked me up at 7 p.m., as promised, and we spent the evening having a delightful dinner in the old Jaffa area of Tel Aviv. I promised myself that one day I would return. I arose early on the Tuesday morning for another inspection of the Moxys before catching my lunchtime plane. To my surprise Zavik was in reception when I came down. He handed me a telex message saying that I must telephone Moxy in Norway immediately. My heart sank as I knew it would not be good news. At the first opportunity, when I knew it would be after 8 a.m. in Norway, I telephoned Svein Stafos.

'Listen, Gordon,' he said, 'you must fly to Molde tonight. I need to speak to you. We have problems to sort out.'

'I can't come tonight, I've got meetings in London tomorrow. How about our meeting in London?' I knew that with the ridiculous amount of time it took to get from anywhere to Molde there was no chance of my getting back to London to meet my commitments if I did what Svein wanted.

'What about Oslo? Can you get to Oslo? I could meet you there,' he asked.

After some hectic telephone calls, I arranged to catch the 2.30 plane via Vienna and Copenhagen and arrived in Oslo that night at 10 o'clock. Svein and I then discussed the problems at Moxy until 2 a.m. His argument was that he had exhausted every possibility within Norway to keep the company going and to my surprise turned the tables on me by saying that I, or rather Browns in England, had a moral responsibility to do something, the implication being that as I looked after marketing and there were forty trucks in stock, we should immediately take them to England and pay for them. This would give the factory the cashflow it urgently needed to continue production while he sorted things out.

I counter-argued that due to the irregularities that had been taking place within the management in Norway there was no way that I could convince my brothers to commit themselves to these forty trucks. I was really trapped between a rock and a hard place because being a director of Moxy Industrier I wanted to help, but on the other hand I could only burden the Brown UK operation with these trucks if I could get them at a knockdown price. This would enable me to dispose of the units more easily in the UK in the likely event of the factory going bankrupt yet again. After speaking to Trevor Gurney and considering my position both at Moxy and at Browns, I decided to leave the trucks where they were, taking only one or two at a time, when I was sure that we could dispose of them at the proper transfer price to avoid being drawn into any conflict of interest. However, this was not good enough for Stafos and at 2 a.m. when we finally went to bed he insisted that he should come to England and lobby my two brothers himself.

I set off for England early on Wednesday 29 September. The following days were taken up with an endless round of meetings between Ron, Trevor, Freddy and Willie. I was drawing up a contingency plan which I did not want to enact. I met Allied Irish Finance, Commercial Credit Finance, St Margaret's Trust and SocGen Lease, lining up ways in which, if I had to, I could finance the forty trucks in stock to give the factory some relief.

In early October I had yet another round of meetings in Oslo and Molde with the Moxy Industrier board to try to lift some of the mounting pressure they were under from creditors plus the unresolved problem of the missing cash from Paye & Brinck. A great deal of time was spent in meetings, trying to clarify our legal situation with regard to events which had taken place in Norway and it was eventually agreed that I would have to fly back to Molde the following month, when the full Moxy board was going to meet yet again.

The saga continued throughout the rest of October with meeting after meeting and with Stafos making his final appeal by flying to England on 27 October with proposals that he felt could save the factory. It was one of those rare occasions when we were all in a sombre mood and I arranged to have dinner at home where we could discuss the problems in peace and quiet.

Sadly his journey was in vain as we could find no common ground for a rescue. Stafos had entered the Moxy camp too late to save it; he was a man with good intentions but we felt that we could take no further risks in this direction. The whole Moxy Industrier set-up was ill conceived. The local board members in Molde had lost our trust. Monies the company needed had been misappropriated. Work had been carried out by companies associated with the local directors on a 'jobs for the boys' basis, and to cap it all, ridiculous expense accounts had been submitted to the point where the share capital had long since disappeared. It was a complete sham. Although Stafos's final appeal to the Browns was well intentioned, we could not forget that he was also trying to save his own skin. He had left a secure job with one of the largest companies in Sweden only to find himself up to his neck with problems; his previous experience had left him ill equipped to cope with a company with a cash crisis of this magnitude. Sadly, Stafos left England with the door shut firmly in his face. Soon after his arrival back home on Friday 29 October the expected telephone call was put through to me. Stafos would not tolerate the situation any longer and had called an extraordinary board meeting for 2 November. It wasn't long before rumours started to flow through the factory; people were already 'gathering wood for the funeral pyre'. But it was not until I arrived home in the evening that I started to receive telephone calls from colleagues in Molde saying that Moxy was already in receivership. One caller stressed that he knew for certain that this was the case because he had heard it from a friend of a friend of a friend of a lawyer in Molde – so it must be true. As far as I was concerned it was the calm before the storm: Monday was not a day I was looking forward to.

Saturday morning ticked over as normal; Tracey, the receptionist, chatted to our customers on the phone; I could see the forklift truck rattling across the yard and I watched the men flock sheep-like towards the canteen as the tea-break buzzer sounded at half-past ten. Life at Riffa went on as normal. I could not help thinking: 'If only they knew'. But it was important to put a brave face on the situation; everybody would find out soon enough. Sunday was a supposed day of rest. I remember spending it with my family at Rufforth Park, watching Simon and Tina with their ponies. Freddy had done a good job of nurturing their interest in horses and on most Sundays Liz would take them to a local show. I rarely accompanied them, but for once I did.

Monday 1 November was taken up with final consultations with Ron, Freddy and Trevor Gurney and our lawyers before my 5 p.m. departure for Molde. The wind must have been blowing towards Norway that night as the journey only took 2 hours 22 minutes from take-off to landing. Not only did this faster journey time give great pleasure to myself and the company cheque book but it also gave great pleasure to Captain Ray Hughes. He would record our flight time on every journey from Leeds-Bradford to Molde and worked extremely hard at conserving fuel. On every flight he would be in constant contact with air traffic control, often requesting permission to fly higher where the winds were more favourable and always calling well in advance to Rexton control to ask if we could cut off the corner instead of flying up the Molde fjord, which was a notoriously bumpy ride due to the varying air conditions over the mountains and the fjord.

When Ray and I arrived in Molde, we checked into our familiar room at the Alexandra Hotel. To save cash, Ray always slept on the en suite settee and never complained. He was a true companion, always in high spirits, a man with a passion for flying. On Tuesday 2 November, I made my way to the factory knowing that this was not going to be a very friendly meeting. When I arrived, I went upstairs to the MD's office to find it stripped of the usual desks and chairs. Instead there were three rows of chairs. I had been expecting a meeting for just the usual six of us, but it was clear that there were going to be many more. Svein was already there and by 9 o'clock the whole entourage had arrived: Alf Lau with his lawyer, Kirsten Bergo with his lawyer, Inge Pettison with his lawyer, Lars Pette Ose with his adviser and what seemed like every other Tom, Dick and Harry (each with his lawyer) squeezed into the room.

The meeting began with Alf Lau explaining the gravity of the situation and that the meeting would be conducted in Norwegian with Jan Vidar Nerland translating for me. The whole day was spent exploring every conceivable avenue, for we were all desperate to find some form of rescue if we could. Everyone seemed to come up with at least one good idea but every suggestion that was made needed the two ingredients that we no longer had: time and money. They would spend an hour explaining how it could be done, only then for the lawyer to stand up and take three minutes to say what everybody knew, that there was no time left. The company was trading illegally.

The end was nigh. In the late afternoon, after a day of fruitless discussions, the bank managers arrived, bringing with them their hand-picked executioner, Mr Larhammer. Once again legal rituals were undertaken but at 8 p.m. the vote was taken by the board to put Moxy Industrier A/S into 'konkurs' – receivership – and offer the running of the company to Mr Larhammer and Mr Agil Wold, the lawyers chosen to be the equivalent of a receiver in the UK. The only difference was that a Norwegian 'receiver/lawyer' was generally some local village chap with more experience in handling divorces or defending sheep rustlers than dealing with receiverships.

The meeting broke up that evening at 9 p.m. Jan Vidar had spent some time in explaining to me in his translation that this was not the end, but once again it was simply the beginning of the end. Mr Larhammer and the bank concerned had already prepared a statement to the workers and the press that Moxy would continue as normal the next morning, and that everyone would be reassured for the time being that their jobs would continue. This statement is the one issued by receivers worldwide and is lifted straight out of any old lawyer's guide to receivership. To anyone familiar with their industry it is a legal light. What they are really saying is that, 'We want everyone at work tomorrow while we work out how many redundancies we are going to make on Friday'.

The meeting broke up and I shook hands with those gathered in the office; it was a moment of doom and gloom. Molde's dream had ended, and we had lost our 'golden goose'. As I walked down the stairs, Jan Vidar Nerland offered me a ride back to Molde, only a seven-mile drive from the factory. We set off out of the car park and down the straight road away from the factory. Jan Vidar told me that this definitely would be the eventual end of Moxy, a statement with which I could not disagree. I remember thinking that Paul Hallan, the smart bank manager who had featured so strongly in the negotiations only six months earlier, must have been choking with laughter at our expense. He and his bank had got out relatively unscathed, his formula for success had turned sour and here we were 'holding the baby'. I asked Jan Vidar to stop the car so I could take one last look at the factory that had become my second home over the last six months. I felt certain that this was it; I was going home to England to get on with whatever business we had left. After all, the gaping hole left by Moxy now had to be filled. Jan Vidar dropped me back at the Alexandra Hotel. That evening Captain Ray and I entered the dining room in sombre mood. I can still remember what we ate: we started with *blomshell* (cauliflower) soup, followed by an excellent peppered steak. Ray, though quieter than usual, soon rallied when the food arrived. There were only two passions in his life that could outstrip flying: and they were talking and eating, both of which he did in abundance that evening. As usual, he was a tonic.

The evening was rounded off with a couple of glasses of wine, and some entertainment from the local live band. The music was excellent and it masked the tinnitus which constantly rings in my ear. The next morning was to be an early rise. As usual Ray went off ahead of me to file his flight plan and ensure that the aircraft had had its final checks before take-off. I was in the breakfast room, having an ample supply of curried and pickled herring, a food which I had taken a fancy to over the previous five years. Suddenly my thoughts were interrupted by the sound of the tannoy: 'Would Gordon Brown please go to the telephone booth'. Mr Larhammer was on the phone. 'I trust you slept well. Are you returning to England?' he said.

I told him that I was leaving immediately. He begged me to wait and then asked me to come out to the factory as he wanted to talk to me. He had already arranged a meeting for 1 p.m. for us to meet Mr Brandeggen at the bank in Molde. So, here I was again, only six months down the line, playing the same game with the same rules, the 'let's find another mug to buy Moxy game. It was all becoming a bit repetitive. However, I still knew it was essential for us, as the most important dealer, to stay involved if we could. So, once assurances had been given that the bank would provide money to keep the factory going I took off for Leeds-Bradford at 4.50 p.m. The journey home was long and bumpy, the wind was against us. The turbulence reflected my mood; I had more than three hours to mull over our new-found state of affairs and the words of the men at Moxy kept haunting me. They had implied that there was only one buyer for Moxy, and my problem was not that we might be the only runner in a one-horse race but rather the fact that I now had to go home and convince Freddy and Ron that we should have anything more to do with this nightmare scenario from across the water. How was I to convince them that buying Moxy might be a worthwhile investment? I had already convinced myself that we had not lost £125,000, but rather made our first downpayment on our latest venture.

CHAPTER 13

We Finally Take Over at Moxy

ONCE BACK in the UK, I knuckled down to my domestic UK work. Our October year-end management accounts indicated that turnover was now up to about £18 million with net profits at £500,000 after paying our usual interest burden and absorbing extraordinary costs associated with Moxy. The net worth of our group had risen to £2 million. Most of this had been accumulated from 1978 onwards. We had transformed ourselves from being an agricultural-based business in Yorkshire to a national organisation dealing in a small number of high-value goods. Our growth policy was paying dividends and there was no doubt in our minds that it was a policy we should continue.

Freddy continued to operate at a local level with our traditional agricultural business, while Ron presided over the tractor sales and machinery business. It was our 'bread and butter'. Increased profits had been achieved through our construction-equipment sales sector, though stability had never been its strong point. It was the high-profit, high-risk area of our business.

Our newly acquired Fiatallis franchise was regarded by most people, other than the dedicated Fiatallis users, as an enormous challenge. We knew it was a challenge, but we felt optimistic about our chances of success. Though we had so far sold only a few units, the profit margin per unit was high. In addition, the support coming from Turin was a great spur. Fiatallis wanted to increase their share in the UK market and we wanted to help them.

The Fiatallis man assigned to support us in our quest to succeed was a personable young chap by the name of Paul Moore, nicknamed Paulo Mooro, as we believed that to speak fluent Italian you simply had to stick an 'o' on to the end of each word. So dedicated was Signor Mooro to the Fiat product that he was a constant source of inspiration whenever he visited us. Many people considered the Fiat product to be inferior, mainly because of a lack of confidence in the organisation rather than the units themselves. Over the years, the UK market for Fiatallis construction equipment had crumbled time and again due to the continuous restructuring of its Italian parent organisation. However, with the enthusiasm of Paul we felt that the only way was up.

It was decided that with Moxy gone we would have to rely more and more on the Fiatallis product for our living. Willie Dalrymple in Scotland was making big inroads into the market and Ron was busy moulding the Selwood/Fiatallis dealership depots into our organisation. We were in two minds: one was mourning the loss of Moxy, the other was praising our intuitive decision to cover for that loss by extending the Fiatallis business. It had been an exercise of foresight but it had also stretched the group financially. Once the decision had been made the integration went forward very smoothly even while Moxy was collapsing around us.

No sooner had we satisfied ourselves that there was life after death and that business could go on without Moxy, than my diary shows that from mid-November the meetings to consider our outright possible ownership of the Moxy plant in Norway gathered momentum. Trevor Gurney's name appears time and time again. With our balance sheet showing that our net worth was strengthening all the time and our projections for 1983 showing turnover climbing with the possibility of a net profit line of £700,000, we began to believe in ourselves again and in our ability to acquire Moxy and to give ourselves and it stability once and for all.

All bids had to be in by Monday 13 December and I flew with ours the day before. When I arrived that Sunday evening it was clear from the social gathering in the Alexandra Hotel that it was not going to be quite the one-horse race that I had been led to believe. A dark horse was coming up on the outside. Svein Stafos was fighting his corner; he too had prepared a bid and it seemed that everyone in Molde knew the exact details of it.

I had set off from England with the authority to bid NKr. 33 million for all assets, fixtures and fittings and of course the factory. The rumour circulating that evening was that my rival bidder had made the mistake of having his bid typed up by a local resident and within half an hour of the person switching off the typewriter, everybody knew down the grapevine that he too was bidding NK. 33 million. I made it my business to listen and probe to the point where I felt that the information was quite accurate. It became clear to me that NKr. 33 million had to be beaten. Fortunately, Liz had left me a space in which to write my final bid: this practice of leaving room for adjustment had been one that I had adopted years before with our water-board tenders. In the old days, I would hear that so and so was going to tender *x* amount for the job. Not to be outdone, I would fill in my bid as I climbed the town hall steps.

The next morning as I delivered my bid to Mr Larhammer's office I filled the blank space as NKr. 33.5 million. My bid was promptly delivered at 8.30 a.m. on 13 December and I retired to my room at the Alexandra Hotel to await the outcome. The expected telephone call came in the late morning with Mr Larhammer inviting me to a meeting with the bankruptcy board at 2.30 p.m. Although he did not give too much of the game away I could tell from his voice that we were the successful bidder, but there was still a long way to go.

The 2.30 p.m. deadline came and I went to Larhammer's office to find the panel waiting for me. Mr Larhammer, in true legal fashion, opened the meeting by saying that my bid was receiving favourable consideration but was not to be interpreted at this stage as being the successful one. There was the usual clarification of the bid which was to include all stock, fixtures and fittings, and all intellectual property, patents and so on. In addition, the bid had to include the fixtures and fittings of a small fabrication factory on an island off the coast of Norway.

Mr Larhammer stated that certain government loans would be written off with the exception of one small loan on the property which we would service until it had been repaid. In addition, we had to satisfy them that we had adequate banking arrangements and an adequate management structure. His final request was political. Larhammer asked if we would give an undertaking never to sell the company outside Norway. This undertaking was discussed afterwards on a number of occasions and I said that I would do whatever I could to ensure that the company stayed within Norway. This personal verbal undertaking was to come back to haunt me in later years.

My diary notes continue to emphasise the daily to-ing and fro-ing. One significant note is on Thursday 16 December which states 'Engaged Jan Vidar Nerland to act on our behalf with regard to Moxy negotiations'. At that point in time he was actually still working for Lars Pette Ose. However, from that day forward, Ron and I relied heavily on his expertise. Trevor Gurney and Jan Vidar worked furiously to meet the conditions imposed upon us by the bankruptcy board. I was hoping that everything would be sorted out so that I could enjoy a traditional Christmas and a well-earned rest, but it was not to be. My diary notes say that Monday 20 December was to be the day when we were to receive formal acceptance of our bid, but procedures were not running as smoothly as we had hoped. Another meeting was set for Tuesday, but again the deadline passed and the meeting was rescheduled for Wednesday. Again the deadline passed. Larhammer was having to wrestle with two problems, one of which was public opinion and the other an illness in the family. The local paper, the *Romdals Budstikke*, continued to question why there was no Norwegian solution, and they were sceptical as to what the Brown brothers' intentions really were. The most dominant rumour was that we would get control of the factory and immediately move production to England. No matter how I explained to the journalists that we had no intention of moving the plant to the UK, adverse speculation increased the sale of the local newspaper and there was no way I could stop it.

I flew home to England at last. This time we must have had only a small headwind as we achieved the crossing in 2 hours 55 minutes. A board meeting had been arranged at Riffa with everyone present including Trevor Gurney. Despite my continued negotiations I could not categorically tell the board that we were the new owner of the Moxy plant in Norway. All the indications were that this was so but it was not until the morning of Friday 24 December that Larhammer telephoned me at the Riffa office to say that the bankruptcy board had accepted our bid and he believed that all conditions had been met. We would finalise everything immediately after Christmas.

We could not have wished for a better Christmas present. Now we could control the operation from start to finish – the product's design, production, quality control, sales, marketing and so on. The ball was firmly in our court, exactly where we wanted it to be. No longer would there be the embarrassment of problems with the units. We could now be sure of having the support of the factory in rectifying them. There was still a long way to go but the Brown brothers had taken their first step towards a major development: no longer satisfied with being a truck distributor, we were going to become truck manufacturers.

It was time for a celebration and we had just the party to go to. Ron and I packed up for the day and got ready to go to Ernest Crabtree's Christmas bash – an annual 'spirited do' put on by Ernest for clients and friends. The party was held in a hanger at the airport. The planes were pushed out, the doors closed and the heating turned up. Ron and I with the benefit of Ernest's hospitality celebrated in style. It was events like this that made it difficult to understand Ernest. Throughout the year he was a Yorkshire businessman, as tough as they come; then there would come this sort of gesture of thanks to everyone who supported him. It would seem to be completely out of character unless you knew the man.

After all the traumas of that year Christmas was a welcome break, with Christmas Day falling on the Saturday. We now had a complete Saturday to Saturday shutdown, which was becoming more and more traditional in the construction industry, so that we could take some annual holiday in this low productivity period. Once again it allowed a lull before the storm because although Mr Larhammer had accepted our bid and we had agreed terms for taking over the factory, I went home for Christmas knowing that all the verbal promises from banks and financial institutions, insurance companies and so on had still to become reality.

The new year began with Trevor Gurney and me flying to Molde once more. Ironically, Forretningsbank run by Mr Hallan and Mr Hals, now pledged its support for our project. I like to think it was the confidence and trust that was built up during the receivership of the year before, which persuaded Mr Hallan to come back in and support us on our own eighteen months later.

While we were sorting out the banking and the insurance and taking over Store Brands existing loan there was ever present the nagging dilemma as to who was going to be managing director at the factory. I had Svein Hjelle pencilled in as my candidate. Ron and Freddy had an open mind but our negotiations proceeded on the basis that there was an overlap situation at the factory and that we would choose someone in the fullness of time.

While I had been an admirer of Svein Hjelle, Ron was sceptical of his abilities and the bank managers would not even consider him as an option. The more I promoted Hjelle the more obvious it became that if he were to be selected, the bankers would withdraw their support and the promised bank facilities would not be forthcoming. Reluctantly, I had to accept that the only man I felt could do the job was not an option and unfortunately I had no other immediate solution.

From previous experience I knew that choosing a managing director could take anything up to four months. We could not wait four months, we needed an MD straight away; the only other possibility was to pick a potential leader from the existing workforce. Ron and I had no alternative but to go to Norway and see if there were any suitable candidates amongst the existing personnel.

With the formalities of banking and financing almost in place, Ron, Willie and I planned to go over on Wednesday 19 January. However, a phone call from David Brown, owner along with the Ogden family and chief executive of DJB Engineering, a dumptruck manufacturer seventy miles up the road in Durham, soon knocked that idea clean out of my head. Although we were competitors, we were in different leagues at that time. The Moxy truck was six-wheel drive and made from road-truck components, whereas DJB was producing a four-wheel truck and also a six-wheel truck, but this only drove on two of the three axles and made from Caterpillar components.

Over the years we had had little to do with one another; occasionally we had said 'Hello' at exhibitions but other than that our paths did not cross. We had been distributors, he a manufacturer. David invited me up for lunch on Friday 21 January. I really needed to get myself over to Norway, but I thought it would be more than beneficial to listen to what David had to say, so I accepted his invitation. David spent a lot of time that day lecturing me on the trials and tribulations of being a manufacturer. He told me that being a distributor was one thing but becoming a manufacturer was quite another. He was respectfully saying, 'Be careful, but good luck'.

I remember leaving the DJB factory at 3.30 that afternoon and getting a telephone call from the temporary managing director at the factory, asking what was going on. He complained that they were without direction. I promised I would be at the factory at 7.30 on the Monday morning, ready to take over. So with Sunday lunch out of the way, on 23 January, Ron, Willie and I left for Molde, not knowing that the events of the next two to three days would change the whole direction of our group. When we set off we intended to finalise everything, sign the banking documentation, sign for the company and choose a temporary managing director and to return to England in mid-week.

During the course of the next three days the jigsaw came into place on a daily basis with the exception of a suitable managing director. Over dinner each night we mulled over the problem. If we did not make some drastic changes, the whole thing would tumble the same way as the two previous Moxy organisations except that this time it would be our cash and our reputation that would go up the spout.

It was eventually decided that, for the time being, Ron would stay and run the factory. I would more or less relinquish any responsibility for operations within the factory although I would continue to deal with finance. In short, Ron would concentrate on creating an efficient production unit and I would go home and put my back into creating a worldwide Moxy dealer network. My main concern was to convince as many people as possible to become Moxy dealers in as many countries as possible throughout the world and to ensure that every truck we produced had a home to go to. As for the rest of the business, Freddy would step in where Ron had left off and run the agricultural sector, and all the sub-managers would move up a notch.

This had the affect of overcoming all immediate problems. I was immensely relieved that Ron would be taking over the factory as it had been the one aspect of the entire takeover which had really worried me. With everything in place, Willie and I returned to England, leaving Ron behind with the daunting task of revitalising morale and getting production up and on to a profitable footing as quickly as possible with the added burden of not being able to speak the language.

However, before I could get down to sorting out the Moxy dealership network, there were a few other pressing problems that needed to be resolved. As part of the bid for Moxy, we had struck an all-inclusive deal with the receivers. As well as the NKr. 33.5 million deal we had agreed to take on forty-two completed trucks as well as to straighten out problems with regard to a Deutz engine. This had been one of the factors which had swung the whole deal our way. There was also a problem of six trucks and boxes of spare parts on the docks in Portugal.

These units had become the subject of a dispute. They were due to be paid for on the same day as Moxy Industrier A/S went into receivership. The dealers in Portugal, Barata, in view of the situation at the factory in Norway, had decided not to pay. Moxy's lawyers had become pretty heavy handed but had still failed to recover the money. We had agreed, as part of the factory purchase deal, to take responsibility for these trucks and to pay the bankruptcy board in full. As I took this responsibility on my own shoulders I felt sure that I could win where the legal monsters had failed.

I had met Mrs Cetano, an important person in the Barata organisation, on two previous occasions and had come to the conclusion that she was a person who could be trusted. In all, there was about £350,000 riding on this issue, enough to pay the factory salaries for two months. I wanted to resolve the dispute as soon as possible. So on Sunday 30 January I caught the Varig flight down to Lisbon, and arranged to meet Mrs Cetano on the Monday morning. As arranged, we met and she listened attentively to what I had to say. I knew that the six trucks were crucial to our immediate capacity to survive and emphasised this point to her. She repeatedly asked for reassurance that the factory was going to continue and I was able to reassure her by pointing out that Ron was now in charge there. I had a letter from the bankruptcy board stating that I could pass title for these trucks.

She asked for time to discuss the situation with her co-directors and I can remember spending a nerve-wracking evening in the Sheraton Hotel in Lisbon, hoping for our sake that she would be given the authority to pay us. I knew that business was not easy in Portugal at that time; money could not be borrowed or moved without good justification. Nonetheless, I believed that if she had the wherewithal to pay for these trucks she would.

The following morning she joined me for breakfast at the hotel and explained that she had persuaded her co-directors to take the units on my assurance that there would be no more setbacks. I heaved a hefty sigh of relief, though I was aware that we were a long way short of the home straight. There was still another major hurdle to overcome, that of convincing their bank to transfer the money. We decided to tackle this hurdle together. So we went to the bank. She said she would try gentle persuasion; I would offer reassurance through documentary evidence. After a little persuasion, the bank manager finally agreed to transfer the disputed amount with my personal guarantee that upon transfer of the funds the trucks could be collected immediately from the docks.

I headed for the plane home, relieved and delighted not only that my perception of this lady had proved correct but that my belief in the value of face-to-face discussion had been reinforced. We had achieved what the legal sledgehammer had failed to bring home. The Barata organisation and Moxy of Norway had solved their dispute through amicable discussion. Both parties were content and a business relationship had been established. If we had tried to battle it out between lawyers we would have succeeded only in spending an astronomical amount of money as well as alienating or losing a successful dealer.

Over dinner the previous evening, Mrs Cetano had spent time trying to explain to me that she was the sister of some close relative of the previous president of Portugal. However, I am afraid I had paid little attention to that part of the conversation as I had been concentrating only on the problem of compensation. Only much later did I realise that Mrs Cetano is a member of one of the most important families in Portugal.

Back in Norway, Ron was moving fast, and within a month he resolved a number of problems at the factory, including the Deutz engine dispute. The main challenge now was to convince suppliers to believe in us again. Understandably, we were not having to barricade the factory doors in order to keep out those desperate to supply. To have betrayed their trust once would have been perhaps excusable, to do so twice would be unacceptable. However, we had to win them back. This meant an endless succession of meetings with Scania, ZF, Clark, all the people who supplied our engines and transmissions as well as steel suppliers and so on. We had to convince them that Moxy had potential and that we would turn it into a force to be reckoned with. It was essential that we regain their trust for without their credit for the production line, manufacturing Moxys would have been extremely difficult.

When we took over the reins at Moxy our immediate task had been to dispose as quickly as possible of the forty-two trucks we had bought from the Norwegian receiver on a ninety-day finance plan. We had spread the finance between two or three finance companies in the UK. With the Barata affair out of the way, it was now a case of six down, thirty-six to go and we had only eighty days to do it in. On top of selling those thirty-six units, we also had the formidable task of preparing to go to BAUMA, the international heavy plant and equipment fair in Munich, This show took place only once every three years and Moxy had to be there if we were to stand any chance of establishing ourselves as a worldwide truck manufacturer. With only seven weeks to go, our first task was to persuade the organisers to let us in; as usual the fair had been booked up months in advance.

At about the same time as all this was going on, we were in the process of selling Cessna BCSV and that weekend we accepted a bid of £80,000 for our good old faithful aircraft. It was not a bad deal when you consider that we had run the aircraft for eighteen months and got all our money back. The sad news for me was that the new owner insisted that Ray came as part of the package deal. The aircraft we intended to purchase to replace Cessna BCSV was a turbo-prop not a petrol-prop, and Ray was licensed to fly only petrol-prop aircraft. We had no choice but to let Ray accompany the old plane. He had been a wonderful comfort both in good and bad times and I was extremely sorry to see him go.

Having got the whole Moxy operation digested by the end of February I wrote in my diary just how many good business friends had 'mucked in' to help me, as they say in Yorkshire. Every day I made a personal visit to people whom I regarded as potential buyers and explained my situation. Each time I ended by saying, 'Come on, give us a chance, I won't let you down but I have thirty-six trucks I have to sell before the end of April'. In my diary I see names like Barton Plant – 2 Moxys 15 February; Gamble Plant – 2 Moxys 16 February; P. J. Burke – 3 Moxys; Cedarmain in Wales – 1 Moxy; Reynard Plant, Tony Rial at Bayford and Co. – 1 Moxy each; and so on and so on. During March and early April I kept up the momentum and before the month was out, all thirty-six trucks had been cleared. Another hurdle had been overcome. The finance companies had been paid off and it was now time to relax a little. It was these transactions which later became the subject of so much controversy in Molde and with the local press in Norway. It was not long before someone at the factory did a quick calculation and decided that we had obtained the factory for only 3 krone, apparently a statutory amount which we had had to pay.

There is no getting away from it. The whole deal had been a calculated risk. You had only to look at our liquidity at that time to see that we did not have the cash to buy Moxy for NKr. 33.5 million. However, we might not have had the cash but we did have excellent credibility with finance companies in the UK. We had an unblemished record of borrowing and repayment. Our credibility with the finance companies proved to be the key to our purchase of the Moxy factory. It is true to say that we sold the forty-two units for roughly the same price as we paid for the factory. In addition, we paid £200,000 for all the manufacturing equipment. Perhaps we did get the company very cheaply. However, if I am not mistaken, our critics in Molde had the same opportunity but they did not take it. Besides having the guts to take the factory on, we also had the marketing expertise; we were the ones with an established customer network. Whoever took over Moxy would have needed our help to dispose of trucks. The bottom line was the sale of those completed units, and whether another buyer had come along with NKr. 33.5 million or not is irrelevant.

By mid-February most of the major issues were out of the way. We had set 1 April as the formal takeover day and after one and a half years of uncertainty we could finally get down to establishing a proper management structure once again. With the exception of our Fiatallis franchise our destiny was entirely in our own hands and although we did not attach too much significance to it at the time we had now become an international company. It became even more important to get it right as the destiny of others, all the Moxy dumptruck dealers around the world, relied on us.

The first formal meetings took place in Norway. It was our intention to set up a system of management which both Ron and I believed in. Norwegian law stated that we had to have local nationals on the board and we were in favour of this. We involved senior management in the day-to-day decision-making and tried to carry them with us. It was a two-way traffic for obviously without the senior management's co-operation we would be in difficulty.

Another important aspect of these meetings was to establish a new identity and name for what had been Moxy Industrier A/S. To give the factory credibility with our suppliers we decided to create a completely new image, to promote the fact that a company with twenty years of experience and successful trading had taken Moxy over. 'Twenty years of experience' was the crucial part of our promotion: we were not 'fly-by-nights'. The suppliers had taken two batterings in a very short space of time; they now wanted the comfort of a little continuity. In order to convey stability and credibility, we put our name to the Norwegian factory. The name Brown Engineering A/S was soon nailed high above the door.

We also discussed the location of the marketing office. I was all in favour of having the marketing department established in the UK. However, this suggestion did not go down too well with the Norwegian management as they felt it signalled the first step towards transplanting the Moxy operation to Great Britain. Though we explained we had absolutely no intention of doing this, only time would show that we were sincere. Eventually I won the day as it was only common sense to have at least the marketing effort operating out of the UK. We had no problem leaving the administration within the factory but geographically Molde in the north of Norway was no commuter base for a world-wide dumptruck salesman. From our Harrogate office access via Heathrow to the rest of the world was much more convenient and much less costly.

Having got this decision out of the way, the next task was to appoint a sales manager. This was not going to be a problem. At construction-equipment exhibitions, we had met an impressive individual with a memorable name. In March 1983 Paul Crapper was appointed to work alongside me on building up a world-wide dealership network. Paul was soon to be thrown in at the deep end. We had successfully wangled a stand at BAUMA; it was small – only big enough to house two trucks and an office – but it was adequate.

More important, we would have a presence at the world fair. Paul's first task, therefore, was to organise the stand so that it conveyed the image of a world-class dumptruck manufacturer. With Paul alongside and Clive Wadsworth handling the UK administration, life was beginning to take on a more settled routine.

While most of our efforts during the past eighteen months had gone into sorting out Moxy's problems, we had not abandoned our other activities. We were constantly mindful of the fact that our main money-spinner, Moxy, might just possibly let us down badly. Consequently we had put a great deal of effort into broadening our horizons. If Moxy could not be secured, we had to have something else to cushion the blow.

The main area of diversification at this time was in Kevin Murphy's department. Due to the ever-increasing union-led rumbles in the mining industry, power stations were making themselves less dependent on deep-mined coal, and coal-washing had become fashionable. We had two coal-washing plants in operation and we had just won contracts for three to four years' work. Kevin Murphy had done most of the exploratory work and during the latter days of the Moxy negotiations he had asked me to meet the Bullen brothers in Lancashire where the remains of the old John Pit waste-heap were situated. By then we had cut our teeth and gained some experience on two smaller sites. Our negotiations with the Bullen brothers were quite unusual by today's standards but not unusual in the early 1980s. We met over a pub lunch and after the usual two telephone calls to Ron and Freddy the deal was struck at the end of the meeting and signed on a beer mat. It was a deal that would give Kevin's department prosperity for the next three years.

Elsewhere in the group Jeff Phillis was broadening his plant-hire base and was getting more of his machinery into stable work as the pipeline era was over. Freddy's transport fleet was one of the most modern in the area. He was running a fleet of predominantly MAN trucks instead of the Volvo fleet which we had had before getting involved in the Moxy project. We could not be seen to be hypocritical. It would not have been too clever if on the one hand we were telling potential customers that Moxy was a superior product to Volvo and then on the other we were seen to be running a fleet of Volvo eight-wheeled road lorries. Consequently we had to change the fleet from Volvo to MAN.

Everything was in place. Transport and plant-hire were doing well, and so far as Ron and I were concerned Moxy production was now in line with Moxy sales. With harmony at the Brown Group, I decided it was time to slip away for four days skiing with my family – a brief break before flying to Munich in April 1983 to establish our product at BAUMA. I arrived out of the mountains on the Saturday to find that our humble stand had not even been started. As usual, cash was the problem. But even after the cash situation had been straightened out it seemed unlikely that we would be ready to open on the Monday morning.

Then a bigger bombshell awaited us. While I had been away relaxing with my family Ron had been wrestling with our new bank in Norway. The NKr. 8 million credit limit which was supposed to be in place when I left on holiday had not materialised. Ron had kept this from me during my frequent telephone calls to the factory in order to ensure that I had a few days of peace. When I learned of our setback, it was panic stations all round. I can remember thinking of our production plan, of our suppliers whom we had spent hours convincing that nothing more would go wrong, that we would provide stability at last. Stability, my foot. If we did not do something quick we would all be in desperate trouble again. We couldn't look to the UK for cash: we were stretched to the limit there because of the difficulty we had had in getting together the money for the opening share capital (we had had to scratch around for it everywhere we could think of).

On Monday morning Ron and I sprang into action. While we should have been showing off our Moxy 5200 and 6200 to the troops at the front of the stand, we spent the first two days locked in the small office at the back desperately trying to sort things out. Here we were, ten days into our new manufacturing life with no working capital. Paul Crapper did a sterling job holding the fort for two days, appeasing the prospective dealers and bull-shitting as to our whereabouts. However, by Tuesday afternoon, after a number of telephone calls between Trevor Gurney in the UK, Paul Hallan for the bank in Norway and numerous lawyers and accountants from both sides of the water, our credit line was in place. With our NKr. 5 million share capital and NKr. 8 million credit line and all our stock of trucks sold out we had reason to be fairly optimistic. It was all down to us now: we were, it appeared at last, firmly in the driving seat, but life would not be easy and every egg would still have to produce a chicken to ensure that we did not go the same way as our predecessors.

We did not exactly come home from BAUMA with a fistful of orders. People were reluctantly inquisitive about our product. Let's face it, the company that had manufactured the Moxy had been bust twice within twelve months and such a formidable record of failure didn't exactly enthuse construction people to dash out and buy a dozen Moxys. However, at least the fair gave us a chance to reacquaint ourselves with the old dealers and make contact with potential new dealers. It also gave us the opportunity to sit down and assure the dealers that Moxy would not be a joke in the future.

We explained the importance of actively promoting the Moxy again. All in all, we had as good an exhibition as we could have expected.

When I got back to England I was confronted by two distressed salesmen. Willie Dalrymple and Ray Chapman, the sales manager responsible for our north-east depot at Gateshead, had told me on several occasions over the past nine months that they were finding it increasingly difficult to sell hydraulic excavators. We were still competitive on wheeled loaders, bulldozers and crawler-loaders but for some reason we were way out on pricing in the excavator market. As far as they could see, the Japanese product was gaining ground and they were losing deal after deal to these well-priced excavators – we just couldn't compete. It was not as though they were missing the deal by just a couple of thousand – they were miles out, missing every deal by £10,000. We were asking £28,000 for a twelve-tonne excavator, while our competitors were taking the deals from under our noses by selling Japanese excavators at only £17–18,000.

With Leo Gerbus, our American Moxy dealer, at Conag in Las Vegas.

CHAPTER 14

Brown Group International is Born

WHEN WILLIE AND RAY had raised the problem of Japanese pricing, I had passed it off as 'salesman talk', as excuses. But still, I could no longer ignore the fact that our excavator sales were practically non-existent now. Realising the situation was serious, I decided to check up on a few facts. I looked at the market share of Hymac, the market leader, and immediately noticed that it had plummeted by half in three years and the other two predominant UK manufacturers were suffering a similar fate. Slowly, after much probing, it came to light that Hitachi, Kobelco and Komatsu had risen from nowhere to almost market domination on a month-by-month basis. Hectic meetings were taking place with all other excavator manufacturers to try to find some solution to the rising Japanese problem.

Because of my immersion in the Moxy project I had not really grasped the scale of the crisis. I was certain that the manufacturers of our excavators could not be so inefficient. I could understand it if we were only a couple of hundred pounds off the mark, but we were thousands out. There had to be something sinister going on. Down the grapevine, I now heard rumours that an investigative journalist had been probing the matter and had seen an invoice which suggested that the Hitachi excavators were being landed at a UK Port at £11,000 each. The European manufacturers insisted that the Japanese price advantage could not possibly be achieved solely by greater efficiency.

Meeting after meeting was held with Fiatallis in London and Turin and we pleaded with them to do something about the situation, complaining bitterly that we were being rapidly pushed out of the market. Rumours were circulating that Hymac, too, were almost at the point of closure. Priestman were also suffering and the other major manufacturer in the UK was becoming very annoyed with the situation. Such intense competition could not have come at a worse time. We could not fight back. The UK contractors were still dazed by the strike-torn 1970s and only too happy to lap up the cheap deals offered by the Japanese agents. Agents such as Beazer Machinery and Komatsu across the country claimed that the excavators could enter the market at such a deflated price because the Japanese were so efficient in their methods of production. However, this argument did not wear with the European manufacturers. They knew that the components were similar, if not the same, and they also knew that the Japanese had the added cost of shipping their finished product half-way around the world. Taking all that into consideration, it was clear that there was no way that they could be so efficient as to undercut our price so drastically.

Sadly Fiatallis could give us no comfort whatever. They could not and would not lower their prices and in the short time that was left to us, we had no alternative but to try to live with the situation.

Fortunately for us we were cushioned from what might have been a devastating situation by the slowly rising success of our new Moxy. We also had the added success of the Fiatallis bulldozer, wheeled loader and crawler-loader range. One product, however – the excavator manufacturers – was not so lucky. The effect the Japanese were having on their business was catastrophic with Hymac eventually filing for bankruptcy and Priestman being reduced to a shadow of its former glory. The other major UK manufacturer was also cushioned by having other product lines but they were far from happy with the situation.

As the summer of 1983 rolled on, we introduced a more formal structure to our organisation. Board meetings, particularly in Norway, took place on a strict monthly basis and wherever possible we tried to shadow them the following day in the UK so that Ron and I could always commute together. During that summer, two important issues had to be resolved. The first was quickly taken care of. We had now acquired a replacement aircraft for the Golden Eagle which we had sold. Ernest Crabtree played his part and located a Cessna 441 turbo-prop. We settled for compromise as we could not afford to go directly into the jet era. The Cessna 441 gave us exactly the flexibility we needed, without the burden of extortionate costs.

We had already decided to run a lean marketing organisation at Moxy. It would consist only of myself, on a part-time basis, Paul Crapper, full-time, looking after the Far East and Australasia, and Ron taking responsibility for the Nordic countries as well as running the factory. We had also decided that our major marketing feature would be to take prospective customers to see the unique factory in Norway. I used to make a comment that the factory looked like General Motors in the middle of nowhere. The new Cessna 441 aircraft could take eight people in comfort and get to Norway in around two hours which was adequate. It cost us £480,000 and supposedly was more economic to run than the old petrol-prop plane, though I very much doubt whether the word economic and aircraft can ever be used in the same sentence.

Our aircraft was never a perk. It was a tool to assist us in getting to and from the factory in Norway, Fiatallis in Turin, and to our European dealers in the shortest possible time. It enabled us to keep our marketing staff to a bare minimum and I always reckoned that it gave me a bonus of twenty hours per week extra working time and similar economies for Ron. When we acquired the aircraft, we had it in mind to use it all the time, and to this end Captain Alan Gaunt joined us that September not only piloting us on our journeys, but also using the plane as an air ambulance, with the seats out and a stretcher on board. In between times it was also available for private charter.

Until now, we had all had the same goal, to earn a living and to build up a business of which the family could be proud. However, time was marching on. I was still only in my early forties and still eager to be involved in the business, but Freddy was not so young any more and was looking to retire. As the monthly board meetings came around, so came the subject of Freddy's retirement. For many years Ron and I had not taken the subject of his retirement seriously. Freddy had always been a 'fair weather' man. If it rained for one week solid, Freddy would be throwing his hands in the air and threatening to sell up and retire. However, once the sun came out and the clouds dispersed, so too did Freddy's view of retirement. So when he brought up the subject of retirement, we were dismissive. However, Freddy was now fast approaching sixty and we could no longer ignore his desire to work on the farm and enjoy his horses. Equally, Ron and I did not want to raise loans to release Freddy from his shareholding, so we had to think of some other solution.

At the monthly board meeting, Trevor Gurney gave us his own view of the situation. He told the three of us what we already knew. Prior to 1980, we had created nothing that was either saleable or of interest to investors. But with our new activities – Moxy, Fiatallis, coal-washing, plant-hire, and so on – we now possessed a stable and marketable group. In 1983 we expected to achieve a turnover of £23 million and possibly a profit of £800,000, and £25 million turnover was forecast for 1984 with £1 million profit. Profits had risen from £200,000 to £1 million in four years.

Trevor believed that our best bet would be to head for the City to find an investor, thus releasing Freddy from his shareholding. Throughout our growth years we had expanded organically. Generated profits had always been ploughed back into the company in order to support increased bank borrowings. By taking out only our salaries and not dipping into dividends we hoped we were giving the bank increased security; in return the bank gave us flexibility for our seasonal operations. At that time, the early 1980s, the banks were happy to support us with overdraft facilities so long as our profits kept climbing. How things were to change!

So now was the time to find someone with cash willing to invest in our operation. I was selected as the money-rustler. There was no point in Freddy

Our first plane – taking a group of customers and friends to the Moxy factory.

Our second plane, G-Moxy, with pilot Alan Grant and our good customers Stephen Hall and Ken Percival, on another trip to Norway.

taking on this role because no one would back the one who wanted to leave. Ron was his natural successor but he was indispensable at the Norwegian factory so it was down to Trevor and me to see what we could do. Trevor provided me with a set of three-year accounts and packed me off to meet the men in grey suits. Charterhouse Jaffat was our chosen 'investment house' and I received some tips from a friend and customer as to the direction their line of questioning would take.

Initially, I focused on our aims and objectives, explaining that Freddy was sixteen years my senior and ready for retirement. Straight away they picked up on this fact. Why, if everything was going so swimmingly, did the chairman want to retire? Before I could answer, one of the other men in grey suits, who had been glancing through the balance sheet and accounts, piped up, 'Who the devil are Brown Butler & Co. – never heard of them?' That did it. I might as well have gathered my bits and pieces together there and then, because from that point onwards, they decided that the discussion was closed. I tried to explain that Brown Butler, or more to the point, Trevor Gurney and Mr Garthwaite, had steered us through some rocky patches over the previous fifteen years. I told them that it was on Brown Butler's recommendation that we had contacted Charterhouse, but they would not listen.

The man who had originally shown his indignation at our employing 'an unknown' firm of accountants now emphasised his disgust by tossing my carefully prepared accounts into the waste-paper bin. He then proceeded to draw up a plan of action. He suggested that our initial objective must be to change over to a 'known' accountancy firm, one of the 'big six'. He suggested that we get a further twelve months behind us and then return to London to try again. On the train journey home I felt despondent. At least we had not been rejected out of hand, merely told to go home, and apply again in a year's time. I felt dejected at the thought of telling Trevor about their suggestions. Trevor and Brown Butler had done a lot for the Brown brothers. Without them our company would probably not have survived to see 1983.

When I got back to the office, I did not mention the negative part of my meeting and told Freddy and Ron that everything had gone well. When I saw Trevor I told him exactly what they had said. Trevor started to laugh. He told me he was disappointed but not in the least bit surprised and asked me to arrange for him to see the Charterhouse brigade as well. A return match was organised and Trevor and I set off back to London. Once again we went over the same ground except that this time Trevor could hear it all at first hand. As we left Trevor handed out his business card. 'If any of your chaps need some down-to-earth financial advice in the Leeds area, please do not to hesitate to call me.'

On the train back to Leeds, Trevor emphasised that he would not stand in the way of our group's progress and we started to work out a compromise plan that would be shown eventually to Ron and Freddy. So 1983 finished in much the same way as it had started. There was no trauma other than the usual lack of liquidity but we were learning to live with that. We rounded the year off with the annual Ernest Crabtree Christmas bash and then put our feet up for the construction industry's customary ten-day holiday. For the Brown Group, the next three years saw the start of Thatcher's so-called 'Golden Years'. The Group grew from a turnover of £20 million a year to £30 million a year and profits of £1.5 million net were achieved after paying our interest bill and absorbing development costs. We were confident that we were operating in a period of stability; Thatcher was in her second term of office and was demonstrating that she was no mouse when it came to taking on the Unions.

I often wonder whether she was simply the Prime Minister in the right place at the right time, or whether Margaret Thatcher was different. Did it really take the Iron Lady to bring the Unions almost to their knees? Could her predecessors have achieved as much? I also had to ask the question, were we as a nation ready for such a confrontation with the Unions? I think that before 1978–79 we were not. I was happy to go along with the situation in the Harold Wilson era, when the unions were always appeased. Ted Heath made a half-hearted attempt at standing up to their power, but it was the Iron Lady who finally broke their stranglehold. The backbone of her strategy was to amass sufficient coal stocks to last twelve months, thus ensuring that the country had enough energy to provide power for over a year, long enough to at last curb union domination. I think Britain as a whole felt much the same as my brothers and I did. Nobody minds someone getting your arm up your back now and again, but it cannot be tolerated constantly.

I remember during the 1970s I used to travel frequently to Hull and Liverpool docks. Behind me, I would leave the hard-working atmosphere of the farm where everybody would pull together for the farm's prosperity. Within two hours I would be in a totally different and distasteful world. At the docks, twenty men would oversee the tipping of my load. The jcb needed just one, but if the union rule-book suggested that twenty should be present, then twenty it was.

Contrary to expectation, the Brown Group did not suffer badly during the miners' strike. Any adverse effect that the strike had upon us was mitigated by the fact that the factory in Norway had been in production for one and a half years and the market place had expanded beyond the mining industry of the UK to the whole of Europe, with inroads made into America and Australasia.

I remember collecting our US dealer, Leo Gerbus, from Heathrow airport. As we came up the M1 towards the coal-mining areas, each motorway intersection was cordoned off by police. As we approached the junction south of Sheffield, we were ordered to stop to allow a convoy of fifty or more coal lorries, complete with police escort and outriders, to deliver coal to the power stations. 'I thought I had seen it all,' drawled Leo, 'is this what it has come to?'

During this period, good fortune appeared to be on our side. At the Moxy factory we had set production targets of 500 units per year to be met by the end of 1986. This took into account our intention to expand further into the US and Australasian markets. These markets were in their infancy and had previously absorbed only comparatively small quantities of the new articulated dumptruck.

At the around the same time, our Swedish competitor began to run into problems. They had launched a new truck which from the start was beset with gearbox problems. But their loss was our gain and their staunchest supporters became easy prey to our Moxy sales team. C. A. Blackwell, one of the UK's leading earth-movers and Mike Hawkins, one of Britain's top dumptruck hirers, came over to us, willing to buy Moxy instead of the Swedish product. Their factory was slow at identifying the gearbox problem and even slower to rectify it. While financially we could not compete with the Swedes, with Ron at the factory and myself out on the ground we could at least react almost immediately now to any situation.

The matter of Freddy's semi-retirement continued to be addressed and in 1984 the first step was taken to bring this about. Price Waterhouse were appointed to become our auditors. and would work jointly with Brown Butler during 1984, taking over full auditing duties in 1985. Brown Butler would take on their new role, offering day-to-day advice, with Trevor Gurney installed as director on our board, and potential investors were sought.

Dumptruck sales were astronomical, and even the bulldozers, wheeled loaders and track-shovels were selling at a satisfactory rate. But excavator sales continued to be a headache; indeed by 1984 they had all but dried up. But as a company we did not suffer much: our dumptruck sales more than out-weighed our failures on excavator sales. However, from the point of view of potential investors, our excavator sales budget was completely wrong and left us having to make endless excuses when questioned on this subject. Potential investors quite understandably believed that our defence was just sour grapes. Everyone looked upon European excavator manufacturers, though not the Japanese, as both incompetent and incapable; in the eyes of the investors, after all, the Europeans were churning out what seemed like inferior machines at uncompetitive prices. They believed that the technically superior specification of the Japanese product, landed at such a competitive price, was just what Europe needed.

By the end of 1984 the European manufacturers had had enough. Both Hymac and Priestman were in serious trouble now, and the main excavator producer had no financial difficulties but was no longer tolerant of the situation. Luckily for the rest of us they had the financial clout to investigate what was going on. They discovered that excavators were being sold in the UK for less than production costs in Tokyo. Having established that, it was left to the Construction Equipment Manufacturers Association to report the matter to the EEC commission in Brussels. This was a final, desperate measure. The protection that the EEC could provide was an unknown factor at the time. Other cases had gone before the commission, but they had not been well publicised, and we had little idea how successful our attempt might be.

However, in mid-1985 all was revealed. The EEC reported its findings and fined the Japanese excavator manufacturers for their well-orchestrated plot to destroy the European industry. The UK manufacturers suffered worst as Britain was the first country to be singled out by the Japanese as a test market for the dumping of their product. Anyway, as a result of the EEC findings the Japanese manufacturers were penalised by a levy equal to the amount by which the commission found they were selling their products below manufacturing costs. I believe that Kobelco, the worst offender, had a 32 per cent import surcharge placed on their product. Komatsu, Hitachi and other manufacturers had similar surcharges imposed. Sadly this curb on the Japanese activity had come too late for both Hymac and Priestman.

This was clearly a case, in my opinion, where the punishment did not fit the crime. It was proved, beyond doubt, that the well-orchestrated plot to dump excavators on Europe at less than it cost to produce them was an exercise dreamed up by the Japanese to destroy the European business and to ensure that the Japanese became the dominant force. Hymac and Priestman were destroyed by this exercise. They should have been compensated for their loss. The Japanese should have been locked out of the European market for a minimum of five years to allow the damaged companies a chance to pick themselves up and recover. Quite the reverse happened. This incident portrayed the ugliest side of capitalism. One or two British people gained astronomically from this incident, while several hundreds lost their jobs.

So far as the Brown Group was concerned, Europe was coming on nicely and we were gaining ground in Australasia and America. None of this was achieved at the expense of price cutting. We always charged equal or at times a premium for our truck orders to compensate for our lack of volume. Unit sales were increasing, we were improving our economies of scale and profits were becoming easier to achieve. All in all things were looking up.

Our new roles were also proving enjoyable. I was very happy with my main job of fund-raiser and marketeer. Ron seemed to be enjoying life at the factory in Norway and Freddy seemed content with his new-found semi-retirement. However, as the year went on, it was clear that Freddy really wanted to step down as our symbolic head and take full retirement. Ron would be his natural successor, but he was living in Norway and seemed to become more and more integrated into the Norwegian way of life. Added to this, he announced at one of our monthly board meetings in 1984 that he was being divorced by his wife Pauline. During the meeting he went on to say that he felt he should stay in Norway and continue to run the factory. He also said that he did not want to become chairman or managing director as he had pressing factory duties to attend to besides his current personal problems. As with all our family-cum-company meetings, when we met a sticky patch like this in our discussions we always tended to change the subject, to talk about Freddy's horses, or say anything to pretend that we were not aware of the depth of Ron's problems.

Trevor then brought the discussion back into focus. I can remember him asking for Ron's approval and then going on to say that he would like to propose that Gordon become chairman and managing director. This had already been discussed with Price Waterhouse and Ron prior to the meeting and it had their full support. I can remember Freddy finding it difficult to accept this at first for after all I was and had always been his youngest brother. However, he had no problem in going along with it in the end, 'If that is what the City wants then it is not a problem for me; I will be out of it'. After another half an hour's debate, Trevor asked for approval and it was unanimously given.

My first reaction was one of disappointment as I was very much enjoying my role as world market development manager of Moxy and at forty-two I did not really want the responsibility of being chairman and managing director. But neither did I want an outsider to take over at this point in our development. While my new role would not take effect until early 1985 I was immediately given the task of raising the funds to buy half of Freddy's third share in the group plus an extra £2 million for working capital.

With this in mind I searched for ways which would bring me into contact with institutions who had the sort of money we were looking for. Trevor and Price Waterhouse gave me some initial leads and I also made it my duty to attend Conservative Party fund-raising functions where I would come into contact with people such as Paul Sykes and a number of other local business people with money. However, the investment we were looking for came eventually from another source. Brian Thomson, another friend, was to be the one to introduce me to the contact who would eventually have the patience and the tenacity to persuade the Brown brothers to go ahead and get on with a private placing as a pathfinder to an eventual public flotation.

At a meeting one day with Brian I told him of my problem, explaining Freddy's wish to retire to enjoy his horses and my need to raise cash, not only to buy Freddy's shares but also to feed our growing monster. The Brown Group was expanding and our gearing was now high and needed to be restructured. It was by chance that I caught Brian on the day that he had just failed to persuade his partners that exactly the same thing was needed for their group. He had called on someone for help and help had been offered. A tremendous effort had been made, which in the end had come to nothing, and he would be only too pleased to introduce me to his contact at the earliest opportunity in the hope that I would enjoy more success.

A few days later he telephoned me to let me know that he had fixed a meeting for myself and the mystery funder at the Queens Hotel in Leeds on Saturday 21 January 1984. The man in question was attending a meeting the night before in that hotel and would see us over breakfast before dashing back to London. I arrived at the hotel to meet Brian and the mystery money man. I already had an image in my mind of this City man I was about to meet – I pictured him in pinstriped suit, double-cuffed tailored shirt, slick-backed hair, horn-rimmed spectacles, lace-up brogues and minimal personality. He could not have been more different. In the breakfast room, I scanned the tables in search of my banker. There were many 'possibles' but the man who was to leap up to greet us was not the one I would have put my money on. Shaking Brian vigorously by the hand he said how pleased he was to see him again. He then turned to me and shook me by the hand. Within five minutes I knew that this was the kind of chap with whom I would enjoy doing business. He went out of his way to create a relaxed atmosphere, explained that he was dashing off to catch a train but knew exactly what we wanted and that he could get the job done. Neil Balfour had entered my life, the man to whom I would eventually owe so much and be so grateful.

Before leaving Neil made arrangements for us to meet the following weekend. In those early stages Freddy kept well out of the picture and it was left to me to explain to Neil the structure of the Brown Group. For Neil's part he explained that he was coming to the end of his term as a Euro MP and was returning to merchant banking. He had set up York Trust with his partner Michael Abrahams, a Yorkshireman whom I had met twenty years earlier, in my days as a labourer working on a farm at Stainburn, near Otley. Neil went on to explain that he had set up York Trust precisely to help people like us. He aimed to bring merchant banking to Leeds, rather than have Yorkshire business people go traipsing off to London all the time.

Soon after our first couple of meetings, Neil and I were on our way to Norway to meet Ron and look at the factory. Without much more ado Neil assured us that he could undertake the task and suggested ways in which funds would be raised for our group by way of a private placing. Neil was ideal for the job. While we had reluctantly accepted our adviser's opinion that more working capital was needed for the expanding group, none of us could quite come to terms with the fact that this would result in our losing our independence. Funding from the City inevitably would inflict City influence on our business and this we did not want.

My biggest problem was how to handle Freddy. He always approached matters of finance with suspicion. Consequently, I had to strike a fine balance. First, I had to capture Neil's interest in the project and then introduce him to Freddy early in the proceedings, to ensure that Freddy didn't think I was excluding him.

It was one Sunday morning when I finally got Freddy down to Riffa to meet Neil. Neil flew up to Leeds-Bradford and made his way to our office. I explained to Freddy that I would not be in the meeting as his exit from the group was his own affair and I never wanted to be accused of having anything to do with the pricing of his shares.

Freddy always found it difficult to handle a meeting with a business person outside his own traditional circle and I suspected that this meeting would be no different. It was as though he had already made up his mind that he was not going to like this London banker before he had even spoken to him.

Spot on time, Neil drove into the yard in an ageing red VW Golf which did little to inspire Freddy with confidence. Freddy saw the car through the window and buzzed me on the intercom: 'This doesn't look like a man who can find £1.5 million to buy my shares.' I explained to him that he had come up on the plane and borrowed a car to make his visit. In those days Freddy and I had offices side by side. I introduced Neil to Freddy and immediately sensed Freddy's allergic reaction to the banker. I left them to it and retreated to my office next door. Straight away I could hear Freddy's bellowing voice as he forcefully tried to make a point; he was ensuring that Neil knew who was boss and I could hear Neil trying to defuse the situation, explaining, 'If what I have in mind for you and your brothers is not what you would like, I can return to London and we can all be none the worse friends'.

Voices were then lowered and Freddy obviously grew to accept Neil. At the end of the meeting they moved next door to join me and as they entered the office they were deep in conversation about the merits of show-jumping and the wonders of their equine friends. Even Freddy was endearing himself to Neil. After Neil had gone, Freddy yet again probed me about our need for extra funding: he realised that Ron and I did not have the spare cash to buy his shares but he could not accept that we needed more working capital. We used to spend hours explaining that with the work we had put in on Moxy we could not stop now. Ron's production line alone needed more working capital. We used to explain that although we had made £1 million the previous year we needed a further £1 million just to finance the higher volume. There were areas in which we could cut back on our transport business and agricultural business, for example, but we were loath to get rid of our traditional activities. However, there was no doubt that it would have released cash for us to pursue our more lucrative activities, such as Fiatallis and Moxy distribution and manufacture. Freddy would then ask why we couldn't curb production at 300 units a year. I would point out that to produce trucks economically and at a profit, Ron had to produce more units and to do that he needed new technology – it was a costly business. Also I had to be sure that I could allocate sufficient trucks to each dealer to make sure that he could at least cover his overheads. It was no good asking them to invest time, money and effort if we were not going to support them. Everybody had a part to play: each dealer had to have a minimum volume and we had to guarantee the production. As our advisers told us more than once, we had created a tiger and we had to learn how to ride it.

I had to admire Neil. He spent hours explaining, settling the brothers down, allaying our fears about the City's methods – yet hiding nothing. This all went on through into early 1985. The final countdown started in the spring with the eventual placing being made on 11 September. Before this could go ahead there was a final issue to be settled. As I have already hinted Neil realised from the start of his private placing that the Brown Group was an immensely sensitive and proud organisation; while on the one hand he and the City really wanted to make their investment, he had the difficult task of delivering exactly what the City demanded. As is usually the case, finance was the sensitive issue. The City was well aware that the Brown brothers had very much run their own ship and already had a finance department in place. Alan Watson had been Freddy's faithful servant for twenty-two years. Philip Hopkinson had recently joined from our accountants, Brown Butler, as a junior and Arnold Naylor had been with us for only three years. None of these was thought to be independent enough from the brothers and Neil had to appease them by persuading us to appoint a new finance director, one of the City's own.

This issue had been simmering for a year and by July 1985 we had all become pretty well conditioned to our new future. So in the end we gave in and Price Waterhouse were instructed to interview a short list of candidates and eventually a finance director was chosen. They picked a man who had previously been with them and had left for the commercial world. Robert Lawson FCA would join us on 1 August from Cawoods, a well-respected Yorkshire company which had just been taken over by Redland. With the new finance director in place, only the signing ceremony was left to be carried out and that took place in York Trust's offices. Freddy received his cheque; Robert Lawson received a cheque for the new placing, and a glass of champagne was drunk by all. Brown Group International PLC was born and we embarked on a new era.

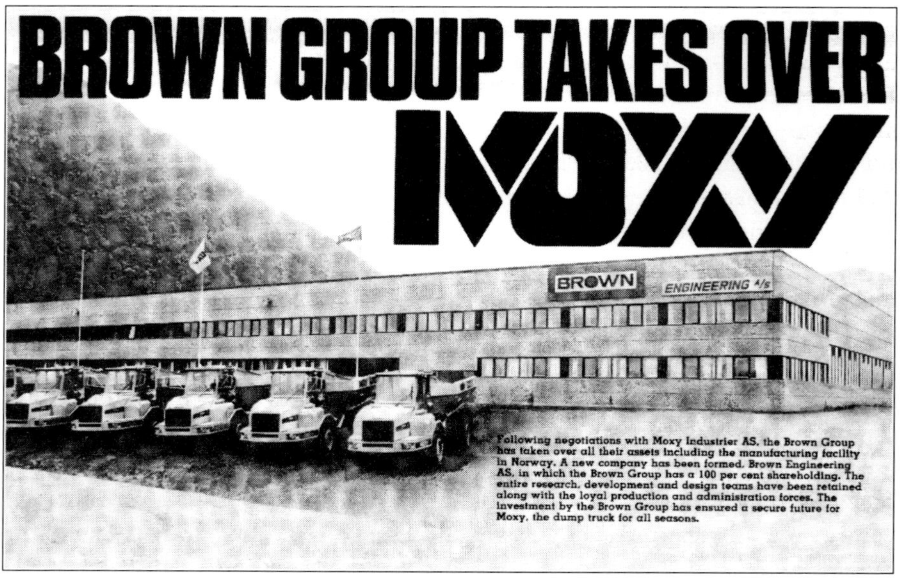

The Moxy factory in Norway.

CHAPTER 15

Komatsu

So the year continued with everything in place. The Japanese had had their knuckles rapped and we were able to sell excavators again. Our truck business around the world was maturing and booming. Our business life was the most fun it had ever been. By economic textbook standards, I suppose we were still not liquid enough. But in our new era at least we could now share this problem with Robert Lawson.

However, during July and August, with all the running around we were doing, from accountants to lawyers to merchant banks and back to accountants again, we had taken our eye off the ball, so much so that we were in danger of not meeting the proposed profit figure that had been submitted in our fund-raising forecast. Turnover had dropped off and we only had two and a half months in which to revitalise our operation. Examining the reason for this shortfall we discovered that one deal for thirty machines to Spencer King in Kent had not matured. While the order was firm and the units were in production, finance had not yet been procured for the deal and we quickly calculated that if this deal could be completed prior to our October 31 year-end, our profit forecast would be met quite easily.

Ron accelerated the production of the trucks and I headed for London in search of finance. After knocking on many doors, I eventually found some that opened and managed to obtain finance for all the machines. Through 99.5 per cent hard work and a little good luck, we delivered most of the machines before our October year-end and closed off with the cash in the bank. I do not think Freddy ever realised how close he was to having to write out a cheque as his share deal was conditional on our meeting a profit target.

Unfortunately, as is often the case, we solved one problem only to be faced with another. This time the problem was an external one. The Japanese were back to haunt us. The industry was still reeling from the devastation caused only twelve months earlier by the unfair antics of our South-East Asia competitors. But not satisfied with that, here they were back again, ready to cast another dark shadow across the UK construction industry. UK manufacturers had only just begun to prosper again when rumours started to circulate in the construction press and in the *Financial Times* that Komatsu was about to open an excavator-manufacturing plant near Birtley in County Durham.

Margaret Thatcher was rolling out the red carpet and wafting a blank cheque in welcome. The headlines in the UK financial press were, 'Japanese to open excavator plant in north-east creating in excess of 500 jobs.' I could not believe it. How could those concerned have been sucked in by these people. I am sure the headlines in the newspapers in Tokyo were saying, 'Plan working well, dumping excavators in the UK has had the desired effect of killing off two of the three major UK manufacturing units and as a bonus prize Maggie's going to give us some grant money – perhaps that'll help us kill off the last one.' Talk about rewarding the villains! I had never seen anything like it. If I remember correctly, it was Roy Sanderson who rescued Priestman from the receivers and, while Margaret Thatcher was licking the boots of the Japanese, Sanderson was going on bended knee to Hull City Council to give him a rate reduction so that he might be able to manufacture competitively priced excavators. So if we examine this logically, Margaret Thatcher was rewarding those who had all but killed off our excavator-manufacturing industry whilst lower down the echelons of power, some of her Hull-based 'yes men' were refusing to help one of the few remaining survivors. It all seemed so illogical, Yes, the Japanese could provide jobs and yes, Maggie would gain Brownie points for engineering such a move but it seemed so short-sighted. Priestman and Hymac could manufacture equipment to sell to the world. Komatsu would be manufacturing only for the European market. What was the point in that? Worse was yet to come. The Komatsu bombshell affected the industry as a whole. Now a thunderbolt from Hitachi was to affect Brown Group International directly. Not only were Komatsu being welcomed in the UK like royalty, but rumours were circulating in Italy that Hitachi were considering a joint venture with Fiatallis to produce excavators within the EEC. Having had to believe the Komatsu situation I just could not believe the Fiatallis/Hitachi situation to be true. The Fiatallis people had had us doing their donkey work, collecting evidence for two and a half years in order to wage war against the Japanese manufacturers until they got the uncompetitive data established and the fine imposed. Now it seemed that they were about to kick us in the teeth.

The rumours were just too strong to ignore. One morning Willie Dal, Ron and I climbed aboard our aircraft and flew to the Fiatallis headquarters in Turin to try to establish what was going on. We arrived at Turin airport to be met by Paul Moore who as usual picked us up in his Fiat 500 and spent the entire journey apologising for the lack of space. Straight away we probed Paul about the Hitachi rumour. However, he was loyal to his cause and refused to be led into conversation on the subject.

We finally arrived at the Fiatallis headquarters and were ushered into Mr Sighicelli's office. Mr Sighicelli immediately set about allaying our fears. He then walked us through the Fiatallis research and development department and showed the next generation of Fiatallis's range of excavators being prototyped. Their organisation needed no assistance and we should not listen to rumours. As with all our visits to the head office in Turin it broke up at about 12.30 to go to the canteen with its yellow chairs which Paul Moore always remarked about whenever we visited, but before this we were allowed a short period of free time.

It was while we were mooching around the reception area waiting to go into the canteen that I took the opportunity to go to the toilet and to my astonishment found three Japanese men alongside me. I thought this is not bad for an organisation which is not supposed to be in touch with Japan or interested in any co-operation. I followed them to the lift and then two floors down, got out with them and followed them into a sub-section where, lo and behold, there were another ten Japanese men working alongside familiar faces from the Fiatallis construction equipment hierarchy. I quickly satisfied myself that what we had been told upstairs was completely untrue and caught up with Ron and Willie at the executive canteen. It was not long before Fiatallis senior management were coming to the door and beckoning Paul Moore and certain individuals out into the corridor for discussions. The cover had been blown but Fiatallis continued for the whole of the visit to deny strenuously that what I had seen was anything more than them having the Japanese to tea!

We did not have to wait too long for the announcement that Hitachi would form a co-operation with Fiatallis's construction-equipment division; and of course this announcement had the effect of immediately throwing Brown Group's senior management into survival mode. One of two things could happen now. Either we would be allowed to continue our Fiatallis distribution which, because of our superior sales performance, by now included the whole UK, as well as taking on the distribution of Hitachi, which would have been a very exciting prospect, or alternatively BM Plant, the existing Hitachi dealers, would become the new Fiatallis dealer, which was very much less exciting. There could not be two winners and there were certainly not going to be two dealers.

The effect of us losing the Fiatallis franchise would make all our seven depots in the UK unviable and about 150 people would be made redundant. We had to fight and fight, as we did throughout the whole of 1986 to try to convince Fiatallis that we should be the single dealer. While all this uncertainty was going on Alan Gaunt, our recently recruited entrepreneurial pilot, was flirting with the airline business. The Cessna 441 was pretty much fully utilised, either transporting myself, Ron and Freddy, with our regular flights from Leeds-Bradford to Oslo or as an air ambulance.

At this point in our business career, neither Ron nor I had any real hobbies and after the long hard days of the dumptruck and bulldozer business it was a kind of relaxation to round off the day listening to Alan expounding his views on how we should take advantage of the gaping hole in the regional airline business. This opportunity was created when major carriers, especially BA, pulled out of regional services.

The Cessna 441 eventually proved totally unsuitable for the Oslo run. However, it was clear that there was a demand for this route and it was Alan's pioneering instinct and our willingness to enter into a new challenge that led us to buy the first Grumman G1 twenty-two-seater passenger aircraft to be put on the British register. The plane was purchased in the US and brought over to Fields at Donnington to be adapted to comply with CAA regulations. This conversion proved to be an absolute nightmare but the plane eventually went into service on the Oslo run and was quite successful.

By September 1985, we had a fledgling regional airline at Leeds-Bradford. But we were made to feel so unwelcome by the airport director that no office accommodation was to be found for us inside the airport offices, though we were allowed to operate out of a portakabin on the aircraft parking area. Right from the start we were clearly branded as outsiders. The next step that Alan took was to apply for the recently mothballed Leeds-Bradford to Glasgow route and after a number of hearings at CAA headquarters in London he was granted a licence to operate this route despite fierce opposition from the established carriers.

In the context of our by now £40+ million annual turnover, this flirtation with the airline business was considered by ourselves and the City to be a sideshow. Prior to the placing our intentions with regard to the airline were put in the prospectus and these intentions were endorsed. By early 1986, we had taken further tentative steps into the airline business and leased a Shorts 330. This ugly duckling was acquired from Jack Walker's Jersey European airline and duly went into service on the Glasgow run on 2 April 1986.

One thing which used to annoy me intensely were those onlookers who were becoming envious of our apparent successes and dismissed the airline as an ego trip. My defence was that I would hardly call a second-hand G1 from the US and a fourth-hand Shorts 330 (the ugliest aircraft in the sky, aptly named on the Glasgow run, the 'vomit comet') an ego trip. It was just about as basic an airline as one could get.

As though 1985 had not been eventful enough, there was still more to come. We planned that 1986 would be a consolidation year, with our effort centred on growing the business organically as we had promised to do in our private placing. However, as the year unfolded, I kept receiving telephone calls from someone who said he had been seconded by a large international construction-equipment manufacturer to approach us with a view to opening discussions. As I was very busy with the private placing, when the calls began, I kept deflecting him. I assumed he was yet another salesman – somebody relentlessly pursuing the chance of a meeting with the pretence that he had something irresistible to offer.

However, I finally agreed to meet him in mid-November at the World Trade Centre in London. The meeting opened with the usual niceties and he went on to point out how well we had done against all the odds with the Moxy dumptruck. He would not disclose for whom he was acting but after a while he asked if Brown Group International would have any interest in disposing of BGI or a part of it. He still would not indicate who his masters were. My first reaction was to say that we were not interested but I had to remind myself that I was now but one of a democratically elected board of directors and not simply acting as one of three brothers.

Having established that I was reasonably interested, a second meeting was arranged for the following week when he would bring along his paymaster. A week later I returned to the World Trade Centre and was shown into a private office. To my astonishment the intermediary was waiting for me with a Japanese man. Having sat down they came straight to the point – Moxy. I quickly established that I was talking to none other than the mighty Komatsu. In view of what had gone on over the previous three years I was not too receptive to their requests but once again I reminded myself that I was now a servant of the board – any personal feelings could not enter into our joint decisions.

Putting my personal feelings to one side, I reminded myself of the rumours regarding the Fiatallis-Hitachi partnership. I already had one big black hole to fill without creating another by selling Moxy to the Japanese. I also had to wrestle with my ethics. As I have mentioned earlier, when we bought the Moxy factory in 1983 I personally had made a verbal pledge that the business would not be sold outside Norway. However, since 1983, circumstances had changed, decisions were no longer taken purely by myself and my brothers, we were now part of a democratic board of directors, and we had to take their opinions and, perhaps more important, the opinion of the City into consideration. I realised that my 'hand on my heart' promise probably would mean little to them.

At the end of the meeting I assured the Japanese that I would put their proposals to the board and that I would telephone them at a later date to let them know the result. Before I had a chance to close the meeting Mr Hagawara sensed that I had too much emotional attachment to the Moxy product to sell the factory, and he offered a compromise. If we would not sell the Moxy factory would we consider building a number of trucks per year bearing the Komatsu badge and in the Komatsu livery. He emphasised that this would be their second choice.

We were now well into the December wind-down period and I discussed the Komatsu proposals with individual board members prior to the Christmas recess. A board meeting was planned for 7 January 1986. Ron and I were, for the first time in our working life together, on opposite sides of the fence. I could understand Ron's wish to go along with the Komatsu idea. Ron was running the Moxy manufacturing plant and had just hit the 500 units target and making good profits. If he could produce another 200 trucks under a different label, it would have a miraculous effect on the overall manufacturing cost of, say, 750 to 800 units a year. The economies of scale were definitely worth thinking about.

From my point of view, I had the marketing of the product to think about. I would be introducing a competitor of my own making into the market place: it didn't seem a logical progression to me. Also, I had to consider the dealers. What would they think of us introducing a virtually identical product? Almost certainly they would regard it as a self-inflicted dilution of our own market share. The market was competitive enough as it was without putting further obstacles in the way. It was not a black-and-white decision.

The newly formed board consisted of Freddy, Ron, Trevor, Neil Balfour, Robert Lawson and myself. After a long debate at our first board meeting of the year it was decided unanimously that we should at least convene a further meeting with the Japanese to see if some sort of compromise could be worked out. There could be a deal if we could agree to manufacture a truck under the Komatsu brand name, but the board was still not too interested in an outright sale as it was too close to the private placing for us to make such a big decision so soon.

The next meeting with the Komatsu people was set for the first week in February and because it was a Moxy-factory negotiation Ron became the lead negotiator for BGI. Common ground was found at the meeting whereby we would try to manufacture a truck bearing the name Komatsu. To appease me, however, it was agreed that further distinctions would have to be made between the two products. The Moxy truck would have to have a very distinct livery and be powered by a totally reliable Scania engine. The Komatsu unit would be produced in the Komatsu livery and powered by a Komatsu diesel engine. It was felt that this would give both groups of sales personnel sufficient marketing differences to enable them to justify their claim that the trucks were not identical. Ultimately this compromise would give Ron the opportunity to achieve greater economies of scale, thus bringing the manufactured quantities of our own truck much closer to Volvo's.

CHAPTER 16

Parkers

I FOUND IT DIFFICULT to hide my dislike of the Japanese attempts at industrial world domination. In my opinion, we could have been just as competitive and efficient if we had been operating on the same playing field. If we had received the financial resources and were given as much assistance from our government and other trade organisations as the Japanese received then we could compete as equals. During our numerous meetings throughout that summer, I could not help allowing my feelings to come through.

Ron conducted many of the detailed meetings without me, but I was present at some. At one meeting in Tokyo, the chairman of Komatsu made it quite obvious that he could not understand how a company like BGI could have a chairman who was only forty-three years old. Japanese tradition dictated that you didn't become the chairman of an organisation until you were at the end of your business career. Another thing that annoyed me about the Japanese way of doing business was their obsession with repetitive detail. I found many of the meetings tediously boring as we went over the same point from twenty different angles before confirming a confirmation and so on. Ron, however, was in his element. When we were younger we always used to say, if you asked Ron for the time he would tell you how to build a watch, an approach which went down well with the Japanese!

As negotiations continued beyond the summer of 1986 I was given the task of persuading all our dealers that it would be in their long-term interest to accept our association with Komatsu. I had the laborious task of either getting them to come to London for important meetings, or alternatively, travelling from country to country around the world, explaining the new situation, listening to their questions and reassuring them of certain key matters. First, I reassured them that for the first three years Komatsu would have a pricing disadvantage, thus ensuring that our existing dealers would not be wiped out of the market. I also reassured them that their truck would have many advantages in the market place and third, that the Moxy brand name would remain superior whatever else might happen. It was my task to ensure that each dealer signed a document consenting to the Komatsu/Moxy association. This was done and negotiations finally wound up in a signing ceremony in Tokyo on 21 November 1986. I still have a picture in which the young upstart chairman of BGI is shaking hands with the time-honoured president of the Komatsu construction division.

With ordinary organic growth and the new Komatsu contract we calculated that a turnover of £60 million would be achieved in 1987. We had achieved £35 million of turnover in 1986, but profits had gone flat and our new City partners were hinting that the honeymoon was over and they now wanted to see some growth in the group. We felt confident that having now got a firm grip on costs at the Moxy factory, and with distribution going well in the UK, our profit forecast and our projected £60 million turnover would be achieved.

We could see production heading for 600 trucks a year and plans were afoot now to produce certain special models at our Tyneside depot in the UK. In March of the following year we would reach the pinnacle of our ten-year association with Moxy. We were collaborating closely with our daughter company, Moxy Trucks of America, by exhibiting at the ConExpo World Fair in Las Vegas. We would be showing there for the first time our new 35-tonne 7235 model, as well as our 27-, 25-, 22- and 12-tonne models. Starting out ten years before with one 20-tonne truck we had now achieved a full range that would cover the whole articulated truck spectrum.

Running parallel with our successes was the need now for us to raise our profile and Paul Crapper was allocated a considerable amount of money to ensure that all our dealers were entertained in a style in keeping with that of a worldwide equipment manufacturer. Willie, Ray Chapman, Roger Jay and other senior managers put together a package deal to take established Moxy users from the UK to Las Vegas. This was an expression of our gratitude to our loyal UK customers for all the help they had given us over the years. Without the UK springboard we would never have conquered the US, Australian and European markets, as we had now done.

BGI plc was now living up to its reputation. Our group of companies included Brown Engineering Norway; the Moxy dumptruck producer BASE UK, the distribution arm with no fewer than eight depots; Brown Transport; Brown Plant Hire and Rental; Moxy Trucks of America; and Brown Air, soon to be renamed Capital Airlines. One of the pleasures of being involved in such a group as BGI was that nearly all the engineering managers and ground staff had come up through the ranks and were totally dedicated to the cause of BGI. Everybody was pleased that we had risen from being outright underdogs in the dumptruck business to a ranking equal to Caterpillar and Volvo in this one sector.

As the chairman of BGI I was beginning to hear comments like, 'You're not doing so badly, Brownie, but you can't survive in a world market with a one-unit product line.' More and more chairmen from other major manufacturers used to look us up and congratulate us on our achievements but always rounded off by saying, 'You can't keep your dealers with a single-line product. At some point you'll have to broaden the line, if you want to keep your place in the market.'

It was a proud time for both Ron and me. We puffed our chests out at the world and felt satisfied with our achievements. Together with our US partner, Leo Gerbus, we both believed we had made a real mark on the US market during our four-year presence. But, sad to say, it was at ConExpo that I heard that Brown Anglo-Scan Equipment would be losing the Fiatallis dealership. Our hospitality suite in the Hilton Hotel was opposite that of Hitachi's. One evening, when we were entertaining our guests, the Turkish Moxy/Hitachi dealer tapped me on the shoulder, asking if he could have a private word. He thought he had heard something I should know. He had been standing alongside the president of Hitachi in the Hitachi lounge and overheard him telling someone that the decision had been made at the exhibition to terminate the Brown brothers outfit in the UK. Having had my suspicions confirmed, I felt thoroughly depressed. The news spoiled what so far had been a marvellous week. But as I passed the news to Ron I remember thinking, 'As this door closes, another will soon open'.

The following day I went for a stroll round the exhibition. As I walked between the stands I came up to Parker Engineering of Leicester and I made a point of speaking to one of the representatives whom I recognised from England. 'Hey, I thought you chaps were in receivership. What are you doing here?' I asked. He confirmed that they were in receivership and had been for three months. He also told me that business was booming. The receiver was happy and therefore keeping the company running. However, the receiver had got to the point where he wanted to dispose of the unit. I made a mental note and continued my tour of the fair.

When I got back to England, I discussed the possibilities with Robert Lawson and the rest of the board. With the loss of our Fiatallis franchise imminent we ought to be searching for allied products to fill the black hole. Parkers might be just what we were looking for. The Parker product was something with which we were not completely familiar but I believed that it was now a case of grasping the opportunity when it became available.

After receiving all the documentation for the Parkers crusher-hire division from the receiver of Parkers, Robert and I quickly made our way to Leicester. Our first acquisition of Parker crusher-hire was made within four days. The receiver had exhausted almost all possibilities for the disposal of Parkers as a going concern when we arrived. He quickly showed us that we could acquire approximately £2.8 million worth of equipment at a written down value of £800,000 if we could move quickly. There was no point in turning to our clearing bank for assistance and while we could have probably squeezed the immediate payment from our working capital and existing facilities it just would not have been prudent. So we turned immediately to our old friends in the City, SocGen Lease, a division of Société Générale. We had been borrowing money from these people for ten years on capital equipment and paying it back on time and our reputation and repayment record was unquestionable.

I quickly telephoned the then manager Peter West and told him that we could acquire £2.8 million worth of equipment for £800,000 and it could go to work immediately. Moreover, our projections demonstrated that between £40–50,000 per month profit could be achieved if we were successful in acquiring the Parker crusher-hire division. I think the decision time on this transaction gives some indication of how easy it was to get hold of this sort of money at the peak of the roaring 1980s. Within ten minutes Peter West came back and said, 'You're on, Gordon, get it bought'. A telephone call to the receiver and arrangements were quickly made to sign and take over the company in Cork Gully's office at 10 a.m. the following morning. Robert and I arrived at SocGen's offices at 8.45 a.m. to meet Peter West in the doorway on his way to a meeting at the Bank of England.

'I'm sorry, Gordon, but I haven't got time to deal with it now – can't we arrange a time later on?'

'No, we've got to be at Cork Gully's by 10 a.m. to sign up. If not, there's every chance that it could slip away to someone else. There are quite a few interested parties and now that they know that we're interested, they are accelerating their investigations. We have got to buy it today.'

As our reputation went before us for honesty and integrity with the SocGen organisation Peter West immediately sat down with his managing director, made out a cheque for £800,000 and thrust it into our hands, saying that we would put all the paperwork in order in retrospect in the afternoon. He wished us luck and left for his meeting. An hour later Robert and I concluded the deal with the now-famous Michael Jordan, and Parker crusher-hire was now added to our group of companies. Having acquired the crusher division we spent a day telling the board what we had done and quickly went back to Leicester to appoint Chris Dunn, previously the junior manager, as the managing director and then reinstated his team.

When we had completed the acquisition of PCH division, Michael Jordan suggested that we take a look at the main Parker business. My first reaction was that we had not yet digested what we had already got. He said he was running out of options and it was a first-class business. Further discussions indicated that he was left with only one other serious bidder and that was my arch-rival Roger Shute from the BM Group, one of the people responsible for importing and assisting the Japanese with their excavator campaign in the UK. But he said that Roger was bogged down because of public company formalities, which were inhibiting his progress on the acquisition. Further discussions with Michael Jordan's assistant gave some indication of the pricing before Robert and I left Leicester for home and a peaceful weekend.

On my arrival back at Leeds I was told that Chris Moore, one of our largest dumptruck customers, had rung to say that he wanted to buy some more trucks. Chris had always been an important friend as well as an important customer, but I had not had time to get down to see him and he would not allow me to delegate the matter to our southern area manager, as he said, 'You were keen enough to sell me the first one when there was only you. Now that I have over forty trucks I still want to deal with you.' A compromise was found. Liz and the family knew Chris well and we decided to invite him to join us for Sunday lunch. Afterwards Chris and I could thrash out a deal, This would leave Robert and me free to return to Leicester on the Monday morning to take a look at the Parker main business which we quite fancied now. I put this suggestion to Chris and he thought it would be a good idea, suggesting that he brought his young son Oliver with him as well.

It was a beautiful sunny Sunday morning when the newly CAA-certified Cessna 441, boasting its freshly administered Brown Group livery, set off to collect Chris and Oliver at Black Bush airport, near London. In the meantime, I got on with some paperwork at my office; I never seemed to get a chance during the week and Sunday was an ideal day for reducing the paper mountain; no phones ringing; no people to see. Within an hour or so, I decided to put the paper on one side. It was too nice a day for the office so I got in the car and headed up to the airport to see whether Chris was airborne yet. When I got to the airport I found Adrian Thompson, our newly appointed manager, outside making sure the G1 aircraft was being cleaned correctly. I remember it all so clearly.

I asked if he had been in touch with our Cessna G-Moxy, did he know how it was getting on? Adrian had not spoken to them for some time, so we decided to call Black Bush to see what time they had left. We walked across the tarmac and into the makeshift portakabin. Adrian called the control tower there and I sat beside him listening to a confused discussion with the airport controller. After a short time, Adrian thrust the telephone towards me.

'I can't make head nor tail of what's going on, he says he needs to speak to you for some reason.'

'To whom am I speaking?' asked the controller, authority in his voice.

'What's the problem? Has something happened?' I garbled, sensing that something was wrong.

'If you could just let me know who you are and your position within the company, sir'?

'I'm Gordon Brown and I'm chairman of Brown Air and our plane has come down to pick up a friend and his son, please let me know what is happening.'

The controller confirmed that I was the owner of G-Moxy before suggesting that I sat down. I told him that I already was and could he just let me know what had happened. My mind was in turmoil. I could not let myself think that something had happened to Chris and his son; it would have been too dreadful. What he said next confirmed my anxiety.

'I'm afraid I have some bad news. G-Moxy was attempting to make a landing at Black Bush five minutes ago. For reasons that are not clear, the plane somersaulted and travelled upside down before crashing into woodland nearby. Emergency crews are there now but I'm afraid that I know nothing more than that just now.'

I made him go through it again. 'You're sure that the plane was landing and not taking off?' I asked.

'Yes, sir, it was just coming in to land.'

At least I knew that Chris and his son were OK but what about the pilot. Putting the receiver down, I sank back into the chair. I felt as if I had been hit by a train. The past five minutes had completely taken it out of me. Adrian and I looked at each other in disbelief. I immediately telephoned my wife to share the bad news – but before I could say anything she said,

'Has Chris Moore got hold of you?'

'No,' I replied 'but I know what he wants me for.'

'What happened, Gordon? Chris sounded dreadful.'

I told Lizzy what had happened before calling Chris, who was still at the terminal at Black Bush. He was very much in a state of shock as he described the last moments of G-Moxy. He said it appeared to be making quite a normal landing and got within ten feet of the runway when for some strange reason the engines appeared to roar into life. It turned upside down and flew completely out of control.

We never did find out the reason for G-Moxy and its pilot's end but both the maintenance that had been carried out by an external southern-based company and the pilot's licence was subject to much speculation. The disaster left us all in a state of shock and we remained at head office for the following week as a mark of respect, putting the Parker situation on hold. The week was spent attending to preliminary enquiries with regard to the cause of the accident.

After a week we returned to the Parker crushing equipment manufacturing plant and established the fact that £9 million worth of stock, work in progress and plant and equipment could be acquired for approximately £3.8 million. The whole manufacturing plant was much more complex than our plant in Norway and it immediately struck me that Parkers was an absolute bargain. Straight away I mobilised all the resources available to me within our group. Ron was summoned to come over from Norway, Willie was brought down from Scotland, Neil Balfour was brought up from London, and we quickly convened a meeting at the Holiday Inn in Leicester where the outline of the deal was presented. The following day was spent checking inventory. Robert looked at work in progress and by nightfall the following day we had established that the whole thing was a bargain: £3.5 million of the £9 million of assets was property. In effect we could buy the whole plant for the value of the property which could be sold for housing in the future if need be.

All we had to do then was find the cash. As with the acquisition of Parker crusher-hire, if we could find the money within a day we would have more chance of dictating the price. Jan Vidar Nerland, by now the finance director of our Norwegian subsidiary, suggested Christiania Bank in Norway, who had the previous year persuaded us to change from Forretningsbank and had the utmost confidence in our group. They had even gone as far as to say, if we ever found a 'turnaround' situation like Moxy in Norway, they would be only too willing to help. He made a few quick telephone calls and established that we could acquire bridging finance immediately in advance of getting complete approval from the Christiania board. The manager himself had the discretion to do this and assured us that there would be no problem turning this into a long-term loan should we accept his offer. Our shareholders were, yet again, supportive of the deal.

Once again Robert and I telephoned Mr Jordan of Cork Gully and said we would be in his office the following morning at 10 a.m. to conclude the deal. Ron, Willie and Jan Vidar all returned to the Parker factory to check once again on the viability of the manufacturing unit which was trading quite healthily on the strong Parker name even though the company was in receivership. Once more it was ironic that when Robert and I arrived at the Cork Gully office there was a telephone call waiting for us from Christiania Bank in Norway requesting an account number and transfer details so that they might send the cash. An hour and a half later we moved to Mr Jordan's office to finalise the deal. He told us that he had just had a telephone call from the lawyer of Christiania Bank to tell him that they were holding £3.8 million to our order. All banking documentation was to be completed in retrospect. In fact, as it turned out, it took almost one year for the security documents to be finalised. Anyway, the deal was completed and BGI acquired, in Parkers, one of the most prestigious names in the world of crushing and asphalt plant manufacturing.

All we had to do now was to find a suitable managing director. Parkers was quite a large business and had a complex manufacturing process. Luckily for us, the receiver had kept a comprehensive management structure in place with the exception of a managing director. In the interim we would send a man from our own team. Willie Dalrymple was considered to be the man for the job. All he needed to do was to hold the whole thing together while we searched for a new permanent MD.

Deep down I knew I had no searching to do. Over the previous two years I had got to know a man approaching his fifties who had served the construction equipment manufacturing industry for almost thirty years. I knew that if I could get hold of him – for I knew he was available – he was just the man for the job. I telephoned Ray Mortimer that evening and told him that we had acquired Parkers and that we were inviting him to become its managing director. In his skilful way, like all good managing directors, he did not ooze with enthusiasm immediately. He said that he was contemplating a number of offers of which ours was one. In short, Ray immediately took the high ground. Deep down I knew that he would eventually join us. Within two days, we had finalised his appointment and Willie was allowed to return to his homeland.

In some ways the takeover of Parkers was to be an extraordinary experience. The company had been built up over many years and was one of those rare occasions when the brand name was bigger than the bank, the receiver or ourselves. There was very little impact on Parkers' order book during its period in receivership, which meant that almost all the workforce had been retained. Parkers was one of the last companies in the UK to be taken over under the old system whereby you arranged with the receiver to terminate everyone's employment on the evening prior to taking over, so that the new company could take on the workers it needed. Soon after this the law was changed.

On the morning we took over at Parkers the gates were locked and the process of reinstatement took place throughout the first day with any troublemakers being excluded. This practice is no longer allowed. I believe it is to the detriment of the workforce as under the new system anyone taking over a company like Parkers must undertake to recognise all the previous years of service which figure in any future redundancy.

If the new ruling had applied when we took over Parkers I doubt very much if anyone would have taken the company out of receivership because there were so many workers with such long service records that the contingent liability would have been enormous. This is why I point out that it is one thing to protect the workers' rights, but it can also have a detrimental effect as in the case of a company like Parkers if this sale had been later.

These two acquisitions were my first serious brush with an English-type receivership. Previously my experience had mainly been in Norway, and there receiverships were handled in a very different way. In Norway there is no actual receivership profession. It is a matter handled by a lawyer. I had already made up my mind by that time that neither system had much merit and I felt extremely sorry for the Parker family who had built up a sound business over two generations. They had become one of the world's leaders in mineral- and asphalt-processing equipment and this feat had been achieved from the middle of Great Britain, not Japan. However, unfortunately for them, they had a trigger-happy bank manager who baulked at paying the Christmas salaries and holiday pay on 23 December 1986. Receivership was the result.

Of all the receivership cases I have ever seen I believe that Parkers is one that should never have happened. I can only comment as an outsider, but it seemed to me that its demise followed the pattern of so many other family companies. First of all the bank insisted that the family bring in an outsider to run the business and then it appeared that even he never quite got to grips with the complexities of such a diverse company. Amid much confusion the company eventually became dragged into receivership. Many years after the event it is clear that after all the receivership costs and legal fees and the fat cats had been paid, creditors received not far short of pound for pound. This in itself makes clear that Parkers never should have been a receivership case. If a 'Chapter 11' style receivership, where the management continues, had been applied at the time, as it would have been in the USA, the traumas experienced by so many people in Leicester could have been avoided.

With our first real acquisitions since the private placing out of the way, both Ron and I immediately had to change our management styles. Ron broadened his scope of activity to Group production director overseeing all production. Although his own main operating unit was in Norway, he had Ray Mortimer at Leicester and Alan Keating at Newcastle, where we made our special trucks, reporting to him on all production matters.

My own day-to-day duties became more aligned with that of a chairman and chief executive and the time I spent assisting with marketing matters was minimal, apart from deciding overall strategy. By midsummer in 1987 both Ron and I had decided that we would visit each operating unit at least once a month. We would start off with the board meeting in Norway and then Ron would return with me to England where we would go to Parkers, then to Brown Crusher Hire, before heading up to Yorkshire to discuss the divisions of Brown Anglo-Scan Equipment, the marketing company of the group, with Ray Chapman, Willie Dalrymple and Roger Jay. We would complete our round of visits by seeing our headstrong airline managing director, Adrian Thompson, for a meeting at the airport. As time went by our meetings with Adrian became more and more acrimonious.

Soon we would start our six-monthly meetings with the institutional investors who had supported the private placing. In the past the meeting had been rather a low-key affair but on this occasion we would have good news to report. Our recent acquisitions had brought with them an extra £20 million of annualised turnover. 1987 would see a £60+ million turnover attained, and net profits would reach almost £2.5 million after we had paid our substantial interest bill to the supporting banks and absorbed development costs.

On this occasion the meeting with the institutional investors took place at Parkers where we were able to show them at first hand the bargain that we had acquired. After the factory tour, we answered a round of questions and listened patiently to the cutting snipes which some of them made about the airline. One of the representatives said that he had seen somewhere in the investment textbook that whenever you invest in wings and wheels or in a glamorous airline, it becomes a poor investment. I replied that there was no glamour in our airline; it was a working man's airline.

By now we had switched from the Shorts 330 to leasing two new Shorts 360s direct from Shorts of Belfast. These were most efficient planes and gave a better ride than the original 330 because of the new tail configuration. I used to quip at these meetings that it was easier to buy a Shorts 360 aircraft at £3.5 million than it was to buy a lawn mower. Kleinwort Benson had no hesitation in funding the Shorts aircraft as they came with the Department of Trade and Industry's guaranteed buy-back.

By now Capital Airlines had expanded and was flying the Glasgow route three times a day, and under the direction of Adrian Thompson had pioneered the Leeds-Bradford to Belfast Harbour route which landed passengers within two miles of Belfast city centre as an alternative to Aldergrove, which was a considerable distance away. This route proved popular and we often looked at a full aircraft.

Our airline remained the butt of many jokes. First, we had to suffer the jibes about the original name Brown Air, which conjured up all sorts of unsavoury images. We also had to listen to various humourists who poked fun at our Shorts 'vomit comets'. I thought I had heard just about every comment and every derogatory description of the Shorts aircraft until one day when a group of customers and I were on our way from Leeds-Bradford to the twenty-four hours Le Mans race. As was usual on this type of trip we were overbooked and I had to sit at the side of the pilot on the jump seat. It was while we were circling Le Mans airport in the queue to land that the American pilot right behind us called us up on the radio:

One of the airline's Shorts 360s.

'Hey, guys, what the hell are you flying there?'

Captain Thompson in a this-is-your-captain-speaking type voice gave a full description of the plane:

'It's a Shorts 360 made in Belfast by the Shorts Brothers. It's an ideal commuter aircraft, able to carry thirty-six passengers . . .' On and on he went, giving every last detail on the plane. If the American pilot had not gone to sleep he must surely have been extremely bored. Eventually he butted in: 'That's all very well, buddy, but when ya gonna take the darned thing out the box?'

There was a roar of laughter through the headphones, but Captain Thompson was not amused.

CHAPTER 18

Hymac and Broyt

HAVING GOT OUR SIX-MONTHLY MEETING with our institutional investors out of the way we were still left with the nagging problem of the Fiatallis/Hitachi association. We knew that we were to lose the dealership and the only consolation was that we would receive some compensation for the loss and that all clean spare parts could be returned for credit. We now had six months to sort something out. We had several choices. We could close down six of the depots and leave just two in operation. From these two depots we could just sell the Moxy product. However, it would be difficult to give the level of service which had been the hallmark of our success. The other alternative was to go out and seek another excavator franchise to replace the Fiatallis dealership, which would certainly contribute to a recovery of overheads at each of our depots.

A number of small European manufacturers made contact but their product had little or no immediate presence in the UK and no spare parts business, so the viability of these units was limited. The search then, reluctantly on my part, extended to Japan. Despite my own feelings I had no alternative but to allow common sense to overrule my prejudice.

Kobelco approached us first. They had had the EEC door firmly shut in their face as a result of the dumping racket of three years before. They had two choices. They could either swallow the five-year fine and re-enter the market in 1990–91 or they could do as Hitachi had done and join a European manufacturer and sneak through the back door. The second option was the one they looked at, and we were the chosen European manufacturer. Ron and Jan Vidar headed the negotiations from Norway, the idea being that the Kobelco excavator would be manufactured at our extensive Parker plant at Leicester.

Ron, Willie and I went to Kobelco in Japan in the late summer of 1987 and spent a week studying their manufacturing methods and the viability of the proposed linkup. Kobelco had an excellent reputation for reliability and it would have been heaven-sent for both Parkers and our eight depots to have structured some sort of deal. However, by late summer it was becoming obvious that Kobelco were going soft on the idea and certainly the investment in such a project would have been something we would have found difficult to handle with our UK risk-investor mentality.

By September, negotiations were called off. Dejected, we returned to the drawing-board once more. One evening soon after the disappointment with Kobelco, Ray Mortimer insisted that I go along with him to the construction equipment federation dinner at the Turnberry Hotel in Scotland, where on this occasion it was J. C. Bamford Excavators' turn to be the host, and where we spent a wonderful evening. Speculation was rife as to what the Brown brothers would do to get out of this black hole. We had carried out a few Houdini tricks in the past ten years but with the shrinking of the industry it looked as though we had no way of escape. It was this continuous speculation that evening that gave me the idea.

The BM Group led by Roger Shute had, during the previous year, taken out an insurance policy and bought the salvage and remnants of the once-famous Hymac excavator company in the UK. No one was ever quite sure whether this was an insurance policy or a deliberate policy to force the Italians and Japanese into giving BM the whole franchise.

On my way back with Ray the following morning I took the bull by the horns and telephoned BM Group to speak to Roger Shute. Roger was away on business and I was put through to his marketing director, Graham Hall. I congratulated him, tongue in cheek, on winning the battle. Quick as a flash he said:

Ron and I with William Dalrymple on a visit to Kobelco in Japan.

'You know what you ought to do: buy Hymac and do the same with it as you did at Moxy and what you're doing at Parkers. It's all there up and running. It just needs someone like Ron in there to kick arses. As you know, Gordon, until five years ago it used to be the UK's No 1 excavator business and I am sure its fortunes can be revived by the right people.'

Quite frankly both Ron and I were becoming a little exhausted with these turnaround businesses although it would be unfair to describe Parkers as a turnaround. Under Ray Mortimer's ebullient direction it blossomed and took little of our management time apart from the monthly meetings. However, as the deadline got nearer the Hymac solution looked more attractive. Our institutional investors were asked for their opinions as was Neil Balfour, the director representing the institutions.

We had successfully taken over three companies and returned them to prosperity, and the institutional investors could not see why we should not do it a fourth time. We were given their go ahead to get on with negotiations. One of the stumbling blocks with Hymac was that, since the collapse in 1984, no money had been spent on research and design. In the initial stages, Hymac would only be able to offer us a very limited range. However, we did establish that the Hymac name was still held in high esteem, particularly amongst the Irish community around London and Manchester. After further investigation we were comforted by the fact that we could immediately sell more of the limited range of Hymac than we had previously been selling with the inferior wider range of Fiatallis.

The first tentative discussions took place with Roger Shute towards the end of October and right from the outset it was obvious that this was not going to be an easy negotiation. Roger was just as desperate to sell and make a good profit on Hymac as we were to fill the gaping hole left by Fiatallis. The first round of negotiations started and broke off very quickly. During the following days both parties moved nearer together but as we got further into the discussions it was difficult to make any sense or evaluate the Hymac company as a going concern. It was extremely difficult to assess the real value of the tangible assets because, since 1984, the receivers, and latterly the BM group, had moved them all over the place and it was proving difficult to get an assessment of their real value or even to value the work in progress.

This was proving to be a much more difficult negotiation than the others. There was Roger seeking a premium to net assets while I was seeking a discount. The only real asset was the Hymac name. The factory which was located at Wolverhampton was the old Guy truck factory and it was a tip. The newly produced 12-tonne excavator had been prototyped with Yugoslav components which were of suspect quality. And while Hymac personnel thought it was acceptable, the valve-control system varied from machine to machine. The model 181 was the most reliable in the range but was getting on in years and needed an update.

Negotiations were almost at stalemate when we all attended the Lighthouse Club dinner (the benevolent fund for the construction industry) in London in November. After a few drinks both parties circulated from table to table and inevitably met up together. Helped by the amiable atmosphere we decided that our discussions should continue and we made arrangements to reconvene at 10 o'clock the next morning at the Grosvenor Hotel. Ron had not played too big a part in the negotiations up to that point but he was on the field now. He and Roger were very much alike in some ways. The meeting started with both of them trying time after time to take the high ground while both parties searched for a compromise. Eventually, a basis was established and that enabled us to go forward with our negotiations.

In the early part of December a deal was eventually struck with the BM Group, but this acquisition was to be no bargain. Nor did we feel at the time that we had paid a premium. There were quite a number of excavators on stock and these would be immediately available for our sales team to get their teeth into when we took over in the first week in January. Having made an agreement to acquire Hymac, we still had the problem of under-utilised depots as not only had we lost the excavators but we had lost the bulldozers and wheeled loaders from our Fiatallis franchise.

It was the rumour throughout Europe that BGI had acquired the manufacturing plant and the right to produce Hymac excavators that triggered off the approach by one excavator-manufacturing company which was situated at Stavanger in Norway. It produced excavators of a specialised nature, more up-market than Hymac, in the 30–50-tonne class. As this unit was in Norway, Ron and Jan Vidar took over the negotiations. Once again, on closer inspection, it proved to be the ideal fit with our newly acquired Hymac operation. We would only have a small amount of bridging to do in the middle of the range by building 25- and 30-tonne models to end up with a more comprehensive range to sell than we had previously had available to us.

Negotiations progressed swiftly as this acquisition, unlike Hymac, had the ingredients of a distressed sale. The Norwegian government had been trying to make a partnership work between their Broyt operation and Akerman of Sweden. I never quite knew the exact details, but for some reason one of the parties was in a hurry to sever its ties before the end of December.

The deal was concluded and once again Christiania Bank were more than delighted to be of assistance with funding, emphasising even more the confidence that the bank had in the Brown Group at this time. This meant that they were now financing operations at the Moxy factory in Molde, at our Parker manufacturing facility in the UK, truck stocks at Moxy Trucks of US with some assistance from the Norwegian government, and now they followed us into the Broyt operation. The funding for the Hymac operation came partly from our own resources, but predominantly from the Hungarian Bank based in London, the bank which had recently been in the headlines as the financier of Eddie Shah's printing presses when he launched his newspaper.

In mid-December Robert Lawson went to Norway to assist Ron and Jan Vidar in the final run of negotiations. The transactions were signed and were held to order awaiting our return to work after the Christmas break. It was with immense satisfaction that I broke for my annual Christmas skiing holiday with my family.

It had taken twenty-five years to put together what I sincerely felt would be the beginnings of a European manufacturing force with the ability to fight against the Japanese and US manufacturers. We were no longer a one product line company. We were, with the exception of the airline, an investor's dream. We had been able to acquire companies at bargain prices while staying focused on our core business, the construction industry. The dream ticket brought together a comprehensive equipment range in just over ten years. The fusing of Moxy, Parker, Broyt and Hymac gave us the advantage of synergy. The grand plan was to use the efficiency of one plant to reduce the costs of another. We aimed to produce parts at one factory before taking them to their respective assembly plant for the putting together of the individual branded products.

All in all I could never remember a time when I had left to go on holiday without a worry in the world. I remember New Year's Eve, sitting high up on the mountain side, head back, face turned up to the sun and thinking how blissful my life was. I had my health, my family and the makings of a successful business. I could not have wished for more. Back at work, I took one call after another from our enthusing managers who were saying:

'We've done it, Brownie, everybody had us written off but without exception all of them are totally enthusiastic about our new position in the construction-equipment distribution business.'

No longer would we be hostage to any manufacturer. We sold the products we manufactured. The area managers were particularly delighted; the frustrations of being a dealer for a company like Fiatallis dissolved overnight. Mechanical problems could now be sorted out quickly and efficiently through a BGI office, which in turn would contact the manufacturing unit involved. The positive result was that problems could be solved within hours rather than days. In the past, if we had a problem with a Fiatallis machine we had to battle our way through Italian administrative bureaucracy before we could get anything done.

The Brown Group had evolved over twenty-five years. Initially, the four of us were surrounded by a small dedicated group of people. As time went by more dedicated people joined us and so it went on. BGI was a people's business. Ron and I knew each senior manager personally and tried wherever possible to understand their problems. Neither Ron nor myself were bean-counters; we had come from the shop floor and found this the most enjoyable part of the job. This was where we spent quite a large amount of our time, visiting our factories and talking to the employees. It was not just about pound notes. It was the sheer pleasure of creating something worthwhile and then getting the satisfaction of seeing people gainfully employed, manufacturing our machines.

The year of 1987 had been filled with uncertainty but I believed that we had now fitted in the last piece of the jigsaw and felt satisfied that our decision to go forward with Hymac and Broyt was the right one. If we had not replaced Fiatallis we would have been faced with depot closures, cutbacks and a lower standard of service. This was never really an alternative; not only did I consider it to be a step backwards but also feared that it would do tremendous damage to the morale of the workforce, an intangible spirit that takes years to build and can be destroyed in minutes.

My family had been a huge support during these traumatic times. Simon was now twenty and had left school at the age of eighteen. Rightly or wrongly, I encouraged him to come into the industry. He eventually joined the family business under the management of Kevin Murphy's BGI contracting division, thus ensuring little contact with me. I wanted his apprenticeship to be away from my gaze and for him to enjoy his young years working out on site as I had done, with real people. His first job was driving a wheeled loader and living in a caravan in Wigan on one of Kevin's coal-washing sites.

For my part, at the age of forty-four, it was the right time for one more push. I felt in my prime. With hindsight, we can see now that 1988 was the peak of the Thatcher years and in January 1988 I felt as if the world was at my disposal. Ron and I now took on new responsibilities. There was planning and strategy to be organised. Much of the day-to-day duties that we had carried out in the past had to be delegated. We examined each company and formulated our future plans for it. The Moxy plant in Norway was fully mature and Ron had it going like clockwork. Production levels were at 700 units a year and we had exhausted the local labour force. Brown Engineering (Parker) was now running well under the stewardship of Ray Mortimer. This plant was very profitable and well managed. The crusher-hire division was operating exceptionally well under Chris Dunn and was producing the most profitable return on capital employed in the whole group. The traditional plant-hire, haulage and distribution sections had all our old-established managers in place and none of them needed any day-to-day help from Ron and myself. With everything running so well, it meant that we could channel all our energy into reviving the fortunes of Broyt and Hymac. As we had suspected all along, a major overhaul of the product line and the way in which the excavators were produced would have to be carried out.

Each company had plus points: Hymac had top-quality excavator designers and the benefit of a highly respected name in the excavator industry. Broyt had similar qualities and was the market leader in durable rock-excavator design. Over the years, it had developed a powerful hydraulic system which could develop high torque forces from much lower engine horse-power than that of our competitors. Now plans were made in February/March 1988 to develop a new range of excavators by pooling the best brains and experience from both of these units. Our objective was to develop 12-, 14-18-, 40- and 50-tonne excavators. This objective could be economically achieved by simply adapting and upgrading existing technology. The 30-tonne market was a different kettle of fish. This needed new design, However, with our limited resources we decided to fill the 20–25-tonne gap by badging a unit produced by FAI in Italy and selling it under the Hymac name. This strategy would give us a range of excavators from 12–50 tonnes, sufficient to cover over 90 per cent of the market.

PART 5

Receivership: Conspiracy or Incompetence?

CHAPTER 19

The Last Golden Year

THE EARLY PART OF 1988 was our honeymoon period. Order books were full and the forty-five excavators which we had taken over from Hymac had already been sold in the January-February period. This performance outstripped any previous sales record we had had with Fiatallis's equipment. Now we had to turn to Robert Lawson and his team to establish whether our strategy and cash requirements could be transformed into reality. The budget that we had set for 1987 had to be reworked; after all much had changed in a short period of time. Our revised calculations were sent to the City. The budgets suggested that we would achieve a turnover of £100 million in 1988 and profits would rise to £5 million net after interest and development costs. By this time the net worth of the group had risen from £1 million in 1982 to £23 million in 1987. We were delivering exactly what our institutional investors had wanted. We had more than doubled our net worth since they had come on board in 1985. All we had to do now was consolidate, control costs and seek profit where possible. Everything was in place for us to build upon. We had the full support of our banks, Christiania Bank in Norway, Standard Chartered in the UK and the Hungarian Bank which was involved with Hymac. They were falling over themselves to lend us money. They seemed attracted to our breed of entrepreneurial flair and had become accustomed to our style of taking on a duff company and turning it round to prosperity.

Armed with revised budgets and forecasts we met with our institutional investors in London. They were delighted by the performance of BGI but suggested that we should beef up the balance sheet by way of another private placing. This would protect the group and give it further liquidity. Ron and I had begun to feel comfortable sharing our group with the City. Having listened to their suggestion, we were only too willing to accept their recommendation. There had been no pressure from our bankers to take this course of action; in fact quite the contrary. They encouraged us to continue with our high gearing and keep much of the shareholding for ourselves. In short, the banks had no hesitation in coming up with more money if and when it was needed.

However, I remember Neil telling me that the time to raise money from investors is before the banks tell you that you have to. We took this advice and a further £3.68 million was injected into the group by way of another private placing on 8 August 1988. Virtually all of our institutional shareholders subscribed for more shares.

While Ron and I had been deciding strategy and ensuring that refinancing was in place, we had also come across another problem concerning the management at Broyt. With the exception of the managing director, other managers were proving to be totally uncooperative, particularly at the German subsidiary. One of Ron's specialities was getting to the bottom of situations when he could not get a satisfactory explanation. The more he examined the books at Broyt the more suspicious he became. They did not seem to have been under what one might term strong control. To offer some explanation for this, one had to look at Broyt's past. It had been owned originally by the Soyland family who had fallen on bad times in the early 1980s. Broyt had survived on a menu of government handouts, bank support and ultimately a mismarriage arranged by men in grey suits. Quite foolishly Broyt had been linked up with its main competitor, forming an uneasy alliance. Broyt sold the Akerman product in Norway and Akerman sold the Broyt product, along with its own machine throughout the world. To cut a long story short Broyt drew the short straw and the fudged alliance left it on the brink of extinction.

The alliance had the result of chipping away at morale. Some employees were more interested in their own gain than in the success of the company. It looked as if they had indulged in a champagne lifestyle on a lemonade income. Now, as Ron delved deeper into the background of the company, he found that some employees were getting a little hot under the collar. What might they be worrying about?

It is ironic that the first real brush with the management arose over the controversial issue of South Africa and apartheid. The Brown brothers were the subject of a ridiculous story started by the Norwegian press. They claimed that we had been supplying Moxy dumptrucks to South Africa in spite of the ban imposed by the Norwegian government on any trade links with the Republic.

We finally got to the bottom of the rumours and discovered the true extent of Norwegian investigative journalism. So-called 'watertight evidence' had been unearthed from the cover of our own brochure. Because, of course, if you were going to participate in the illegal trade of selling dumptrucks to South Africa you would most certainly shout about it in your brochure, wouldn't you? We had produced a brochure on the Moxy product. On the front of the brochure were arrows spanning the world, indicating our international coverage. One of these arrows pointed directly to South Africa when in reality it was implying the African continent. The Norwegian

Combining business and pleasure. BGI sponsored the world sidecar champions, Webster and Hewitt.

journalists decided that they need look no further; what more did they need? Here was their conclusive evidence.

There was of course the matter of three Moxy trucks which did exist in South Africa but they had been supplied prior to the ban. One of Broyt's managers was winding Ron up one day and making asides about the South Africa issue. 'We don't find it too much of a problem dealing with South Africa' (nod nod, wink wink, know what I mean). 'Perhaps the largest number of Broyt machines in the world is in South Africa, and without the parts business, Broyt would have been dead on its feet, It was in our interest to find a way round the embargo problem.

Ron had immediately retorted: 'What d'you mean? How are you doing it?' Back came the answer: 'We put them through our daughter company in Germany'. 'But,' Ron said, 'it's a 100 per cent owned subsidiary under your direct control. How can you be so stupid? This practice must be stopped immediately. I would sooner go broke than go to jail.' As far as he was concerned that was the end of the matter.

A few weeks later, when Ron was at the German subsidiary trying to get to the bottom of what had really been going on, he could hear the telex machine pumping out a wonderful parts order. He was about to congratulate the management on the 2-metre-long request when he noticed that it was from South Africa. He was livid and left no one in any doubt that this underhand business had to stop immediately.

So, we established that a little hypocrisy was going on. On the one hand, we were accused by the Norwegian papers of shipping Moxys to South Africa based on the aforementioned 'concrete' evidence. We were doing no such thing. However, on the other hand, a Norwegian company, in which the Norwegian government had an interest, was exposed as supplying parts to South Africa through a wholly-owned German subsidiary. Such hypocrisy left us with a bad taste in our mouths.

The shipment of parts to South Africa was stopped from that day onwards but still there was a great deal of apparent wealth, particularly among Broyt's senior managers in Germany, and whenever they were questioned on the subject there was an air of unease. Both Ron and I were amazed at how these people had carved out such a lifestyle on the sale of one dozen excavators per year. We suspected there must have been something amiss and the people involved were quick to gather this fact. Shortly afterwards senior management in Germany and the accounts staff in Norway left without pressing any requests for compensation. It did not take them very long to realise that the management style of the Brown brothers would be very different to the unaccountability of the past.

Jan Olov Nilsson was then appointed managing director. Ron and I took an instant liking to this man and felt sure that around him we could build a management team. With Nilsson at the helm, Broyt soon started running smoothly, but, still in the early stages of its development, it was not yet profitable. We had decided to have their new range completed by 5 April 1989, ready for the next BAUMA Fair. We were going to achieve in one year something that would take our Japanese competitors much longer.

Barry Clark was now the managing director at Hymac and he had claimed this position by sheer hard work and dedication to the product. He had started out with Hymac in its old Rhymney days as an engineer and had come right up through the ranks, had been messed around by subsequent regimes but had been appointed managing director by us. Apart from Barry having an in-depth knowledge of the excavator business he had one other noticeable asset. He had the enthusiasm of an eighteen-year-old and appeared to be enjoying every minute of developing the new range. The same went for Broyt. Jan Nilsson was just as full of enthusiasm and it was refreshing to be in his company. With the attitude of these two, neither Ron nor I was confident that our new range would be ready for BAUMA.

We were now approaching the end of 1988 with no end to the boom in sight. Sales and turnover continued to rise and we calculated that we would achieve a record turnover of £113.5 million, with profits of almost £8.8 million before interest at the year's end. The net worth of the group was now approaching £23 million. People applied the PE ratio to our achievements and were conservatively valuing our group at £35 million were we to decide on flotation.

Meanwhile in my home town of Otley, changes were taking place. The Ogden family, whom we had worked alongside, and from time to time against, announced that the brothers were selling out and going their separate ways. The group that had been started from the Timble Inn near Otley was to be broken up and disposed of to larger groups in booming Britain. It was with a little sadness that the people who for so many years had been our measuring stick would no longer exist in their corporate style. We would miss seeing their fleet of lime-green vehicles proudly carrying their logo driving through Otley.

The year was rumbling to a close. While there was not yet talk of a recession a few dark clouds were on the horizon. In October the stock market experienced Black Monday. We, as a company, were unaffected as we had not achieved quoted share status. However, I personally had a lucky escape, not through any clever share-dealing but through sheer good fortune. During 1987, along with others, I had listened to the continuous banter from Margaret Thatcher and her compatriots about share ownership and how it should be spread to the masses. Prior to 1987 I had abided by my father's old adage, 'The best person to look after thee brass, lad, is the'sen'.

During 1987 I was tempted to dabble in stocks and shares by the ever-growing band of telephone stockbrokers who used to call me in my car as I went from manufacturing plant to manufacturing plant. Towards the end of September, a broker called me, suggesting I invest in this, that and the other. I politely put her off by saying I was a little busy and could she call me back later. She persisted in calling me throughout the day. By 3 p.m. I thought to hell with this, then rang her back and told her to sell everything; I instructed her to do it the following day and she did. Four days later was Black Monday. There was no skill attached to these decisions; I made a small gain but nothing major. However, I have that woman to be grateful to. If she had not harassed me to the edge of insanity I might have lost money rather than gained. I did wonder for a little while whether I would get a cheque but I have to admire the trust of the City. Thirty days after the sale of my shares, my cheque arrived.

Black Monday sent shock waves through the financial community: bank managers and merchant bankers ran round like headless chickens. Along with many of my colleagues I could not understand their panic. So far as I could gather only the paper value of the shares had changed and given time and patience the whole thing would recover as it did not long after. However, bankers are brought up differently. They arrive at a value by putting a line across the page at 5 o'clock every night. Maybe one day someone will sit me down and show me how a bank manager's mind works.

However, the rumblings continued and more and more I heard people talking about the 'overheating economy'. The only sign was the half per cent rise in the interest rate which was now introduced on a regular basis. The talk of recession continued but I suppose you have to live through one to be able to identify the warning signs. Like many others, I had never experienced a recession on the scale of what was ahead.

Our order book had never been so full. We were heading into 1989 with a forecast turnover of £150 million with £7 million profit after interest and development costs, and if there was to be a recession it certainly was not yet obvious in our industry. I remember thinking that we had created a company that was practically immune to recession. At the Moxy factory we were no longer dependent on the Moxy outlets and had broadened the scope of the factory by introducing Komatsu machines as another outlet.

At Brown Engineering (Parker) 65 per cent of their production was destined for overseas markets from China to Africa and Australasia. Surely these markets would not turn down on the same day? The only companies which would be affected by recession in the UK were distribution, plant rental, transport and Hymac which accounted for a small percentage of turnover. To my mind this was not a recipe for disaster whatever the economic climate.

As the spring of 1989 began to turn to summer the excitement surrounding our achievements increased. We had put a considerable amount of thought and effort into our presentation at BAUMA. For the first time all our products would be presented in corporate livery. Each brand would bear its own logo but the overriding theme would be a small badge on each machine which simply said 'A Brown Group International Product'. The BAUMA fair was the world's shop window, the disadvantage being that prospective customers could look in only once in three years. We had to make the most of our opportunity, and to give our product a professional backdrop we decided to invest in a really prestigious stand that would equal those of Liebherr, O. & K., Hannimag and other European producers.

Paul Crapper was made responsible for appointing someone to design and build the stand and to watch the cost. As it was a tri-annual event our public relations machine swung into action and arrangements were made to ferry groups of customers from the UK to the event, giving them the opportunity to inspect at first-hand our new range of equipment.

Meanwhile at Capital Airlines, business was booming. Adrian was a most difficult man to manage, but while I found his attitude abrasive, I had a

Our prestigious stand at BAUMA, 1989.

healthy respect for his ability to put together an airline. His work ethic was second to none. He was there early in the morning to see his planes off and there late at night planning strategy and endless campaigns aimed at maximising seat utilisation.

The airline had grown from four Shorts in 1988, turning over £4.5 million, to six Shorts with a turnover of almost £10 million by the end of 1989. Under Adrian's stewardship the airline gained an enviable reputation for professionalism and cleanliness. But by early 1989 our institutional investors had become disenchanted with the airline. I thought their lack of enthusiasm was unjustified. Unlike other airlines which had emerged during this period, we had not accrued great losses. In fact, throughout the early part of our development period we had operated at better than breakeven. In 1989, we achieved a profit of £600,000 which I considered an achievement for an airline at that stage of its development period. Unfortunately this trend would reverse during the year due to a price war with our competitors on the Irish routes.

The Shorts 360s would take off from Leeds-Bradford airport at 7 o'clock in the morning en route for Glasgow, Belfast, Dublin, Southampton, Cardiff and Bristol. On their return they would be met by dedicated ground staff who took out the seats of one or two of the units and turned them into mail planes for a night shift. They would arrive back at 5.30 the following morning to have their seats replaced ready for the day shift.

We had managed to keep it very much a 'working man's' airline. But then Adrian began to put the pressure on us to invest in two British Aerospace 146 aircraft and utilise them on the routes which had developed beyond the capacity of the Shorts, the Luton/Dublin and the Luton/Belfast connections, for example. In addition to the daytime flights, the planes would be used throughout the night on holiday flights (commonly known in the trade as 'bucket and spade' trips).

Apart from the economics of this venture which Adrian, in his usual manner, managed to present as extremely viable, there was another aspect which he felt was important. Neither Ron nor I agreed. It was becoming difficult to keep pilots. We had a mixture of young pilots coming up through the ranks and older pilots nearing retirement age. Adrian argued that we could lift the profile of our airline immensely, make a profit and also settle our junior pilots down if they knew they could be promoted onto the BAe 146s. He had a point but, as a board, we were most reluctant to enter the jet era and made a strong case against it.

Negotiations took place through 1988 to acquire the two BAe 146 aircraft. They ended in London, in our lawyer's office, at the end of December. I went into that meeting determined to ensure that my criteria for obtaining these aircraft would be so uninteresting to British Aerospace that a deal would not be crystallised before their deadline of 30 December. However it was not to be. I had a mandate from the board of BGI to go ahead with the deal on our terms and our terms were fully satisfied. Reluctantly I signed the documentation that would see us enter the jet era in the spring of 1989.

As I have already mentioned, we were never welcome at Leeds-Bradford airport and though the relationship had been fairly cool between the mild-mannered Alan Gaunt and the airport director, it became explosive when Adrian Thompson came along. They were like oil and water. Time and time again I was summoned to the airport to mediate over the most petty of conflicts. While Adrian's ability to run the airline could not be questioned, his man-management skills were awful.

It amuses me that rank is so important in the airline business. Captains spoke down to first officers, first officers spoke down to hostesses and in turn hostesses spoke down to ground staff. The bickering that went on was unreal. In the rest of the group 1,500 people went about their daily tasks in relative harmony. But at Capital I was once summoned to the airport to decide who should wipe the flies off the window of one of the planes. By the time I arrived at the airport I was seething. An ex-BA pilot proceeded to tell me that at BA such a task would be seen to by the ground staff, to which I retorted:

'At Capital Airlines, if the pilot wishes to see where he is going and there are no ground staff available, I suggest he grabs a sponge and wipes them off himself. If that task is beneath him, I suggest he runs off back to BA and we'll find a pilot who will.'

By late 1989, this sort of petty bickering had become a daily chore that we could do without, and the Brown Group board began seriously to consider disposing of the airline. However, before we could do that I wanted Capital to have its own reservation centre and maintenance hangar.

Throughout 1988, Capital was made to feel unwelcome at the airport. We were eventually allowed to move into the main building, but our offices were suitably unimpressive, and referred to as the dungeons as they were below ground level. At this point we were accounting for about 40 per cent of the entire airport's traffic and yet we were still unwelcome. The ultimate humiliation came when the airport allowed an airline, landing only four flights a day, to have their own gate complete with hospitality lounge while we, with over thirty landings a day, had to herd our passengers through a gate that was more like a sheep pen.

It was this intolerable situation that forced us eventually to turn to a small air charter and aircraft maintenance operation on the opposite side of the airport, owned and operated by the ebullient Ernest Crabtree. He felt it was time to retire and his hangar, office space and so on was up for sale. By November 1988 he was in little doubt that he had more than a captive customer in BGI. We desperately needed what Crabtree had available and by the end of December we had acquired Ernest's Northair Aviation Company. By adding Northair's facilities to our airline we took another step towards our ultimate goal of selling Capital as an operating unit complete with its own reservation centre and maintenance hangar. Indeed, by August/September 1989 we had started negotiations with three airlines wanting to acquire Capital Airlines and these negotiations would continue throughout the winter period.

Meanwhile, back at the core business, apart from one or two last-minute hitches all the equipment for the BAUMA fair was assembled in the week prior to 10 April 1989. Our most prestigious chipboard stand, decorated to last a week, was in place and I would fly out on the Saturday afternoon before the fair to make a final inspection on the Sunday. Before that Ron and I would be hosts at a dinner on the Sunday night for all our managers who had put so much effort into our exhibits. It was with immense pride that I stood back and admired our display of equipment at 6.30 on the

BAUMA, 1989. At last, a stand to be proud of.

Sunday night before rushing off to host the dinner where I made one of my very rare speeches and thanked all involved for their extra effort, especially Barry Clark at Hymac and Jan Nilsson at Broyt, who by other manufacturers' standards had achieved the impossible.

It was one of the proudest weeks of my business life. We met customers from all over the world. Our order book that week swelled even more and we had the usual entertainment of watching delegation after delegation from Japan with their cameras crawling all over our equipment. As one of our customers said to me, as I watched yet another group of Japanese engineers snapping every detail of our stand, 'Those people only ever invented one thing, Kamikaze pilots, and it never caught on.'

I have to hand it to the Japanese. They have demonstrated the fine art of stealing other people's ideas and improving on them. They set higher standards in their engineering products before British manufacturers got round to it in the late 1970s and that ultimately gave them their name for reliability and helped them to achieve market dominance. But I shall maintain to my dying day that I knew at least twenty British engineers at that time who, given the same financial resources, would have reached the same levels of perfection.

Throughout the Margaret Thatcher regime, if you could not survive and finance your own research and development, then hard luck. Handouts were for foreign visitors wishing to set up manufacturing units over here, not for domestic manufacturers. BAUMA had been a truly wonderful week; we had enjoyed meeting our customers, and I think they had enjoyed inspecting our machinery and receiving our hospitality. All in all, the exhibition had been a success. However, the week's achievements were pushed to the back of our minds as news of the Hillsborough football disaster and the unbelievable circumstances under which it happened filtered through to us.

On reflection, two other things came out of our presence at the BAUMA fair that week: one was certainly worthy of note and the other for the record. The most important item was that for the first time ever we made contact with the now famous auctioneers, Ritchie Brothers, who called at our stand to tell us they had brought their unique style of auctioneering to Europe, had set up their headquarters in Rotterdam and would like us to take part in their June sale. They were a group of people to whom I took an immediate liking and made arrangements to discuss the matter further after the fair.

The other item for the record was far more significant. As I have mentioned previously in my story, Paul Crapper arranged a public relations exercise, ferrying planeloads of our customers each day to BAUMA. One of these was reserved for our institutional investors, our merchant bankers and our clearing bank managers to see our achievements at first-hand. Arrangements were made for them to look round the fair in the morning and a small conference would be held in our stand office during the afternoon. Just before I was due to chair this meeting, Neil Milne from our merchant bank, York Trust, took me on one side and said that I should not miss the opportunity to raise more funds as the investors were so impressed with our exhibit and its potential they would have no hesitation in putting yet more funds into our group.

My first reaction was to hesitate. We had already had two placings which I found tedious and time-consuming and we were in no hurry to plunge into another one at this moment. However, we debated the subject at length at our meeting with all the institutions offering their congratulations and pledging their full support and Neil Milne promoting the idea of another placing.

The Standard Chartered Bank manager, Les Bridger, said there was no pressure from his bank, and the cheapest funding available for any company was from its clearing bank. He went on to say that, at that point in time, he could see no requirement for any restriction. This rather took the wind out of our merchant banker's sails. I must say I was in no mood to press the point and the meeting broke up without a conclusion. To my disappointment the Christiania bank manager was unable to attend due to the changes that were afoot at his bank. There were rumours that our supportive Bank manager from Norway was on the move.

When I returned to England Neil Balfour was furious. 'How could that stupid little banker offer yet more credit? Has he not looked at the Group's gearing? Gordon, he's playing with your reputation and is only interested in this year's Christmas bonus for himself.' However, the prospect of further dilution and months of painstaking documentation effort when it was not immediately necessary was particularly unattractive. To this day I wish we had taken York Trust's advice.

After BAUMA we settled down to the management of the business once again and with the ever-increasing rise in interest rates a new saying was being coined in every organisation – 'Cash is king'. Whilst our turnover continued in line with budget, interest rates, which had risen from 7.5 per cent in early 1988 to 13.5 per cent by December 1988, were now heading for 15 per cent base rate and our monthly interest bill was beginning to erode our margins. In early June 1989 advice was coming from all quarters that we should adopt a new style of management, take the emphasis away from turnover and profit and strive for cash. By now Les Bridger, at the Standard Chartered Bank, who only two months before had said that there were no restrictions on cash from his bank, changed his tune completely. He was now expressing caution and the clear message from his bank was that he wished no more expansion. He suggested that we should consolidate with the emphasis on cash.

We turned our attention to our stock levels and decided that the most instant resource that we had available to us was our stock of used equipment and Ritchie Bros immediately sprang to mind. Their 'no reserve' style of auction would give us the opportunity to liquidate up to £3 million worth of used equipment within weeks and a decision to participate was soon concluded. Approximately £2.5 million worth of this stock was liquidated at the Rotterdam auction in mid-June. Even though much of it was sold at a book loss we were now consistently calculating and balancing off-book loss with interest savings that we would gain from the liquidated cash.

We had not progressed far into July when Jan Vidar called to let me know that our supportive bank manager from Christiania Bank had left and to let me know about the new situation. 'Gordon, the new bank manager from Christiania has been in touch. He wants to visit the plants, and he says he'll start in Molde. Then he wants to visit Parkers, Moxy USA and Riffa; he says he just wants to familiarise himself with the organisation.'

'Sounds OK to me, let me know how you get on.'

The Molde visit took place and after they had left for Oslo Jan Vidar telephoned to inform me that he would arrive with the bank delegation at Parkers on 29 August 1989 and that he would like me to be there.

'What's he like?' I asked.

Jan Vidar mumbled something like, 'He is a strange person', but said that he would reserve judgement.

The Christiania Bank delegation duly arrived on the morning of 29 August after spending the previous evening sampling the delights of London. It was always a source of amusement to the management of Parkers that whenever Christiania Bank paid a visit, it was always a delegation which included the bank managers from Oslo, Molde, and Ollesund, as well as the bank's lawyers and goodness knows who else as well. It must have cost a fortune.

We carried out the usual tour of the factory at Parkers and then after lunch made our way for a meeting round the big square table in Fred Parker's office. This was to be my first meeting with our new bank manager, Tor Honingstad. It was an easy meeting; fully up-to-date management accounts were submitted, and Ray Mortimer with his usual enthusiasm told the bank of his achievements. The order book was good, cashflow acceptable, profits were being maintained: there was no reason at all for any gloom at his factory. The meeting was concluded by mid-afternoon and the Norwegian party enthusiastically departed back to the bright lights of London. Before leaving, we arranged that I would attend a meeting at the main bank office in Oslo the following week.

Business continued to boom in the construction industry and relations at this point were still good with Christiania Bank and Standard Chartered Bank. The head of Retail Banking in the UK had only recently been up from London to congratulate us on our phenomenal success. It was with a spring in my step that I left for Oslo for what was to be a routine meeting at the Christiania Bank headquarters. While Ron and Jan Vidar had previously been to the Christiania ivory tower it was my first visit and I was surprised at the reception area which was divided up into a series of pens, a little bit like a luxury cattle-market.

The receptionist was obviously expecting our arrival and we were asked to wait. It was not long before Tor Honingstad, followed by his troops, came down in the lift and ushered us to a meeting room where Jan Vidar and I were seated with our backs to the street. The Christiania delegation lined up at the other side and at both ends of the room. It was a most uncomfortable set-up.

The meeting began with one or two niceties from Tor Honingstad but he appeared ill at ease. He probed around the way we ran our group and proceeded to criticise the way in which goods flowed from factory to factory on open credit when there were two banks involved, Christiania and Standard Chartered. He then focused on the outstandings due to the Norwegian factory from B.A.S.E. or Moxy Trucks USA, Brown Engineering (Parker) at Leicester and went on at length about how we must stop our practice of allowing the goods to flow through UK and US distribution with cash being repatriated back to the factory when the goods had either been sold or put on local stocking finance. I countered by saying that this had been the practice ever since we had taken over the Moxy factory in 1983 and had been fully endorsed by his predecessor. I could see no wrong in the practice as all three outlets were under common ownership and the best way to dispose of high-value capital goods is to move them as near to the eventual consumer as possible.

I continued to defend the practice: 'Take the UK market, for example. It is a highly impulsive market. When a plant hirer wants two more trucks, he doesn't want them a week on Thursday, he wants them first thing in the morning. We move the trucks to the market place, sell the trucks and send the cash back to the factory.'

I could not understand Honingstad's concern. In the case of Moxy Trucks USA and Brown Engineering (Parker), not only were the companies under the same ownership, they both had the same bank (Christiania Bank) as did Brown Engineering in Norway. The bank had the first fixed and floating charge. This was not the case with Brown Anglo-Scan Equipment but to give Christiania Bank comfort we had given Honingstad's predecessor a cross guarantee, giving him a second charge behind Standard Chartered some time back to minimise the effect of goods flowing under another banker's charge. Honingstad was totally inflexible and would not listen to our explanation, insisting that the practice must stop. I reiterated that his predecessor had been well aware of the process and fully endorsed it. I rounded off by saying I fully understood the nature of his complaint but he must understand that this practice had gone on for some time and we must be given an amount of time to correct it: a complete rethink with regard to financing would be needed. Goods would have to be stocked at the factory and not at the point of sale as had been the practice for the last seven years. I also reminded him that interest on any outstanding amounts between the Norwegian factory and Brown Anglo-Scan Equipment Ltd had been calculated on a monthly basis and charged accordingly. Besides, I could not understand what he was beefing about, as BGI had owned the Moxy factory for seven years and had not at any time paid up a dividend to the parent company in the UK. I quickly told him that we could soon correct this imbalance by paying a dividend from the accumulated profiits from seven years' trading. Of course, this action would ultimately trigger a tax demand by the Norwegian revenue. I also pointed out that trucks had always been transferred to the UK company at the same transfer price as that which applied to all other European dealers. Ron had always insisted on the aforementioned terms to ensure that no one could criticise the way he had run the Norwegian company.

After what I felt was a reasonable debate, in a very abrupt manner Honingstad said: 'I demand £25 million of extra cash into this group from your shareholders immediately.'

Jan Vidar's mouth fell open and he looked aghast at the statement ... but this was only the start. While Jan Vidar and I were still gathering breath from his last statement, Honingstad blurted out, with pure venom in his voice: 'The first thing you can do, Mr Brown, is put back into the company all the monies that you and your family have taken out over the years. I am sure you have some cash available somewhere.'

I was livid and turned to Jan Vidar in amazement. I could not believe what I was hearing. I almost hoped that something had been lost in the translation and prayed that Jan Vidar would back my theory up but he was as ashen-faced as I was; putting his hand on my arm, he told me to calm down and listen to what Honingstad had to say. Honingstad proceeded to imply that my family had had a good run out of the Norwegian company and that Freddy had cash in the bank. By this time my anger had built up I was not going to listen to any more of this.

'What in hell are you trying to say? What sort of insinuation is that. Let's put the record straight, shall we? I can assure you that neither Ron nor myself has ever had one penny piece out of the Brown Group other than our salaries and running expenses. Freddy's nest egg came from selling shares in the Group to outsiders. None of us has ever had one penny of dividend from the company.' There is one issue we can get out of the way right here and now. The Brown brothers have no personal money to put into BGI.'

Honingstad shook his head in disbelief: he too was very angry. He mumbled again in broken English, and I remember him saying that he would tidy up BGI '... even if it breaks you personally, Gordon Brown.'

The meeting headed for a speedy conclusion with Honingstad repeating, 'You had better convey the message as soon as possible to your board of directors and shareholders. My demand is £25 million to be put into the company.'

I still could not believe what I was hearing. I struggled to keep the meeting going, as a desperate attempt to bring him round to our way of thinking. How the hell were we going to raise £25 million? I had to get him to change his mind, see our point of view. I brought to his attention the unethical nature of his demand:

'When we submitted our group budgets to Christiania Bank last November, your predecessor was pleased with our projections. £150 million turnover, £7 million profit after interest – I can't see what the problem is ... Just explain to me why you suddenly need an injection of £25 million? On what basis does your opinion differ so greatly from your predecessor?'

'My predecessor had his way of controlling your company and I have mine. I do not have to justify my actions to anyone.'

As soon as I got out into the sunlight of the street I turned to Jan Vidar: 'Did I hear correctly? Did I hear that bastard say that he was going to break me and my family?'

Jan Vidar's reply was well thought out: 'Yes, you did hear him correctly but calm down, Gordon. I think you should give him the benefit of the doubt. You know that sometimes the meaning is lost in the translation.'

I looked at Jan Vidar's face and knew full well that I had not misread Honingstad, nor had anything been lost in the translation. The Norwegian bank manager knew perfectly well what he was saying. This man was dangerous and he meant what he said. I understood he was envious of what we had achieved and that we had achieved it with a Norwegian asset for which we had paid very little.

Jan Vidar took me straight to Oslo airport and I headed back to London to convey the news to Freddy and Neil Balfour who in turn conveyed the message to the shareholders. Yet again my business life was about to go through a dramatic change but I had no idea just how dramatic that would be.

Back in my office at Riffa my days rapidly became just a run of telephone calls between Jan Vidar, Neil Balfour, staff at York Trust and Honingstad who frequently telephoned demanding information on progress. Neil Balfour reported back that he had telephoned round those institutions who already held a shareholding in BGI but he had received a very lukewarm reception. How very different this was from only five months earlier when they were all pledging their support. As is quite normal in such cases Honingstad's unpredictable course of action had had the immediate effect of being alarmist. Neil went on to say that all the shareholders wanted to be supportive but feared that Honingstad knew something they did not. And so the vicious circle began.

I sat and discussed our problem hour after hour with Robert Lawson who had now become firmly established as a loyal colleague. His single status meant that he had no other calls on his time and so was able to devote all of eighteen hours a day every day to the problem. Wherever possible we carried out our normal day's work but more and more time was taken up in supplying masses of information to Price Waterhouse our auditors, the banks and institutional shareholders.

While I had turned first to Neil, as our merchant banker, for his wisdom in this matter I had also opened up a second front. I was now becoming familiar with looking into black holes. My experience was that it was prudent to try to have as many options as possible. Over the year I had received a number of telephone calls from Drexell, Burnham and Lambert, expounding the virtues of the junk bond market and how it was ideally suited to our type of business. Robert and I went off to London to meet these people at the first opportunity, complete with five years of up-to-date accounts and management accounts. Over a pleasant lunch I gave them a potted history of our company, telling them where we had come from and where we wanted to go to. Our meeting was as brief as possible as demands on my time were now becoming incessant.

I will find it difficult to forget the restaurant where we had lunch. There I was in the depths of despair trying to persuade Drexell, Burnham and Lambert to put us together a junk bond in twenty-one days only to be confronted by the restaurateur who, as part of a feature of his restaurant, gave a lesson in the history of wine while you waited for your first course. However, even with the turmoil going on in my mind I did at least learn one thing from him. Until that day I never knew that Russia was the biggest producer of wines in the world.

To my delight, Drexell, Burnham and Lambert telephoned me a week later saying that they had run all our numbers through their computer and they would have no difficulty in raising the £25 million and only needed another fourteen days.

By now we were heading towards the end of September 1989. There were further meetings with Drexell, Burnham and Lambert which Ron and Jan Vidar attended, and hey presto, two days later, a confirmed offer letter arrived in the post from them offering us £25 million junk bond with a deferred redemption date five years out from draw down. The interest rate was not too prohibitive but the sting in the tail was that for arranging the bond Drexell, Burnham and Lambert needed a small equity kicker which they were persuaded to reduce to 5 per cent.

In the meantime Neil and his staff had spent almost the whole of their time trying to drum up cash from institutional sources. They had little success with our shareholders who I do not feel ever grasped the urgency of the situation. At that time Jan Vidar and I were the only ones who had seen Honingstad eyeball to eyeball and all I could see was vengeance. He spoke with controlled dispassion in his voice. His daily interference with the company was becoming more acute; he was telephoning Jan Vidar on a regular basis and becoming more and more involved in the running of the group. His telephone calls to me became more threatening as October arrived, and his interference was taking its toll on our efficiency. However, in the rest of the economy the boom continued. We had no lack of orders for our products with the exception of Hymac where domestic demand was proving a little slow.

Interest rates would rise the following month to 15 per cent base but for the time being, much to my annoyance, this was one issue I could do little about in the short term. My short-term objective had to be to get £25 million into the company as quickly as possible. With that accomplished, we could make the necessary decisions to prune our organisation.

It was with immense satisfaction that I was able to announce to Neil Balfour that I had found an immediate solution to our problem and showed him the letter from Drexell, Burnham and Lambert. Much to my surprise it was not received with much enthusiasm. He was, I thought, rather too dismissive about Drexell, whom he described as 'expensive gunslingers', but he admitted that we should not leave any stones unturned. Secretly I suspected that Neil was anxious to protect York Trust's position. Raising £25 million via Drexell, Burnham and Lambert put no smoke up his chimney and he and his staff had just spent a month of their time searching for ways in which to provide £25 million of which they would receive an introductory commission which would cover their expenses. Neil pointed this out to me but I replied: 'Neil, we are talking about survival here.'

Being the sort of chap he was, Neil immediately said that he would not stand in the way of the junk bond if that was to be the only solution. I was now trapped between the baying wolves at Christiania Bank and two institutional solutions, the junk bond deal led by Drexell and the interests of shareholders, led by Neil.

By now the alarmist tactics of Honingstad had alerted Standard Chartered to the difficulties our group was facing with the Norwegian bank but unlike Honingstad the head of Standard Chartered's risk department was most supportive and was already in dialogue with Honingstad. He suggested that to calm the waters immediately he should put in a team of independent accountants who would produce a report on behalf of both banks. While this was being prepared he suggested the group should be run by its directors in the normal manner as he could not see any need for the crisis tactics which were being adopted.

I thought this would be a bad idea. Men in pinstriped suits crawling all over the place would only make matters worse. Alarm bells would start ringing, rumours would abound, creditors would become nervous and the whole thing would spiral out of control. We did not need any more pressure on our cash resources. Standard Chartered tried every way to be helpful even to the point of suggesting that they allow our own auditors, Price Waterhouse, to prepare the report, but first of all we would have to have a meeting with all interested parties round the table and this would be convened the following week at Christiania Bank's headquarters in London.

In the meantime I was still carrying my secret weapon, the Drexell, Burnham and Lambert junk bond. I persuaded Neil to present it to our existing shareholders. Their lack of enthusiasm for this idea was such that we could only get them together in small numbers so Neil Milne and I travelled round various locations presenting the proposal. Eventually it was rejected by the bank's shareholders. Both Robert and I were devastated but while the shareholders had rejected the junk bond option, they had agreed to put the money up themselves. Neil also told me that it was not entirely the size and cost of the junk bond the shareholders had rejected, but it was the small equity kicker they could not bring themselves to accept.

In the meantime, the early October meeting had been arranged at Christiania Bank in London where we were to learn that the two banks had come to the decision that Gordon Horsfield, a senior partner from Price Waterhouse, should be appointed to submit a report on the current position and the future prospects of the company. By now both Robert and I were becoming exhausted with the endless round of producing more and more information and I was beginning to feel a second-class citizen of little importance to anyone. I was rapidly beginning to realise that our twenty-six years of experience in building our group counted for nothing.

At the meeting Gordon Horsfield and his assistant sat alongside the Standard Chartered banking director, Eric Harrison, and Honingstad sat opposite. Ron, Jan Vidar, Robert and I were placed like convicts on trial at one end of the table. The problems of the Brown Group were debated at length with neither Ron nor I allowed to have much input. It was almost as if a much cleverer person had now been found to run the Brown Group and our experience would no longer be needed.

Gordon Horsfield was appointed to start his work on 6 October 1989. He sat waiting for his turn to address the meeting. In his own mind he had already decided that Brown Group was a casualty department case and told us how he was a dab hand at turning round companies like ours. I was so incensed by this remark that I asked him to 'name me a few'. He immediately replied that his ethics did not allow him to but he had seen one of his casualty cases that day in the *Financial Times* as he came to London which was now doing nicely and suggested that if I looked in the paper I might be able to pick it out.

The meeting ended leaving Robert and myself deeply dejected. Gordon Horsfield had told the meeting several times that he must avoid at all costs any possibility of being identified as a shadow director; the message was equally clearly conveyed that he would act as policeman over cash movements from that day onwards. My role would be reduced to one of carrying the responsibility of chief executive and chairman but without the authority.

As we moved towards the end of October Price Waterhouse were getting on with their report but it was the way in which it was produced which annoyed me intensely. At the meeting in London, Gordon Horsfield had given everyone the impression that he would be carrying out the study himself. In fact he was rarely seen. It was left to an assistant from Price Waterhouse to compile the information but it was the Brown Group accountants who had to prepare all the figures for him. So much for the independent report which Christiania Bank and Standard Chartered Bank would receive.

While this was going on Neil Milne and his team had been going round the institutional shareholders and had worked out a conditional offer to demonstrate to Christiania Bank that the shareholders were supportive. As all the signs at the time were that our budgeted turnovers were being achieved our only problems were that our margins were being eroded by high interest rates. But in spite of this we would still turn in a profit as a going concern to October 1989. York Trust and the institutional investors they represented would immediately raise £5 million equity on condition that Ron and I expressed confidence by pledging our existing shareholding which was in excess of 50 per cent to York Trust as security. We had no hesitation in doing this, pending a more permanent solution, as the documentation stated that our shares would be returned to us when proper funding had been procured.

For sometime my day-to-day input into the running of the group had been reduced to almost nothing. My responsibilities had been taken over by Willie Dalrymple, Ray Chapman, Ray Mortimer and the other managers who, under the circumstances, did an absolutely fantastic job.

Because Ron, Jan Vidar, Robert and I were now locked in meetings, which the bankers and accountants thought so important, the direction of the group was going awry. It was dreadful to watch a group, which had thrived over all these years with clear-cut decision-making now floundering like a sailboat without a sail. In November, a small boost to our morale arrived: £5 million was injected into the group as a demonstration to the banks of our investors' confidence in BGI. However, a more permanent solution still needed to be found. The thinking behind the £5 million gesture was that this amount, coupled with the small profit of £2 million, would equal the £7 million budgeted profit. By achieving our forecast figure Christiania Bank would have one less piece of ammunition to use against us. If they were to behave ethically for the time being they would have no grounds whatsoever to be precipitous. With the £5 million injected and the Price Waterhouse stage 1 report issued there was to be a calm before the storm. This would allow Ron and myself to apply a little management time to the group though it only lasted through to the new year.

As I am concerned in this book to write about the people who failed, for the good of BGI I feel bound to expose the manner in which the Price

Waterhouse report was compiled. Gordon Horsfield was rarely seen on the case, though the fee charged for the report did little to reflect this fact. BGI was charged £200,000 for the time of a senior partner when in fact the job was delegated to an assistant and many of our own staff. Certainly the observation by all our senior managers at the time was that for Gordon Horsfield's assistant to dash round six locations in two countries and to compile a report in less than one month was downright dangerous. Hence the initial inaccuracies with which the report was filled.

A panic call from Robert Lawson in the last week in October alerted me to the fact that he had been summoned to Price Waterhouse by Gordon Horsfield to help conclude the report. He was agitated because he knew his presence was needed more than ever now back at Riffa but he said the report contained so many inaccuracies that if it went to the two banks without correction it would have a detrimental impact. He said that even the simple arithmetic showing the net worth of the group was out by £4 million. What was he to do? We decided there was no alternative as we wanted to present the most accurate report possible and Robert stayed there the whole day.

I joined him the following day. I was now beginning to seethe because for twenty-seven years we had run a tight ship and now I found I was watching £200,000 going down the throats of yet another fat cat, money that was badly needed for creditors.

I was further incensed when Gordon Horsfield, having presented 'his' report to the bank, which incidentally suggested that at most the Group needed an injection of no more than £15–20 million, arrived at our office demanding payment. I was in Robert's office at the time and I remember reminding him that over the last three months he had advised us of our directors' responsibilities. Did he not remember the rule that we should show no preference to individual creditors? Something about people having to be paid in accordance with the company's sixty-day terms? He had said that such a practice should be imposed to avoid the directors falling into the trap of fraudulent preference. Here he was demanding his cheque, stating that it had been authorised by Standard Chartered Bank. A telephone call ten minutes later from Standard Chartered Bank instructed me to give Price Waterhouse their cheque in preference over other creditors. Both Robert and I expressed our disgust at this demand. We had been scratching around for cash, and this amount would have gone a long way to filling many hungry mouths rather than paying for what amounted to little more detailed commentry on the company's own set of professionally presented management accounts. It was instances such as this and others I could mention which had come to symbolise the culture of excess and greed that had been cultivated and encouraged towards the end of the Thatcher era.

Honingstad once again started his rumblings in mid-January, insisting that the further £20 million be injected into the group as soon as possible. He was now aided by the Price Waterhouse report which clearly stated the obvious – an extra £20 million in the group would certainly assist liquidity. We had not needed to spend £200,000 to come to that conclusion.

At this point the whole affair took an unusual twist. We were advanced in negotiations to supply 150 Broyt excavators and 200 Moxy dumptrucks to Libya. At the time, Norway had no restrictions on trading with that country. Christiania Bank had been aware of negotiations throughout and had been appointed to make substantial advance mobilisation payments. We had not made a song and dance about the deal as Libya was a very sore subject politically at the time. While they were classified as mobilisation payments they were really payments to oil the wheels to make sure that the transaction ran more smoothly.

It was at one of our meetings in Paris that I felt it was only fair to mention our difficulties to their chief negotiator, Mr Blockwitz, immediately seized upon my problem, went away from the negotiating table and returned after half an hour saying: 'Your Group's funding will not be a problem. Meet me next week in Zurich and I will take you to a broker who will handle the funding.'

I went along initially alone with Mr Blockwitz as I felt that as yet this offer of funding had little substance. On arrival I was introduced to Petter Hans of Petter Hans Treuhand who had already inspected our proposal which had been sent in advance, and he had no hesitation in saying that the transaction was already agreed and he would purchase shares to a maximum of £15 million.

I kept this transaction private, sharing my findings initially only with Ron, Jan Vidar and Robert. A few days later I returned to the Petter Hans office in Zug whereupon, in Robert's presence, a contract was signed confirming that the injection would take place on 13 April 1990, which in fact turned out to be Good Friday, rather an unfortunate day to choose. On arrival back in London we went to the York Trust office and showed Neil Balfour and Neil Milne our contract to purchase shares in line with the criteria set out at York Trust.

Neil Balfour immediately telephoned the banks involved and said that the problem of the cash injection was solved as £5 million had already gone into the company, a further £15 million would be provided by Petter Hans Treuhand and the remaining £5 million he would procure from the institutions. The initial reaction from the banks was one of disbelief. Over the ensuing hours there were a number of frenzied telephone calls from the York Trust office to try to establish who Petter Hans was. References were supplied and one of them was a major bank in Zurich which gave him a good reference.

The entire matter had now become one of intrigue. A compromise to appease all concerned was worked out which involved Robert and myself returning to Zug. This time we would take with us Gordon Horsfield from Price Waterhouse and Morris Cowan from the lawyers in Leeds, Booth & Co. We would revisit Petter Hans's office, a contract would be re-signed and the two representatives from Price Waterhouse and Booth & Co. would be there to authenticate the event on behalf of the banks.

When we arrived in Zurich we first took up the references and again no adverse reaction was received. Our delegation found the Petter Hans offices and explained why we were there and asked if he would reconfirm the contract. Both Morris Cowan and Gordon Horsfield had to accept that we had done as much as we possibly could to confirm our contract and spent the rest of the afternoon in a very pleasant wine bar on the lakeside awaiting our plane back to England.

This transaction was reluctantly accepted as authentic by the banks and once again all involved waited with bated breath until Friday 13 April 1990 when the money was expected to be transferred. No money arrived. A number of telephone calls were made to Petter Hans and his explanation that all the banks were closed because it was Good Friday seemed reasonable. He assured us that the transfer would be made on the Monday. I spent a tense weekend at home, waiting for Monday to arrive. Monday arrived but still no money; Tuesday came and there were still no funds; Wednesday and Thursday passed without any sign. By Friday, Petter Hans had stopped answering the telephone. We never did get to the bottom of what had gone wrong. York Trust and our legal advisers just said there was no point in chasing after him with the signed contract. This would have to be addressed at a later date. The only saving grace I had from the enormous personal embarrassment that this caused was that both Morris Cowan and Gordon Horsfield had been present and that they too had been totally convinced that Petter Hans Treuhand was a bonafide investor.

With the hope of rescue by Petter Hans Treuhand now in the past, BGI was once again thrown back into turmoil. Honingstad phoned us relentlessly insisting that the cash be sourced at once. I pleaded with him time after time to reconsider but he had set his course of destruction and he was not going to change direction. By now the net was being spread even wider and people such as 3Is and the Electra group were taking an interest. Once again we would be subject to a two-three week diligence exercise. Every day Robert, Ron, Jan Vidar or I had a meeting with one institution or another who claimed to be potential investors with money burning holes in their pockets.

By now York Trust were considering other advisers, in fact anyone who could assist with the situation in which we now found ourselves: and Neil Milne had a chance meeting with a newly formed financial service organisation by the name of Gartland & Whalley Securities. There was absolutely no possibility of doing a day's work for the company now. It was hard to believe that only a year earlier we had been basking in the fortunes of BAUMA, enjoying the favourable reaction to our comprehensive range of equipment and our full order books. Who would have thought that twelve months on there could be such chaos? I thought back to my days on the farm, the times spent with Tony on contract farming. I remembered our highs and our lows. We had had our lows but never anything like this. This was something I had never imagined could happen. It was becoming a desperate struggle for survival and while I and those around me had the will to survive, it seemed that Christiania Bank had already decided that we would not.

My days at the office were no longer a pleasure: I felt as if I was biding my time on death row. My time was spent listening to one adviser after another, and in between listening to the hellbent demands of Honingstad in Norway. Towards the end of April a meeting was held at the offices of Electra in London: Honingstad had become extremely impatient and had threatened to take precipitous action unless York Trust came up with the remaining £20 million. Electra, Gartland & Whalley, the institutional investors, and Robert and I all appealed for more time. A responsible investment organisation could not be expected to help until they had had time to investigate further.

Three weeks earlier York Trust, as a gesture, had suggested that as an interim measure they could raise a further £6.5 million. It had been little more than a gesture of confidence from the shareholders to gain a little more time until institutions such as Electra and the 3Is had reached a decision: it was not yet a firm offer. However, Honingstad decided differently, insisting that the promise of £6.5 million should be carried out there and then.

The representative from Electra supported the Christiania Bank, saying that it was his interpretation that the £6.5 million was a firm promise and would be injected into the group as an interim measure. This was obviously a ploy for him to gain more time for more analysis. Sadly, the ploy was to be at York Trust's expense.

Tor Honingstad insisted that he had documentation that supported his claim that York Trust had promised to inject £6.5 million into the group immediately. Neil Balfour refused to accept this and asked to be excused. A phone call to his office cleared up the situation within minutes. Five minutes later Neil arrived with the documentation to disprove the Norwegian's allegations. The wording used clearly indicated to Christiania Bank that £6.5 million was mentioned only as a possibility and nowhere in the document was it stated that this funding had been promised.

When this document arrived Honingstad flew into a rage. Putting on his coat he spluttered: 'If £6.5 million is not raised within fourteen days I will put the Norwegian company into liquidation.' Or to use his language he would withdraw the Christiania Bank loans which amounted to the same thing. At the end of the meeting Neil Balfour was grey with anger. They had been bamboozled into an intolerable situation through no fault of their own. I had been at all the meetings and they had operated ethically throughout.

I rode back to the York Trust office with the two Neils. We simply could not believe what Honingstad was doing. And for why? He was slowly but surely tightening the noose around our necks. But if he wanted rid of us, he was still going to have a fight on his hands. When we got back to the York Trust office Neil summoned every friend he had in the industry. Tony Gartland and Jeff Whalley were there to offer support and advice. They made it quite clear that at the time they were not willing investors but were willing to assist in structuring a master plan to secure the future of BGI.

As the days passed the two Neils were able to convey to institutional investors that one of the best and most respected industrial turnaround companies in the country, Gartland & Whalley, were now on the case and felt it worthwhile raising a further £6.5 million to stave off any precipitous action by Tor Honingstad.

Gartland & Whalley went back to Yorkshire to structure a master plan which would be presented to the banks as a once-and-for-all solution to the BGI problem. In the meantime Neil would put together a £6.5 million emergency injection which would buy some more time. With the injection of the second £6.5 million, the bank would grant a further six weeks to raise the remaining £12.5 million, making a total of £24 million. York Trust approached every source they knew in the business and eventually were in a position to inject £6.5 million on 16 May 1990.

During this traumatic period my daughter Tina had the misfortune to celebrate her 21st birthday. I say 'misfortune' because her birthday was on 12 May, just days before the threatened day of receivership. A party had been organised for the following Saturday evening, 19 May 1990, at Rudding House near Harrogate. On the 12th I got on the train from London and headed north for home. A table had been booked at the Dusty Miller restaurant in Summerbridge. Unfortunately, I was in no mood for celebrating anything as the £6.5 million had not yet been secured. However, I tried to put a brave face on the situation having already made up my mind that, whatever happened, my daughter was only going to be twenty-one once and BGI or no BGI we would have a good time. Fortunately the injection of £6.5 million during the course of that week ensured that my spirits were well and truly lifted in time for the party the following Saturday night and Tina had a birthday to remember.

However, this was once again to be the calm before the storm. All the big guns lined up against Honingstad, including even the Standard Chartered Bank which appeared disgusted by his uncompromising stance. At least Electra and Gartland & Whalley had secured their six-week stay of execution while they formulated their plans.

By this time, I had spent a substantial amount of time with Tony Holmes, a man who had the rare ability to talk about a blade of grass for an hour. I never quite understood Tony's role with regard to Electra: I was never sure whether he was an employee or a consultant. However, one thing I was more or less sure of was his anger when Gartland & Whalley came on the scene.

Vulture-like, he had been circling his prey for quite some time, watching BGI grow weaker and weaker. He was none too happy when a rescuer in the guise of Gartland & Whalley appeared on the scene. Under Tony's plan the family shareholding would have been wiped out and at best I would have been kept on at the company for my knowledge of plant and equipment. From the beginning it was obvious that Tony was not acting in the best interests of BGI or its shareholders. Straight away he had aligned himself with Honingstad and Christiania Bank. Earlier on they had a couple of cosy meetings and many telephone conversations from which we and the institutional shareholders were excluded. It was conniving and, in my opinion, unethical behaviour by both parties.

Gartland & Whalley were regarded by the City as superstars. During the 1980s they had created a company called FKI, merged with Babcock, and then masterminded a brilliant financial manoeuvre whereby they de-merged the company and soon after relinquished their responsibilities, rendering them free to start their own merchant bank, Gartland & Whalley Securities. Anyway, Tony Gartland and the chairman of Electra knew each other well and before long they had short-circuited Tony Holmes, putting him back into the shadows.

We were now fighting on three fronts. There was Electra, Gartland & Whalley and of course York Trust, who had now been joined by a fund called Renaissance, led by Nicholas ('Nicky') Branch. Mr Branch, whose friends were specialists in turnaround situations, sensed that the group was strong enough to survive and prosper. From the moment he came on the scene, he seemed to take the lead in putting together the £6.5 million refinancing package. The investors who came in (some old, some new) believed Electra would, after conducting a bona fide investigation, inject the balance. Mr Branch and his friends certainly stood to do well if we came through with Electra and Gartland & Whalley support. Branch and Renaissance, like the rest of the City, believed Gartland & Whalley would bring the secret ingredient. Everybody now believed the banks wanted us to survive.

I was assigned to take Jeff Whalley and James Barker, the financial strategist from Gartland & Whalley, around each plant and interview each managing director and finance director. At first I was sceptical as to how I would get along with Jeff and James but I had no need to worry as we hit it off immediately. They treated me with the utmost respect and were most sympathetic to Brown Group's plight. During our ten days together, Jeff and I established that we were both from a similar type of background and I felt very comfortable in his company. I learned a great deal from these two men. Throughout my nine months of turmoil, I had spent countless wasted hours in the presence of so-called 'advisors'. I now considered 99.9 per cent of them to be a complete waste of time. However, my meetings with James and Jeff, and of course with York Trust, were constructive. These men were two of the three advisors whom I respected. They had an in-depth understanding of industry and production, and of both series production and bespoke production. I found that we could relate to each other easily on all subjects connected to our business. After a couple of weeks with Jeff I felt I knew him well enough to comment on the fact that his nickname was the 'smiling butcher'. He had gained this reputation during the 1980s when stripping the fat from companies in an effort to make them lean and profitable.

During the following three weeks, as Electra and Gartland & Whalley spent more time in conference on the Brown Group situation, I was excluded more and more from the final meetings. Gartland & Whalley revealed their plan of action first to York Trust and then, one by one, the bankers and institutions were informed. I was included in this most demoralising of exercises.

Under the plan, as I expected, Tony Gartland would emerge as BGI chairman and Jeff Whalley would be managing director. I would become marketing director and Ron would continue as production director. However, by this time I was so battle-weary it did not worry me. I was now more concerned with ensuring that the 1,600 people who worked for the

Brown Group had continuity of employment. The plan would give me a job, although it would be much less interesting. Anything would be better than Honingstad's plan of bankruptcy. I can remember telephoning Liz that night to say that I now had no problem commercially deciding between what was right and wrong, as the alternatives available to me were only 'bad' and 'worse'.

The final meeting was arranged for Monday 24 June 1990 at the Russell Hotel in London. Gordon Horsfield of Price Waterhouse would chair the meeting with Christiania Bank, Standard Chartered Bank, Hungarian Bank, Gartland & Whalley, York Trust, Electra and Mr Branch representing our institutional shareholders.

Roughly ten days before the meeting, Gartland & Whalley met with Electra to see if they could establish any common ground. Jeff Whalley by now had become a real friend of mine and I could see that from time to time he was trapped between the emotion he felt for our plight – he knew that we had spent twenty-seven dedicated years building our business – and his professional duty. Before the meeting, he told me that I would not be allowed in and warned me not to build my hopes too high. After what seemed like hours, Jeff telephoned me with the bad news that they could find no common ground and Electra were pulling out.

Neil Balfour was incensed on hearing this news. However, the departure of Electra was not as disastrous as it might have been. Prudently, Neil had been working behind the scenes with Renaissance to secure the life-saving £12.5 million. Electra may have turned tail but we now had Renaissance to back the Gartland & Whalley plan.

Jeff and James had no hesitation throwing in their lot with Neil and the new funding from Renaissance, However, Tony Gartland seemed more hesitant, which was hardly surprising in view of his special friendship with the head of Electra.

On Sunday 23 June 1990, I had packed my bag and said farewell to my family. I left feeling quietly optimistic that we were going to be saved from the gaping jaws of the receiver. On the way down to London, I picked up Jeff Whalley and we travelled down the M1 together. It was a relaxed journey. Both Jeff and I felt everything was in place; we had managed to secure the funding and to meet the demands of Honingstad. £11.5 million had already gone into the company. Initially Gartland & Whalley would be subscribing a further £1 million of their own cash towards their shareholding in the company. After nine months of scouring the globe for cash, we felt we had succeeded.

We spoke about working together and although it had been a horrendous nine months for me I was looking forward to the future. I had gained a healthy respect for Jeff's judgement and felt that he would be someone I could get along with.

On Monday 24 June we convened at the Russell Hotel at 9.30 a.m. with Gordon Horsfield introducing all parties and explaining the reason for each one's attendance. We finally had to bring to an end whatever grievances anyone had with regard to the future structure of BGI.

Honingstad appeared to be extremely ill at ease throughout the meeting. His expression can only be described as that of a bulldog that has just swallowed a wasp. On this occasion he actually brought an English lawyer with him. Each group was allowed to speak in turn establishing their position. Gordon Horsfield had the job of intermediary; it was for him to reiterate or make clear what others had said.

Honingstad stated again that he wanted £25 million in the group and a substantial part of it to be transferred to Norway. Throughout the meeting, the main dialogue was between Christiania Bank and Standard Chartered Bank with little attention being paid to the presence of the Hungarian Bank. In the course of the afternoon a formula was worked out around the Gartland & Whalley plan. It was about 5 p.m. when Mr Branch of Renaissance, speaking on behalf of the institutions, made his demands.

He stated that his institutional group would willingly inject the further £12.5 million into the company, on the understanding that Christiania Bank would issue a letter making it clear that they would not interfere with the company as they had done over the last nine months. The English lawyer pointed out to Honingstad that this was not an unreasonable request. Standard Chartered Bank backed up this statement. They too had had enough of Honingstad's request.

Indeed all who attended the meeting, including Gordon Horsfield, got the impression that Honingstad agreed to the letter and that the drafting of it would be dealt with the following morning when the meeting reconvened. The meeting broke up and Robert, Jan Vidar and I went back to the White House Hotel totally convinced that the battle was won. However, we stopped short of buying champagne. We telephoned Ron who at the time was with the Komatsu people in Japan, launching our tunnel truck version of the Moxy. He like ourselves was 'over the moon' that a solution had finally been worked out. We all wanted this whole nightmare scenario to be over, so that we could get on and work in the battle-weary group that remained.

We reconvened the following morning in good spirits. But it did not take long for our bubble to burst. It was apparent that Honingstad was in a very agitated mood. Gordon Horsfield had already set the agenda. We expected simply to clarify certain points – dot the i's and cross the T's. We had not been seated five minutes when a nervous Honingstad blurted out that he was issuing no letter. He had been on the telephone to Oslo for most of the night and his bank would not agree to such a demand. The bank wished to reserve its right to interfere whenever it pleased them. I simply could not believe it. Was this man hellbent on wrecking us? Once again we were in deadlock.

The entire morning was spent searching for ways to break the deadlock. Gordon Horsfield immediately arranged two separate rooms ushering Christiania Bank, their lawyer and delegation into one and York Trust and Gartland & Whalley into another. He then spent his time darting between the two meetings trying to find some common ground but Honingstad was immovable. By this time, everybody in the York Trust camp was extremely suspicious of Christiania Bank's intentions. What exactly did they want? Only nine months ago they had voiced a most unreasonable demand for an immediate injection of £25 million; this we had finally met and now, at the eleventh hour, they had decided to shift the goal-posts. It was not as though Mr Branch was making an unreasonable request; no one could be expected to relish running a company under their destructive scrutiny. It was an unbelievable turnaround. The evening before everything had been agreed. Now it looked as though Christiania Bank were determined to force a bankruptcy, refusing any compromise.

Gordon Horsfield continued to mediate backwards and forwards between the two camps. Tony Gartland was feeling under the weather, suffering from a bad cold and was thoroughly fed up with the entire proceedings. He hinted once or twice that for two pins he would go home as he had wasted enough time on the case already. He was just about to comment again when Gordon Horsfield's assistant appeared at the door saying that Honingstad demanded our presence in Christiania Bank's room as he wanted to make a statement. Tony Gartland was not impressed:

'No one demands my presence. They can request it but no one demands it. How dare he! Anyway, I don't feel very well, I'm going.' And with that he put his coat on. Before he left, he said that his departure need not stand in the way of a successful outcome. He would delegate all his responsibilities to Jeff Whalley and James Barker.

My heart sank, I felt absolutely devastated, I simply couldn't cope with people walking out on meetings, I needed to know that these people were rallying round me, not deserting a sinking ship. Jeff looked at me and read my disappointment.

'Don't worry, kid. Tony has not felt well all day. Leave it to me.'

In a way, I was glad that Jeff was taking over. I felt that his manner might be more appropriate given the volatility of the situation.

We all trooped up the corridor and congregated in the room occupied by the two banks. Mr Harrison of Standard Chartered Bank was now desperately trying to hold the whole thing together but I think that he was realising that there was more to this matter than the initial request for £25 million. Even he felt that York Trust and everyone concerned had done their utmost to obtain a solution. Added to this two of the most respected men in industrial Great Britain were offering to take over the running of the group.

Once again, Jeff Whalley, James Barker and Gordon Horsfield all protested to Honingstad that BGI was not a receivership case. If anything precipitous happened he would have to bear a substantial part of the responsibility. This was like water off a duck's back. I often wondered if he really knew what he was doing because most of the time he seemed to be either under instructions or in the clouds. He had little input into any reasonable debate.

Around 2.30 p.m. Gordon Horsfield took Honingstad and the bank delegation back into the main conference room in one last attempt at mediation, leaving James, Jeff, all the York Trust delegation, the shareholders, including Mr Branch from Renaissance, and myself in the small room with the balcony window overlooking Russell Square. Out on the balcony, I watched the world going by, people going about their daily lives and thought how mine was crashing down around me. I am sure that Jeff Whalley kept an eye on me as he thought that in my state of mind I was likely to jump over.

Mr Branch had postponed going on holiday the day before, deciding to stay for the final drafting of the letter and to ensure that he was there to pledge the extra £12.5 million. He was beginning to get a little irritable and hinted that his wife would not be pleased if he did not catch a plane soon to the south of France. I was afraid that he too would soon leave. Without him, the Brown Group would have no future. I can remember starting to tell my old young farmer jokes as a way of giving myself some light relief and also to try to stop anyone else leaving before Gordon Horsfield had made one last attempt at Honingstad.

Everyone trooped back into the room around 3.30 p.m. and Gordon Horsfield proceeded to sum up the position of both parties with regard to the letter. Honingstad started to shuffle and look more uncomfortable than ever. The expression on his face was one of anger. I thought he might erupt. Suddenly he jumped up, instructing his delegation to get to their feet. He announced that the matter was closed. He went on to say that before he had left Norway he had put the wheels in motion that would eventually put Brown Engineering in Norway into bankruptcy: he had already started the process of withdrawing Christiania Bank's loans. With that he and his delegation abruptly left the meeting.

I was absolutely devastated – stunned. I just could not believe the inflexible nature of this man. Jeff Whalley turned to me and said:

'Well, I reckon that's about it, kid. We can do no more. His mind's made up. He seems determined to push us over the edge. I'm so sorry.'

The meeting was adjourned with Gordon Horsfield giving what sounded like the last rites. Robert was sent up to Leeds to be at head office the following morning. He could see no reason to stay on in London. However, there was just one last chance of a solution.

York Trust appealed for everyone to have one last think overnight and reconvene at their office the following morning at 10 a.m. We all appealed to Mr Harrison of Standard Chartered Bank as he was the only one now who might just be able to produce a satisfactory solution. He was asked to try to persuade his colleagues to provide the cash to take out Christiania Bank in Norway. Mr Harrison promised that he would go back to the bank that evening and discuss the matter with his colleagues; and Jeff Whalley would telephone them around 7.30 p.m. to find out what conclusion had been reached. Mr Harrison gave Jeff his home telephone number.

Jan Vidar decided that it was time to desert the sinking ship – I could not entirely blame him. He asked if he could leave, saying that he could do nothing useful by staying. He was heading to the airport to catch up with the Christiania Bank delegation. He believed that from lunch-time the following day, when BGI would effectively enter into administrative receivership, his future would no longer lie with us.

The meeting finally broke up with everyone in a very sombre mood. I went back to the White House while Jeff returned to the Meridian Hotel near Piccadilly Circus. I did not have the stomach to ring anyone. I already knew that BGI was at an end but this would not become official until 12 noon the following day. I went to my room and telephoned Lizzy. I tried to put a brave face on the situation but explained that it was not looking good.

'What's gone wrong? When you spoke to me last night, everything was going well. I thought it was just a matter of sorting out the letter . . .'

'Honingstad won't agree to it. This is it, Lizzy – I think it's the end and don't say anything to anyone yet. Don't even tell Simon or Tina. I'll call you in the morning.' With that I put the telephone down.

Within five minutes, Jeff Whalley phoned:

'How you feeling?'

'Ah, you know . . . not so good really Jeff, I can't believe what he's going to do to us . . .'

'Why not come round to the Meridian and we'll watch the match in my room and then we'll go out for something to eat.'

I had forgotten that it was the World Cup and England were playing. Jeff's suggestion lifted my spirits a little; I certainly was not looking forward to an evening on my own. I sat in Jeff's room like a zombie watching television. I was in such a state I could not even enjoy Platt's famous goal. All I could think of was that for twenty-seven years my brothers and I and our loyal workforce had striven to build up something that I was really proud of, something that I really loved and enjoyed, a place I enjoyed going to every day. Now it was about to be destroyed by someone who obviously had no emotional feelings whatever, by someone who had no understanding of what had gone into making that business, no feelings for the 1,600 lives he was about to fill with insecurity. He had sealed our fate, we were to become a statistic, a victim of the 1980s. It was hard to swallow. He was set on a path of destruction and there was no way that we could change his course.

Next morning I worked my way from the White House through the London traffic to the Meridian. I purposely left my telephone switched off. I collected Jeff and we proceeded along the Embankment arriving at York Trust's office at 10 a.m. Neil Milne, Neil Balfour and Gordon Horsfield were waiting in the boardroom. Jeff and I went in. On the middle of the table was a conference telephone balanced on top of two phone directories.

Jeff opened the meeting by telling us what we already suspected, Standard Chartered Bank could not save us. We went round the table in turn. The final execution began. I was given my instructions over the conference telephone by Morris Cowan from Booth & Co. in Leeds. He told me to call up each director, including Freddy and Ron, who was still in Japan, and explain to them that they might be in breach of their responsibilities. Our advisers told us that, even though the net worth of our company was still intact, without on-going banking facilities from Christiania Bank the company would be insolvent on the basis that it could not pay its creditors as and when their bills fell due. Added to this, because of the precipitous behaviour of the Christiania Bank and the cross guarantee situation, I had no alternative as chairman and managing director but to seal the fate of the rest of the group. It was like a house of cards. Honingstad had knocked one down and the rest had collapsed on top of it. I was instructed to ring Standard Chartered Bank and ask them to appoint a receiver.

My first task was to call Freddy; it was terrible. Freddy was devastated. I could not get hold of Ron. I then telephoned Willie Dalrymple and gave him the news. I was also briefed that before I rang Standard Chartered Bank I had to telephone Honingstad at Christiania Bank in Norway and ask them for one last time whether their decision had changed. I tried to explain to Honingstad that because of his action, I would have to ask Standard Chartered

Bank to appoint a receiver. As usual he seemed bemused by what I had said, so much so that I put him on loudspeaker so that everyone round the table could hear and experience at first hand the person we had been dealing with for the past nine months. Not once but two or three times he said, 'I cannot understand you doing this. In England you have Standard Chartered Bank. We have no wish to destroy the Brown distribution. We only want the factory back in Norway, the Norwegian asset.'

Neil Balfour took up the running and said:

'Excuse me, Tor. You do not seem to understand our receivership law. Due to your action we have no alternative but to put the whole group into receivership.'

Honingstad countered again that this would not be necessary. He almost appeared to be panic-stricken. However, he must have known the result of his actions; after all we had spent the last nine months explaining it to him. We decided unanimously that there was no point in continuing the conversation. Only time would tell what had really been going on in this man's mind. The receiver was replaced and there was nothing more for me to do but to telephone Mr Harrison at Standard Chartered Bank and request that he appoint a receiver and by that time it was 12 noon on 27 June 1990. The bottom had fallen out of my world.

I then telephoned Robert Lawson and told him to instruct each managing director to do what was best for each company, but that they had to incur no expenditure whatsoever. All that was left for me was to shake hands with Neil Balfour, Neil Milne and the rest of the party and thank them for all their help and effort. As I made my way to the lift, I was close to tears. I felt so alone. Suddenly, Jeff joined me. He had been going to catch the train home but changed his plans and accompanied me on my journey up the M1 back to Yorkshire.

Within seconds of leaving the Finsbury Square underground car park my telephone started to ring. It was quite odd in a way. The first telephone call was from Ray Mortimer, offering his condolences. I was so overcome that I could not speak. I told him to do the best for himself and thanked him.

The next call was from someone overseas who launched straight into a request to buy two dumptrucks, saying they had been recommended to get in touch with me. This was the most painful telephone call and in the end I just put the receiver down.

I received one or two more calls from our managing directors around the country, such as Barry Clark and Ray Chapman, once again offering their condolences. If there was anything they could do, I was not to hesitate to contact them. After a while Jeff reached over and pressed the off button on the telephone:

'Leave it behind you now, kid. You just want to settle yourself down and think about the future. No point in looking backwards.'

I could not help feeling most sorry for Ron as he lay in his bed in a hotel in Tokyo having received the news in the middle of the night and then having to set off on the long twenty-hour journey home to a very uncertain future. He had given all he had to the Norwegian factory only to find himself now without a job and with his home in a foreign land.

Jeff and I discussed all the way up the M1 what might have been; what had gone wrong. Thinking about my own uncertain future as neither Ron nor I had taken one penny out of the company, apart from our salaries. We were not wealthy by any means, but I consoled myself by thinking that I was luckier than some in the same position. At least I had my home which had been kept well outside the Honingstad security net.

Arriving back at Riffa at around 6 p.m. I was met by my family and the ever-faithful Willie. Simon had had a tough nine months. He had been working in the plant-hire division and had to spend day after day denying rumours that the company was in trouble. It was hard for him to pretend that everything was going well, when he knew the turmoil that raged behind the scenes. Tina was temping at ICI at the time and had rung up Lizzy from work expecting to hear that everything was OK. She too was upset and had come down to Riffa to see me. I found her in one of the offices reading an article from the late 1960s which we had had framed. It sang the praises of Wharfedale Agricultural Services, predicting a promising future – the irony of it all! Willie too stepped out to console me. He had been with the organisation for fifteen years now and it was as dear to him as it was to me.

Willie shook hands with Jeff and thanked him for all his help: 'Don't worry about us, Jeff, we'll find ourselves a couple of rich old tarts to look after us, if the worst comes to the worst.' And with that he left the yard for the evening.

Going back into the office, faxes of commiseration had already started to come in and continued to do so for the next few days. News had travelled fast. The words of comfort that I received from customers, manufacturers and friends from all over the world were greatly appreciated.

I was taking one last look at my office when the telephone rang. It was my good friend Neil Balfour: 'Brownie, I'm on the train to Leeds. Can I take you and Liz out for dinner? Some of your old shareholders have asked me to come and convey their deepest sympathy for what has happened. And when you've sorted yourself out, we'll put something together again.'

I thought this was a wonderful gesture after all Neil had been through. Not only was this affair a financial disaster for me, it was also, to a lesser extent, a financial disaster for Neil. However, his upbringing taught him that true friends are there whenever they are needed and he spent his time over dinner encouraging me to pick myself up off the floor and start thinking about the future. He told me that the following day he would be on hand to listen to any reasonable ideas.

I could not sleep that night and was awake early next morning for my usual moorland walk. Over the years I had spent many hours striding over the moors pondering my business, analysing problems, examining strategy and so on. I suppose this must have dated back to my time on the farm. I still felt most comfortable when I was in the country. Now, for the first time in nine months, I had a clear head and was able to stand back, look at the work of half a lifetime and try to see what had brought it all crashing down.

Above all I now had the time to try to work out why Tor Honingstad had been so inflexible. His predecessor at Christiania Bank, Per Kipstard Pettison, had been very satisfied with the running of the group and had always accepted that Ron, Jan Vidar and I were people of integrity. In return we respected his position as our bank manager.

Suddenly we had been confronted with every businessman's nightmare – a trigger-happy bank manager who for the short time we had known him had run around like a headless chicken and in doing so had placed his own bank in a difficult situation. I had no problem with Tor Honingstad wishing to impose new disciplines on the group. It had never been disputed that the English and US companies legitimately owed money to the Norwegian operation for finished goods that had been supplied on extended credit with the intention being simply to move the units nearer to the ultimate market place. This was a practice which was acceptable to Per Kipstard Pettison, but not to Tor Honingstad, who had no experience of this type of export arrangement regarded as quite normal in the construction-equipment industry. Notwithstanding this he had had the over-riding protection of cross guarantees in favour of his bank throughout the group. A banker with real experience should know that a group with approximately £150 million turnover per year cannot change direction instantly but can over a period of time in order to avoid the type of catastrophe that he created.

It was the opinion of everyone concerned that BGI could have pursued both the short-term and long-term plan put forward by Gartland & Whalley, thus ensuring that at least the bank's cash would have stayed intact at the sacrifice of the shareholders, predominantly the Brown family. No one could understand Honingstad's inflexible attitude. In addition, no one could accept that, after his unreasonable demands had been met in their entirety, he still went ahead and terminated Christiania Bank's loans, leaving the directors with no alternative but to put Brown Engineering into bankruptcy.

Events since then have quite clearly shown that Christiania Bank was in considerable financial difficulties. At the time it was not public knowledge that Tor Honingstad was obviously under pressure from some quarter. However, surely this factor alone could not explain his peculiar behaviour. There were further incidents which just did not stack up, such as the fax which turned up in Leo Gerbus's office in the USA in the middle of the night, six weeks before we had gone into receivership. The fax stated that Brown Engineering A/S was in bankruptcy and that as Moxy Trucks USA was a daughter company he could no longer incur any credit. Leo had telephoned us immediately when he had arrived at the office the following morning, wanting to know what was going on and why we had not told him. One or two frenzied telephone calls to Christiania Bank led to the immediate withdrawal of the document and an apology.

However, in my mind this fax opened a whole can of worms. First, who had sent the fax? Obviously it was someone at Christiania Bank and it became obvious to me that, in the eyes of Christiania Bank, there never had been a future for the Brown Group. From that day in September 1989 when Tor Honingstad made his demand for £25 million, our fate had been sealed. Someone at the bank had a gun to our head and was just waiting for an appropriate moment to pull the trigger.

Then there was the unbelievable possibility of a conspiracy on the part of the Norwegians. Did certain members of Christiania Bank, urged on by certain members of the government, want the Brown brothers out of Norway? As it had been suggested that the Browns had got the factory for NKr. 3 after the Norwegian government had spent approximately NKr. 20 million of Norwegian taxpayers' money, could it be that, with the factory up and running and making money, they wanted it back? And was this the only way they could get it?

There was also the unsavoury publication of an article that had appeared on 9 June 1990 in a down-market magazine, *Kapital*. I believe this article probably spurred on Christiania Bank and Tor Honingstad in their ultimate precipitative action. While the article carried a small amount of factual information it was, as is usual with this type of editorial, given out of context and mischievously written so as to imply that misappropriation of cash was taking place at Brown Engineering/Moxy in Norway. At the time neither Ron nor I had the time to defend these allegations as we were engaged in a much bigger battle. However, I was assured by our Norwegian managers that the magazine had little importance and was generally looked upon as a gossip paper. It was certainly our intention to sue these people for their defamatory statements, but as events unfolded, their article became submerged in all the rest of the skulduggery.

My story was to end at this point as a disillusioned, demoralised chief executive who had done his utmost, in the first place quite selfishly, to protect his own shareholding and the shareholdings of others, but, in the end, sacrificed his own shareholding and job in favour of the Gartland & Whalley plan which would have saved the group and all the workplaces within it.

However, even with all these sacrifices and compromises Tor Honingstad and Christiania Bank continued their precipitative action. But certain events which have unfolded since then have left me with no alternative but to add another chapter to my story and let the public at large try to resolve the mystery.

The past: A Moxy dump truck.

CHAPTER 20

The Receivership

DESPITE WARNINGS, the bankers immediately proceeded to make their first big mistake. It was well known to the banks that BGI was a vertically integrated company. The factory in Norway was a daughter company of the group, as were the distribution outlets based in Great Britain, USA and Germany. These three outlets accounted for approximately 40 per cent of all dumptruck sales.

To preserve value it was essential that the group remained as a whole. The bank's decision to appoint a lawyer in Norway and KPMG in the UK to look after the receivership would only have worked if the banks had insisted on BGI being disposed of as an integral group. Unfortunately, this was never the case. The two receivers had a brief meeting in Oslo during the first week of the receivership. However, little common ground was established. A quick solution was not of interest. Both parties could gain more by prolonging the receivership. As a result of their procrastination, the Norwegian lawyer ended up with a factory with a capacity to produce 800 trucks a year, but with 40 per cent of the distribution network already in doubt, while KPMG in the UK had a distribution network to sell but with no certainty of supply. It became obvious almost straight away that this action considerably devalued the group within the first seven days. So much for the 'professional' approach.

I expect the reader will have gathered by now that administrative receivers are not my favourite section of the accountancy profession. I would go further, and argue that in many respects their activity is contrary to the well-being of society. It is a fact that when a company is in receivership the creditors and the employees are always likely to be the losers, while the banks and the receivers will invariably gain. A radical rethink of the whole concept of administrative receivership must be made. Unfortunately, so long as this lucrative trade enjoys the luxury of self-regulation, there will be little incentive for change.

Having said that, during the early 1980s steps were taken to try to change the system, to move a little further towards the US 'Chapter 11' way of doing things. However, the level of success was minimal. A committee was set up to look into ways of dealing with companies who found themselves in trouble and this brief flirtation with change was doomed from the start.

The committee's independent chairperson was an official receiver and so was hardly independent.

As sure as Christmas Day falls on 25 December, while self-regulation persists, this present lucrative system will continue. Can you imagine what it would be like if other businesses were self-regulated? What would people have thought if Arthur Scargill had been allowed to decide the miners' salaries? Or what if our truck drivers were allowed to decide how many hours a week they could safely work? Surely even administrative receivers should be regulated by an independent higher body.

In a nutshell, an administrative receiver claims to be someone to whom a bank or indeed anyone involved in an insolvent company can turn for advice. Their function is to administer the affairs of the company after the bank had appointed them generally at the request of the directors in order to avoid trading insolvently The receiver is supposed to be the 'guardian' of the company, representing the interests of the creditors (in order of importance), with the initial aim of disposing of the company as a 'going concern' and preserving jobs. Failing that, he closes the business down, sacks all the employees and sells the assets at auction.

In reality a receiver is a servant of the appointer, the bank holding the charge. His initial objective is to get the bank's cash back. Secondly, he has to ensure that there are sufficient funds to pay his own fees (or maybe the other way round) and thirdly, if there is any money left in the pot, it is divided between those at the bottom of the pile, the unsecured creditors. If a receiver does his job well, he may never even have to meet one. Oh yes, they do a lot of legal huffing and puffing on the first two days of their appointment and push out a lot of circular letters designed to create the impression that they are acting in the best interests of the creditors, but that is about the last you will ever hear. Once they have got that job out of the way they set about getting in the cash as quickly as possible, issuing credit notes and getting rid of assets at knock-down prices.

Apparently, in the early 1980s, the receiver's committee, under pressure to adopt an American-style 'Chapter 11' solution to these problems, did come up with a half-way compromise. This solution amounted to little more than window-dressing – the changes were subtle to say the least – and the new alternative, Administration, is rarely implemented since, before Administration can go ahead, the Administrator has to be assured of continuing cooperation from the bank. The chances of this being gained are usually remote.

It is my opinion, having both bought from administrative receivers and fallen victim to them, that on the morning of 27 June 1990, when our group, BGI, went into receivership, the directors and I should have been able to appeal to a higher authority for a three-month or longer stay of execution. This US-style remedy allows for a cooling-off period where management can seek a solution which would be in the best interests of everyone concerned and also guard against the wild card bank manager.

It is a great shame if a system cannot be worked out to protect a company such as Brown Group International, a company built up over a long period. We had done everything Margaret Thatcher had wanted. We had employed hundreds of people, paid salaries, contributed in all ways to the economic system of Great Britain plc. Surely the state could allow at least a period of ninety days before calling in the administrative receiver. Such an act could only benefit all those involved. The present system benefits only the bank and the receiver.

If assets must be disposed of and debts collected with frantic speed, surely it would be better to leave the management structure in place, allow the court to appoint a supervisor and allow the business to continue in an orderly manner, disposing of assets and collecting debts over a period of time, pound for pound. Under the present system, Joe Bloggs, the man in the street, knows that he can get something for nothing, and he has the upper hand. He knows the receiver wants to get the cash back in the bank, he knows that the receiver will be looking to cover the bank's debt and those of his firm. Why pay the full price, when you can get it for as little as half its true value at the receivership sale!

Brown Group International plc was a victim of this destructive profession and its receivership was to be no exception. I found it most disturbing that while we had been spending week after week, constructively trying to find a solution to the problems of BGI, others, particularly KPMG's insolvency section's marketing manager, had been actively lobbying the banks involved, expounding the virtues of getting in to the company early to achieve the best results for the bank.

An administrative receiver was appointed to handle the receivership of BGI at noon on 27 June 1990; the staff and the public at large were informed soon afterwards. However, no representative of the receiver actually turned up to administer the company until 1 p.m. on 28 June 1990. This twenty-four-hour no-man's-land gave rise to looting. I began to receive telephone calls from the depots telling me that looting was rife. Our Riffa-based elder, Len Baxter, came to my office in the middle of the morning to tell me that it was a free for all in the workshop. What could be done? I explained that I was no longer in charge and we were awaiting the administrative receiver. Apparently this state of mind amongst the workforce is not unusual. The rationale is that they will not get paid, so they should grab what they can. Even the plug sockets disappeared.

By the time the receiver arrived I was reliably informed that there were not many grinding units, sanders and welding sets left in any depot – so much for protecting the creditors. I would have thought that part of the receiver's drill would have been to dispatch a security company immediately to each depot to ensure that this type of thing did not happen.

Soon after the receivership was announced, I received a phone call, requesting that I turn up for work as normal the following day. However, I was not to make any decisions or incur any credit. When the receiver arrived on 28 June, I have to say I was pleasantly surprised. I expected to be treated like a discarded boot, but quite the contrary. I was shown the utmost respect and asked to stay for the foreseeable future. Apparently on their way from London the receiver and his staff had called to see Gordon Horsfield who had suggested that they should break with tradition and instead of firing the chairman and chief executive in the first hour, they should keep me on. He felt that I could be useful as I knew my way around the business.

For the first time in my life I had the luxury of drawing a salary without the headache of responsibility. The previous six months had been traumatic to say the least; now I had time to twiddle my thumbs. For the first time in my life I had time to go out for lunches with business colleagues and friends. We commiserated and talked about old times, the days spent on the farm, laying the pipelines in Scotland, the prosperity of the oil-boom, the buying of Moxy and so on and so on. They, like many others, had watched and helped BGI grow from an acorn into an oak only to see it prematurely hacked down. It was a sad time for all of us.

Not many hours had passed into the receivership before I heard talk of 'cash'. However, before they could concentrate on hauling it in, they had some redundancies to make. All receivers assume that a failed company is badly run, overstaffed and unproductive. BGI was assumed to be no exception; therefore, the opening rule of the receiver's handbook must be implemented: fire 25 per cent of the staff regardless. This demonstrates to everybody an air of efficiency. This miserable task accomplished, the question of 'cash' was addressed once more. How quickly could the receiver get the cash back for Standard Chartered Bank? This should not have been a problem. There were plenty of book debts, lots of stock and, above all, had the business been sold pound for pound there would have been (in the best case scenario) £25 million of surplus cash. Perhaps this is an overly theoretical assumption but, even if they had had to issue credit notes to those who required them, they should still have been able to get the bank all its money back and pay all creditors. But no such luck. The speed with which they could get the cash in became the overriding priority and to this end all stocks had to be liquidated as quickly as possible with no regard whatsoever to any representation of true value.

All sales representatives were summoned together on the second day and were told quite clearly that the receiver would accept any reasonable offer for any stock. BGI was renowned for employing quite a number of bright lads and with the exception of one or two they soon spotted that there was an opportunity here to operate a two-tier market. A number of them initially went out looking for a trading pal, which was not too difficult to do. They had many more connections than the receiver. Then they would pick up a machine worth, say, £60,000 which they could easily sell via their friend for £45,000. It was not long before the pal was ringing the receiver offering £30,000 for the machine, number so and so, and with the dash for the cash well and truly on, the reply used to be, can you bring a cheque in today? If he could, the machine was his. Poor old unsecured creditor. Another £30,000 gone, representing 50p in the pound of value loss.

One week prior to receivership I had agreed a deal to ship £1 million worth of equipment to Nigeria. All the information and documentation was in place. I continued to handle this deal on behalf of the receiver for a number of days after his appointment and the transaction was going through the normal channels. However, his impatience led him to take direct control of the deal himself and he had concluded it within a matter of minutes. For the £1 million of equipment he accepted £600,000 of cash there and then. In a trading situation prior to receivership this would have represented at least a 30 per cent trading loss.

How can these people claim to be acting in the best interests of creditors? This particular customer was captive. He was legally committed to the equipment and yet they still ended up giving it to him at a big discount. This pattern of events was to be repeated over the next few weeks, and it was the same with credit notes. If a customer could think up any constructive reason why he should receive a credit note for 50 per cent of his invoice it was usually met with a sympathetic ear and 'I will issue a credit note today if you will leave a cheque'. Within weeks the receiver is getting congratulatory telephone calls from the bank while the unsecured creditors are left struggling to keep their businesses afloat. They will receive daily rebukes from their bank manager, telling them that they are abusing their overdraft and to get their cash in quickly.

If it was not bad enough watching your empire being destroyed brick by brick, there was worse to come. In Norway, a lawyer, Jens Kristian Thune, had been appointed to act as a receiver for the Norwegian side of the business. Taking his new role to the extreme, he had gone out of his way to appear on television and radio programmes, openly calling into question the integrity of Ron and myself.

Having moved into what would be termed, in parochial Norway, a glamour bankruptcy, J. K. Thune was basking in the press and television adoration that goes with it. After all it was a major crisis in a country twice the size of Britain with a population of only about 5 million. The problem seemed to stem from the fact that the lawyer appeared confused between monies owed from daughter and parent companies as a genuine debt and misappropriation of cash. And he immediately started making loose statements to the press suggesting that there was NKr. 160 million missing from the company. He made asides such as 'as soon as I get the company tidied up and running correctly I will go after the Brown brothers in search of this cash'. The press scrambled this message, so that headlines such as 'NKr. 160 million missing at Moxy' began to appear above statements such as 'Moxy lawyer will go after the Brown brothers to recover the NKr. 160 million.'

On hearing these reports Ron and I telephoned each other expressing disbelief, and then we telephoned our colleagues at the factory in Norway: 'I know what you mean, Gordon. We are all reading the same thing here. It is a joke but you cannot tell this man anything. He has made up his mind that you are another Rexton (Rexton was a controversial company which became a scandal in Norway in the late 1970s and early 1980s) and he is convinced that you have misappropriated cash throughout your complex group. No matter what we say we cannot convince them that the Brown brothers were not that sort of people.'

Ron and I were relieved to hear that we had their support and this ridiculous rumour was certainly not coming from the factory, only from the office of the lawyer handling the receivership.

By now I felt most sorry for Ron as he was right there in the midst of it. Until that day I am sure the majority of people in Molde thought the world of him and marvelled in his achievements at the factory and the employment that he had created for the local community. Ron did not have a sound grasp of the Norwegian language, nor did he have the same access to the press. He was in a foreign country, receiving body blows from a prominent Norwegian lawyer and felt powerless to defend himself against this blatant defamation of character. Not surprisingly the Norwegian public believed their own man; he was a lawyer after all and it would have been a pretty irresponsible statement to make if it were not true. It had to be true.

We both telephoned Thune and insisted that he correct the untrue statement but by now, carried along by the media, his head was in cloud-cuckoo-land and he was in no mood for withdrawing any of his controversial statements, as this would have had the immediate effect of diverting the media attention which he was enjoying so much. Ron, people at the factory, and I were amazed that even when it was brought to his attention that there was no cash missing or misappropriated in any shape or form, he still refused to retract the statements that he had made. He used a very careful structure of words, leaving the Norwegian public in no doubt that what he really meant was that Gordon and Ron Brown had stolen NKr. 160 million.

In an attempt to correct the situation I appeared in a television programme and emphasised to the Norwegian public that there was no misappropriation of any cash and that only with the fullness of time would it be demonstrated that not one penny was missing. Thune also appeared in the same programme, still continuing to make innuendos with regard to the NKr. 160 million of supposedly missing cash.

Setting aside Ron's and my integrity, the same receivership pattern began to emerge in Norway as in the UK. Trucks were being sold daily at substantially less than their real value to satisfy Christiania Bank's thirst for recovering their cash as soon as possible and to hell with the unsecured creditors.

Ron had been told to leave the factory almost immediately. Soon after, Jan Vidar was also asked to leave. As far as Thune and his party were concerned, Jan Vidar had become a loose cannon. He did not like the way that Thune was portraying the Brown brothers as villains and told him so. Indeed, it is true to say that he sacrificed his job in defending Ron and myself.

Meanwhile back in England, the receivership plodded on. In July the receiver came to see me to let me know that a Nigerian client of BGI was on the telephone. We had had a successful business relationship with this man, Chief Ogundoyin, for three years and trusted him implicitly. He had contacted us to confirm that he had another consultancy contract for us, the value of which was $5.5 million and the payment terms were as before, payment with a mobilisation deposit and then monthly in advance for up to ten consultants. This had been the most lucrative contract that BGI had had over the past three years.

I was absolutely astonished when the receiver jeered at the Nigerian chief and said:

'You what, work in Nigeria, never, no – I want nothing to do with working in Nigeria.'

I was just about to point out to the receiver what a lucrative contract this was and that we had spent six months negotiating it when for the first time I had reluctantly to accept that my twenty-seven years of loyalty to BGI was at an end. The receiver had already refused the contract and put the telephone down, so why should I bother?

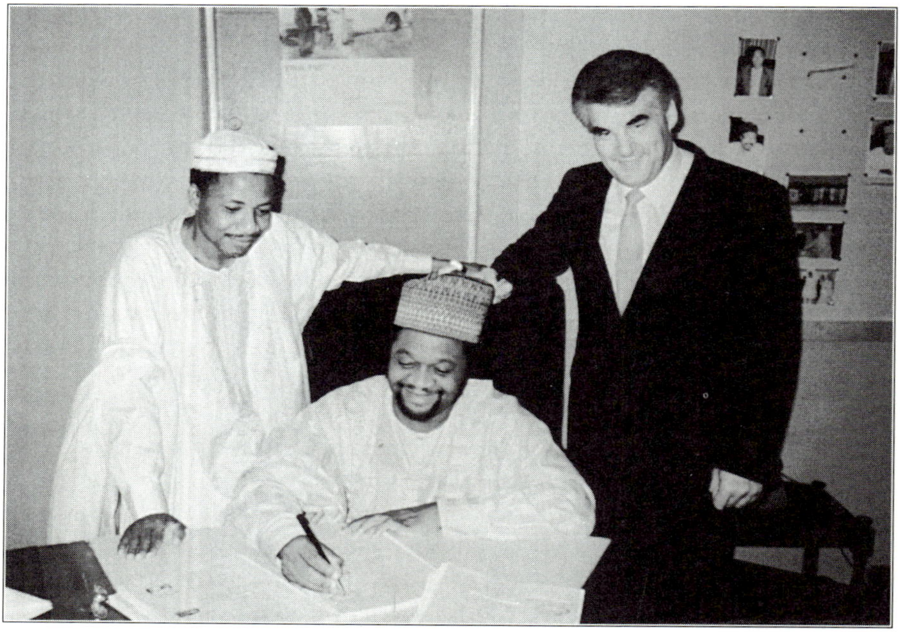

Chief Ogundoyin and I behind the head of the water authority
for the Nigerian irrigation project.

Soon after this, hurt and embittered, I said I would like to resign as soon as possible. A telephone call from the receiver's office soon followed telling me, in his words, that this was the job he least liked doing but he had to tell me, as chairman and chief executive, that I would no longer be needed from the end of the telephone call.

With some relief and trepidation and without being consciously aware of it I was starting to put together my broken empire. My first call was to my good friend Chief Ogundoyin in Nigeria. I asked if I might take up his offer of a new contract as it had been turned down by the receiver. Within a matter of hours I was on the next plane to Lagos. I signed a new contract with the Chief to provide a team of consultants to construct another series of small irrigation dams with the promise of an advance payment of $500,000 to be paid on mobilisation. By the second week in August I was opening an account at the Bank of Scotland in Leeds with a deposit of $500,000 which would be the only funding to start our new organisation. Chief Ogundoyin died suddenly soon after the contract started, but I shall be eternally grateful for his help.

While the Nigerian contract was being mobilised by one of our consultants during the first week of August I slipped away to Houston, Texas. I had received a telephone call from a business colleague whom I had known since the early 1980s called Malcolm Stockdale. Malcolm had accumulated considerable wealth by selling his business interests. He told me he wanted to mount a buy-out of BGI from the receiver. He had already assembled his team which included a top lawyer from New York and a top firm of accountants based in Houston. The missing link was that he wanted a chief executive, someone familiar with the Brown Group. Whilst I was compiling their bid in the peace and quiet of a Houston high-rise office, Saddam Hussein was on the other side of the world mobilising his troops in Iraq.

A plan was formulated to buy BGI back in its entirety but it would have to be carried out in stages. The first step was the acquisition of the Moxy and Broyt factories in Norway. A bid of NKr. 280 million (approximately £28 million) was forwarded to Thune for his consideration and arrangements were made for the buy-out team to transfer their operation to London during the following week. The Clifton Ford Hotel in London was to be their headquarters.

Malcolm Stockdale was the first to arrive over the weekend, closely followed by his New York lawyer, Carro Spanbock of Kaster & Kuiffo, and his team of accountants. The first day we spent being briefed by a production consultant from KPMG. He had been appointed to look round all the manufacturing plants and submit findings prior to our final negotiations. Once everything was in place, we decided to reconfirm our bid. We all assembled and the New York lawyer telephoned Thune.

He outlined our bid of NKr. 280 million and went on to outline that we would be willing to meet both ZF and Scania as it was essential that they continued production. We had already formulated an ongoing paydown plan which would enable them to recover the money owed to them by Brown Engineering A/S.

However, we were astonished to discover that Thune appeared not to be impressed by our continuing interest in the purchase of the Norwegian factories. He immediately started putting ridiculous obstacles in the way, saying, for example, that the Houston team of accountants was from the same company as the team of accountants that he had employed at the factory in Norway, and he felt sure there would be a conflict of interest. All the time he was making it quite obvious that our bid was most unwelcome.

We arrived at a point in the proceedings where Thune asked if he could speak to our lawyer without anyone else being present and the call was transferred to another room to allow privacy. About ten minutes later our lawyer opened the door and beckoned Malcolm Stockdale into his private room where the conversation continued for another twenty minutes or so.

When at last they returned to the conference room, where I was sitting chatting with the rest of the party, it was to say that they had no alternative but to pull out of the bid. Thune had explained to them at great length that Gordon and Ron Brown, because of their actions while running the Norwegian office, would not be allowed either to own or be a director of a Norwegian company in the future, and he added that a lot of information would come to light later which would confirm his allegations. He went on to confirm that he would not accept a bid where Gordon Brown was destined to be chief executive of the new group.

You can imagine my total disbelief at this unprofessional behaviour. How could one lawyer in Norway take it upon himself to refuse a bid from these people who were ready, willing and able and had the cash waiting? How could he take it upon himself even to pretend that he was acting in the best interests of the creditors and turn down NKr. 280 million. We had even offered to pay back in full the two major suppliers. I could not believe it. Thune had struck again, and succeeded in turning another set of people against us.

While Malcolm Stockdale had not been a close friend, I had known him for twenty years. When he returned to the room, he gave me a piece of his mind: 'You should have told us there was a problem before we went to all this expense. It has cost me a lot of money so far and it is all for nothing because I am not willing to proceed without you there as MD. You know the company inside out. No one else does. So the deal is off.'

And with that his team packed their bags and went back to Houston. I sat in my hotel room that afternoon feeling shell-shocked. Thune was slowly but surely beating me into the ground. Not only was this man discrediting me and my family in Norway, he was also discrediting us overseas. There were no grounds for his accusations.

While travelling up the M1 back to Yorkshire on the Saturday morning, Stan Wayland telephoned me from HMC Holdings in Australia. He had heard that the Americans had pulled out of the deal and asked if there was any chance that I would be prepared to transfer my allegiance to HMC? I would have transferred my allegiance to Mr Blobby if he had offered to help me buy back the Brown Group! I pointed out that all I wanted was to be involved and have a job and some shareholding if possible. I went home, got a clean change of clothes and immediately returned to London. We set up another office at the White House Hotel where Robert and I worked day and night with Stan Wayland compiling a new bid – it was September by this time and the company's assets were diminishing in value.

Stan Wayland was already well aware of Thune's attitude towards Ron and myself but he attached no relevance to it at all. He had known and dealt with us for the last five years and knew that Thune was talking rubbish.

With HMC's negotiations I had no access to the bidding. This was carried out by Stan and his German lawyer, Herr Strack. My job was to assist them in compiling their bid with a promise that, if they were successful, I would be reappointed managing director. I understood that HMC's bid was more complex than the US bid but it was still in the region of NKr. 240 million for the remaining assets and Wayland and Herr Strack had already visited Scania and ZF to make sure that they suffered no loss on goods previously supplied to the Moxy factory.

During September it either leaked out, or else Thune suspected, that HMC could not be so well versed with everything that was going on within the Brown Group without having had some personal contact with Gordon or Ron Brown; and finally Stan confessed that I was involved. Once again Thune proceeded to slander both Ron and myself.

On this occasion I was able to hear more of the detail of what Thune was saying because Stan came back to London and discussed fully with me the seriousness of Thune's statements. Stan told me that Thune had used the word 'crooks' on several occasions when talking about the two of us. This favourite word of Thune's was already becoming familiar to me as I had heard it from Tony Holmes and others who had telephoned me.

Thune had told Stan Wayland that no bid would be accepted if either Gordon or Ron Brown was involved; he even put it in writing. When Stan Wayland showed me the letter he had received from Thune I couldn't believe it. What right had this man to take it upon himself to be judge and jury? To decide whether or not Ron or Gordon Brown could work as directors or owners in Norway? How could he be allowed to hold his own kangaroo court?'

Surely Thune had stepped well over the mark. And again Herr Strack spoke to me and said: 'If a practising lawyer is making this sort of statement he must have some pretty strong supporting evidence somewhere because if he cannot substantiate these accusations later on, he is leaving himself wide open for a lot of trouble.'

In a letter dated 26 September 1990 Thune wrote:

> 2. HMC must, by 1st October 1990 at the very latest . . . present documentation that first class finance institutions will guarantee full payment of the purchase price as offered by HMC.
>
> . . .
>
> 3. HMC must confirm their previous statement that the previous owners (the Brown family), neither directly nor indirectly has or in the future will have any ownership in the continued operation of the two companies.

With regard to Item 2 I have had negotiations with financial institutions for over twenty-five years and have not come across one who would issue a guarantee along the lines sought by Thune before negotiations had even started. I am not sure whether this item was designed to ensure non-compliance or whether it highlights Thune's inexperience in dealing with such matters. However, Thune did receive letters from financial institutions confirming that cash was available to support HMC's bid but as is normal they were qualified by statements saying that due diligence must be carried out and that any undertaking to supply finance would be conditional upon their clients being satisfied with the deal. Once again this is quite normal. Why should any financial institutions stick out their necks so early in negotiations and give an irrevocable guarantee, whatever the outcome.

Item 3 in the letter astonished Herr Strack as he could not understand how Thune could have any jurisdiction over the livelihood of the Brown brothers either inside or outside Norway. After much discussion and under duress, Stan Wayland, in a desperate attempt to get to the negotiating table, swore an affidavit to the effect that the Brown family would not be involved in his bid.

To emphasise even further the hypocrisy of Thune and his bankruptcy board one should take a look at the letter written to me by Thune dated 7 November after a number of previous communications from me which had not been answered, and compare the statement in the first paragraph:

> I can't see no reason [sic] why you can not act on behalf of a group of investors who would like to purchase the assets of both Moxy and Broyt manufacturing units . . . On behalf of the group you are certainly free to make a bid . . .

with Item 3 of the letter written to HMC dated 26 September 1990. Perhaps it was by this time that the task was proving too much for Thune and some instability was becoming obvious!

As far as Herr Strack and the financial advisers of HMC are concerned, they did everything in their power to reach the negotiating table, even to the extent of Stan Wayland's affidavit, which in the opinion of a number of people was obtained under duress and was deemed illegal. It was now quite obvious that no serious negotiations would be allowed to take place with any organisation outside Norway. It was clear too that Thune and his bankruptcy board felt ill at ease on the international stage. Equally, in my mind I had no doubt that the Norwegian authorities believed their handling of the affair would fade with time.

In the meantime, while I had been away, Tony Holmes of Electra had returned to pick over the bones, but he also found, along with others, that the Norwegian receiver had no intention of co-operating with the UK receiver and, to preserve value, both units would have to be sold as one as they were so interlinked. In short, the golden egg was situated in Norway and the golden distribution network was situated in the UK and the US. To be sure of attaining ongoing viability all units would have to be purchased at the same time but with Thune's attitude this was to prove impossible.

It was only now that I began to wonder what was really happening. Was there a conspiracy being perpetrated by the Norwegians? Initially we had had Tor Honingstad and now we had to contend with Thune. Were his actions those of a loose cannon or, more to the point, were his strings being pulled by a higher authority? Were his actions actually illegal? It was becoming quite obvious that somewhere, someone in Norway had a sincere wish to return the Moxy and Broyt operations to Norwegian ownership no matter how unethical and illegal their tactics were. It was becoming obvious that Thune and the people behind him wanted a Norwegian solution.

In September, after I had met the UK receiver in London at his head office, he told me that Thune had behaved most strangely when they had visited him in Norway. He was puzzled at Thune's reluctance to advertise the business internationally: at that time he had not advertised the Norwegian companies in the *Financial Times* – one of the most important mediums through which such an organisation could be sold. This action alone made it clear that somebody was pulling strings behind the scene and every effort was being made to ensure that there were no serious international bidders.

Meanwhile, back in the UK, observers were gasping with astonishment at the administrative receiver's progress at Capital Airlines. Here again we had a glamour receivership. The receiver was seen posing on breakfast, lunch and evening television on a regular basis either sitting on an aircraft wheel or in a set pose in front of a fleet of aircraft, mopping up every bit of publicity he could. But, oh, what a disaster followed.

In the last months before the receiver was appointed, we had started negotiating with three major regional airlines wishing to purchase Capital Airlines. Honingstad had been kept fully aware of these negotiations and had even been faxed copies of correspondence in the weeks prior to receivership. Now, because of the receivership, Air UK got almost everything they wanted for nothing.

On the afternoon of the receivership Adrian Thompson had been spoken to by Robert Lawson and had been told that Capital Airlines was in receivership and as managing director it was his responsibility to ensure that no further credit was incurred before the arrival of the receiver. As a result of this instruction, during the course of the evening Adrian ensured that all aircraft returned to base, and by mid-evening all units were parked in a line on the hard standing at Leeds-Bradford. As there was no receiver to make a decision on the morning of 28 June, the planes remained parked at the side of the runway and passengers stayed within the gates in the terminal, waiting for the receiver to give an instruction to put the planes back in the air and preserve the value of the airline.

I was never quite sure exactly what happened. All I do know is that the planes did not get back in the air – whether this was due to the receiver's procrastination or an overzealous observation of insolvency law, I do not know. However, what I do know is that by not ensuring that the aircraft carried on with their routine flights, the licences lapsed, and in a matter of forty-eight hours the airline was rendered valueless. Air UK got all they needed and the creditors were well and truly shafted. In the negotiations the value of the airline and its route licences had been put at around £7 million. Now, within hours, the airline was regarded as valueless. On both sides of the North Sea, all interested parties had been and looked and gone away. Now all the receiver had to do was to pick over the dry bones of what was left. All the companies in the group had become only a shadow of their former selves. Irredeemable damage had been inflicted and customer confidence and employee morale were at an all-time low. It was difficult to imagine that anyone would buy what was left as a going concern.

Over in Norway Thune had gone a long way towards achieving his goal. He had one or two Norwegian companies who were seriously interested. However, he still had one wild bidder from the UK to take care of. Richard Lanni, with some former Brown employees, had mounted a bid for what was now left of the Moxy factory and assets. While he had been backwards and forwards trying to finalise negotiations for the factory he was making little progress as Thune was convinced that because he was from the UK, that Gordon Brown would be involved. On this occasion he was totally wrong. I was not involved in Richard's bid.

Now the Norwegian authorities decided to have what I would call a sham auction in the spring of 1991. The auction was to be held for the factory, with the production rights to the Moxy trucks, manufacturing assets and intellectual property all to be negotiated under a separate deal with Thune. In short, one had first to buy the factory and then negotiate the purchase of the rest of the assets, and once again if you were lucky enough to achieve both, you would have a dumptruck factory.

On the evening before the auction Richard Lanni telephoned me. He had been a client of BGI for a number of years, and asked me if I was going to the factory auction in Norway. I said I was, and that I would be a bidder for by now I had found a backer and was going to have one last go at owning the Moxy factory again. This would really put the fairness of the auction to the test. In the interest of saving costs Richard invited me to join him on a Lear jet that he had rented for the day.

Imagine the surprise on the faces of the airport staff when I arrived with Richard in the luxury of the Lear jet. By this time I had been completely written off. Ron still had his house in Molde though he did not live there all the time. I could hear the whispering as I passed through the terminal and the surprised look on everyone's face when Richard and his party took one taxi and headed for the Alexandra Hotel and I was collected by Ron and taken to his house.

Ron would not attend the auction as he knew that most of the people from the factory would be there and quite a number from the town. By the spring of 1991, Ron was tired of the continual press harassment from people seeking answers to Thune's allegations, for still no material evidence had been supplied to substantiate his claims.

I took a taxi along to the auction room in Elnesvagen. I can remember thinking on the way that I was luckier than Ron. I was living in England and did not have to tolerate the day-to-day harassment with people pointing me out at the supermarket or whenever he went for a meal. I was just here for the day.

As the taxi approached I could see a large group of people standing outside and along the short road to the entrance to the sale room. I stopped the taxi and decided to emphasise the fact that I had nothing to hide.

I paid the taxi fare, picked up my briefcase and turned round to a deathly hush. Gordon Brown had come back to haunt them one last time. It was a little bit like High Noon. I walked the last 150 metres to the sale room with reporters saying, 'Tell us where the NKr. 160 million is, Gordon.' I retorted, 'What NKr. 160 million? Ask Thune, he seems to know more than I do about it.'

I arrived at the sale-room door and once again my entrance into the room was met by a deathly hush. I took a seat just behind Richard Lanni, who sat in the front row with his advisers.

The auctioneer explained from the platform exactly what the purchaser would be buying. All had to be clear because some items were fixtures and fittings belonging to the factory and others were a separate batch of assets which I have previously described.

The bidding was started by Richard Lanni. Then came one from somewhere else in the hall. Richard countered again and then suddenly a voice right behind me bid one for one with Richard. It did not take Richard long to realise that the man sitting behind me was bidding without thought or hesitation. Each time he immediately countered and Richard quickly dropped out. The hammer finally fell and the bidder sitting behind me was the winner.

With proceedings at an end, Richard and I discussed the auction. Richard had done his homework and I was not surprised to learn from him that the man behind me was either representing the state of Norway or a department connected to the regional board which in turn was part of the state of Norway. My mind raced: this was yet another confirmation of my conspiracy theory. First, we had had Tor Honingstad, who was immoveable, then we had J. K. Thune, ensuring that any would-be purchaser was chased off the scene, and now for the final scene, the sham auction. It was not long before there came an announcement that the intellectual property and manufacturing rights and remaining assets had all been sold for a figure believed to be NKr. 37.5 million, a considerably lower price than had been previously offered from Malcolm Stockdale in the US or from HMC, to a company called Olivin A/S, wholly owned by the state of Norway; eventually a small shareholding would also be held by Komatsu of Japan. Recently, when I telephoned Mr Thune's office in an attempt to confirm these details, I spoke with a Mr Ottesen, who could no longer recollect the exact details but felt that my figure was correct. Surprisingly, he also told me that the matter had been taken out of their hands in the latter stages.

I must say that along with others I found it incredible that a very profitable and equal-second largest articulated dump truck manufacturer in the world had ultimately to be sold to a rock quarry owned by the state of Norway, with no engineering or dump truck manufacturing knowledge whatsoever. There had to be a question mark. My mind raced once again through the various scenarios of the previous eighteen months. I thought this sort of thing only happened in black Africa when the white man prospected a goldmine only to have it nationalised when it had been matured. I will take a lot of convincing that what we had experienced for the last eighteen months was not back-door nationalisation and I think anyone reading this book will agree that the facts of the matter speak for themselves.

For my part, there was only one more niggling issue to resolve. Thune's innuendos and accusations with regard to misappropriation of cash had to be answered. By this time, the press and media in Norway were growing impatient. Thune had still not pressed charges nor was there any evidence to substantiate his claims. By now he was mildly playing down his original statements but still there was no outright retraction.

Ron and I still had to endure the knowledge that around 5 million people in Norway were clearly of the opinion that we were a couple of crooks. However, a judicial enquiry had already been set up, and to our absolute joy on 17 June 1992, Judge Heidi Heggdal made a statement from the court steps in Romsdal that cleared us of any misappropriation of cash. She announced that she had examined all the financial and legal records of the company and with her staff had interviewed all senior managers and taken statements from all directors. Her judgement was that there had been nothing improper in the way the Brown brothers or the board of directors of Brown Engineering A/S, the producers of the Moxy dumptruck, had conducted their business. It is fair to say that in her summing up there was some mild rebuke levelled at each director for the way in which we had carried out some of our duties, but there was no question of any misappropriation of any funds whatsoever. She concluded that no director would be disqualified from either owning or directing a company in Norway and that included the two Brown brothers.

I was not present at the time in Norway but I felt it a real mark of respect that Judge Heggdal telephoned me and asked that my secretary interrupt a meeting that I was conducting at my new company. She came on the telephone and apologised for the interruption but felt that I should be one of the first to know as she felt sure that Ron and I had been subjected to the most unreasonable behaviour by the authorities in Norway. She went on to say that her findings had exonerated us of any financial malpractice and that we would not be disqualified from directing a Norwegian company in the future. I must admit there was no feeling of relief. The whole matter had dragged on for two long years, and there never had been any foundation for Thune's accusations.

By now it was June 1992. The recession had bitten even harder and nobody knew when it would end. But for the last eighteen months I had started to pick up the pieces of my fallen empire, beginning with the small consultancy contract in Nigeria. Soon afterwards I was able to buy back from the receiver Brown crusher-hire at Leicester and in April 1991, with the help of the City, I purchased the distribution arm of the old BGI.

The new company was called International Machinery Company (IMACO). As a desperate measure to try to beat off the recession, we merged IMACO with one of our competitors and the company became known as Imaco Blackwood Hodge. This was a little bit like taking two sick men into hospital and hoping that we could bring one healthy one out. This business was ultimately sold to Terex Equipment in June 1994. This allowed me to pursue my own family company, Weston Plant & Equipment, and a separate group of companies, Group 2000, which I intend to build up and float on the stock market and my latest venture, DDT Engineering Ltd, articulated truck manufacturers.

Since June 1990 I have tried to have my day in court with Thune. Surely he should have been made to answer for his defamatory statements, which had caused Ron and myself so much harm. But, as yet, there has been no retraction nor apology for his unprofessional conduct. I secured the help of Herr Strack, who had advised HMC, as he was the one person who had heard at first hand Thune calling Ron and myself 'crooks'. We then obtained a number of sworn affidavits from other people who had witnessed his outspoken and untrue allegations.

All that was left was to find a Norwegian lawyer who would act for us. I made a number of visits to Oslo in search of such a person but could find no one willing to speak against Thune. They all claimed that they could not oppose him in a country where the legal community is so small. Without exception they said they would prefer to be excused on this occasion.

Herr Strack accompanied me on my last visit in December 1993 and experienced at first hand the lawyers' reluctance to argue my case. He persuaded me, and in due course I reluctantly agreed, that I should go home and waste no more money on this fruitless crusade. There was clearly no possibility that the Norwegian legal system would turn against one of its own.

As a final twist to the mystery, Christiania Bank found itself in deep financial trouble soon after the demise of the Brown Group, so much so that the Norwegian government had to inject funds to ensure that it could comply with Norwegian banking regulations and could continue.

After this I could only turn to the writing of this book so that the world

In retrospect it transpires that the opinion voiced by the Norwegian media and by the Norwegian professional people involved in the dealings concerning the Brown Engineering A/S in receivership on the subject of the responsibility of the brothers Brown for their company falling into receivership and on the subject of the judgment about the "sinister manoeuvres of Gordon and Ron Brown" against the Norwegian companies and against the Norwegian people was instrumented by Mr. Thune. There is no other source of negative information on the subject of the brothers Brown known to the undersigned to whom the spreading of this information could be attributed.

As to the knowledge of the undersigned all the negative information on Mr. Gordon Brown and his brother which has reached the public and the bidders could be traced back to Mr. Thune.

The final part of German lawyer Herr Strack's affidavit.
Several other affidavits confirming statements made by Thune were also obtained.

at large could be made fully aware of the manner in which these people ultimately destroyed our company.

To conclude my story, let us take a look at the skeletons that this receivership left behind. Despite numerous warnings, Christiania Bank and Honingstad ignored our pleas for a stay of execution. We warned them that any disruption to the production of our product – a product that relied strongly on brand name for its prosperity – would be most detrimental. The warnings went unheeded. We told Christiania Bank that a company like ours could not afford to go through the existing receivership system and we were correct. This is why I stress more strongly than ever that I advocate a system whereby a ninety-day stand-off should be brought into play supervised by an independent third party to ensure a fair and rational solution. The companies involved in the Brown Group have never really survived the traumatic effects of receivership, the loss of confidence and continuity. The airline no longer exists, wiped out in a single day. Hymac no longer exists, except for a small parts organisation. Broyt is a shadow of its former glory, producing around twenty units a year plus a spares business. Parkers at Leicester was sold to Morris Hudson and now operates on a much smaller scale. The Brown distribution arm was purchased by myself but could never shake off the stigma of receivership and is now renamed IMACO and belongs to Terex. The Moxy factory in Norway, even under government ownership, has not yet got back to producing 250 units a year (information from the latest available statistics), which must be a source of acute embarrassment for both Honingstad and Thune after all their efforts. When the Brown brothers were in charge of the Moxy factory, we produced 850 units in 1989 and would have been close to repeating this achievement in 1990.

Now to my brothers: Freddy sadly died in January 1993. His pride never quite got over seeing the ultimate destruction of his lifetime's work. Ron, who suffered most at the hands of these people, has endured ill-health since the demise of his company: he lost his home, his work colleagues and returned to England to try to pick up the pieces of his life at the age of fifty-six. Since then he has had heart by-pass surgery and still cannot come to terms with the fact that you can work hard all your life and have the utmost integrity and still be treated in this way. And then myself – I am surviving. I also had a small heart attack in 1992. This I put down squarely to the stress under which I had been placed. And there was the denting of my pride, something from which I shall take years to recover.

Of course I made some mistakes in my old business life but I do not think any of them were of such a magnitude as to warrant Christiania Bank's ultimate destruction of our group. I believe I tried every way possible to appease them, even to the point of sacrificing my own job when Gartland

& Whalley came along to ensure that the approximately 1,600 people we employed could be kept in work.

In some ways events have overtaken my book as more and more banks are electing to work with management to try to work out company problems together. It is refreshing to see that recently some CVAs (Creditors Voluntary Arrangements) have been put in place. Even this could do with my ninety-day holding period to assist it because until this happens, the company concerned has to exist on a knife's edge.

Often I think back to what might have been. Who nudged the Ogden family and told them to sell out in 1988 at the top of the market, just before the recession struck? I have often spoken to them about it and maybe, after all I have said, there is such a thing as luck!

And now to my hero Joe Bamford, who built his JCB empire over fifty years and to this day stands as a shining example of what British entrepreneurial flair can achieve. I congratulate Joe and his son Anthony for creating their wonderful organisation, a credit to British engineering. The organisation they created was my dream – but sadly it was not to be repeated.

The future: our company's latest innovation – a DDT 630.

The Brown Group of Companies

Turnover

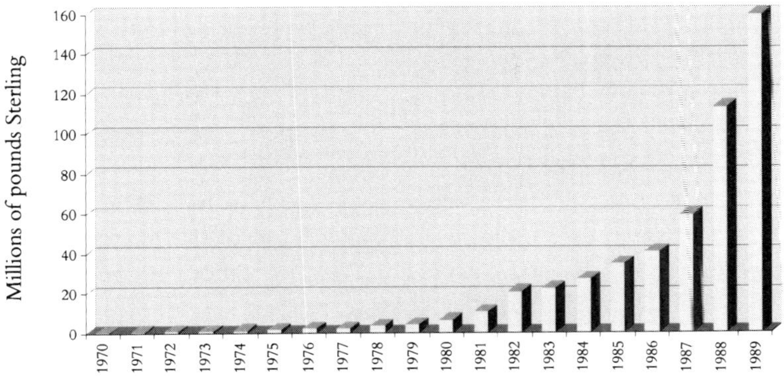

Profit before tax after interest and development costs

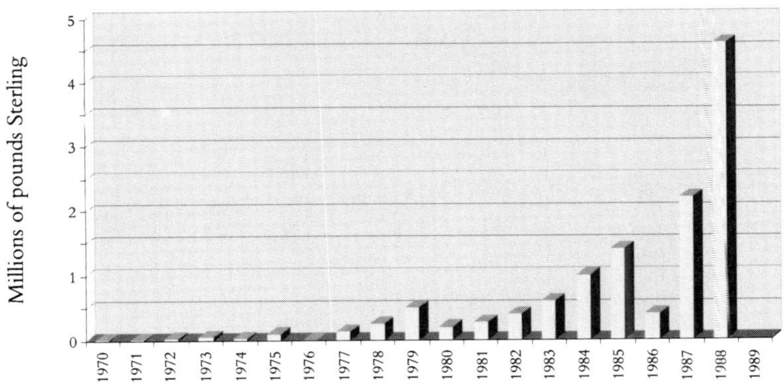

Net worth

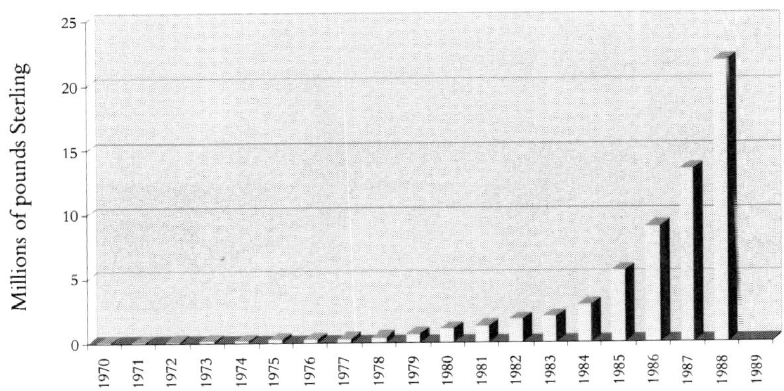

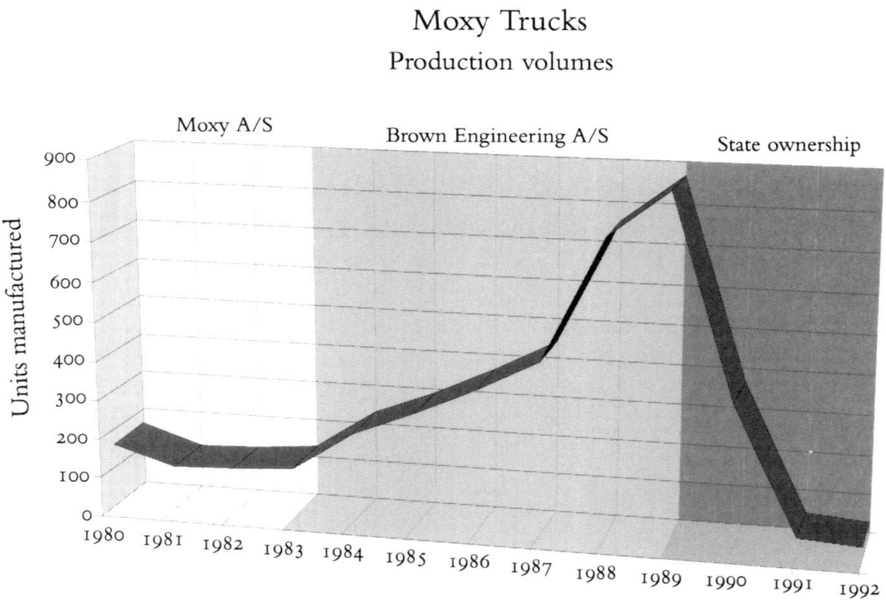
Moxy Trucks
Production volumes
Moxy A/S
Brown Engineering A/S
State ownership
Units manufactured
900
800
700
600
500
400
300
200
100
0
1980
1981
1982
1983
1984
1985
1986
1987
1988
1989
1990
1991
1992

This book is to be returned on or before the last date stamped below.

LIBREX